Surrogacy, Law and Human Rights

Edited by

PAULA GERBER
Monash University, Australia

KATIE O'BYRNE
Doughty Street Chambers, UK

Routledge
Taylor & Francis Group
LONDON AND NEW YORK

First published 2015 by Ashgate Publishing

Published 2016 by Routledge
2 Park Square, Milton Park, Abingdon, Oxfordshire OX14 4RN
711 Third Avenue, New York, NY 10017, USA

First issued in paperback 2016

Routledge is an imprint of the Taylor & Francis Group, an informa business

British Library Cataloguing in Publication Data
A catalogue record for this book is available from the British Library

The Library of Congress has cataloged the printed edition as follows:
Surrogacy, law and human rights / edited by Paula Gerber and Katie O'Byrne.
pages cm
Includes bibliographical references and index.
ISBN 978–1–4724–5124–8 (hardback)
1. Surrogate mothers – Legal status, laws, etc. 2. Surrogate motherhood. 3. Human rights. 4. Surrogate mothers – Legal status, laws, etc. – Australia. 5. Human rights Australia.
I. Gerber, Paula, editor author. II. O'Byrne, Katie, editor author.
K700.S87 2015
346.01'7–dc23

2014049973

ISBN 13: 978-1-138-70173-1 (pbk)
ISBN 13: 978-1-4724-5124-8 (hbk)

SURROGACY, LAW AND HUMAN RIGHTS

This book on the developing field of surrogacy law, across a number of jurisdictions, tackles an intricate and sensitive legal subject. It is one that has grown out of modern biological technology as it interacts with new social attitudes and values. This is a legal work. But, inevitably, the authors address the contested ethical positions that sometimes stand in the way of sensible law reform. The book is timely, well written and interesting. The authors are well qualified and engaged with their topic. This is cutting-edge law: at a new legal frontier where universal human rights law, conflicting religious and moral positions and powerful feelings of human love come together in vigorous dialogue.
The Hon Michael Kirby AC, CMG, former Justice of the High Court of Australia

This collection is a timely addition to the global debates on surrogacy, drawn from a uniquely Australian perspective. The wide range of views and recommendations for reform in Surrogacy, Law and Human Rights *make it a very valuable contribution to the burgeoning academic 'dissensus' on the role of law in responding to the challenges posed by domestic and transnational surrogacy.*
Professor Jenni Millbank, University of Technology, Sydney, Australia

Contents

Notes on Contributors

Sonia Allan has undergraduate and postgraduate qualifications in psychology, law and public health. She is a Senior Lecturer in Law at Macquarie University in Sydney, Australia. She previously held positions at the University of Melbourne, as a Senior Fellow in Law; at Georgetown Law Center, Washington D.C. as a Global Health Law Fellow; and at the Victorian Law Reform Commission as a legal research and policy officer. She is an expert on the regulation of assisted reproduction, surrogacy and related matters. She has published in leading national and international journals and contributed to federal and state government inquiries on these matters. In 2011, she was awarded a Churchill Fellowship for her work on donor conception.

Anurag Chawla is a practising lawyer in the Supreme Court of India and the High Court of Delhi with more than three decades of professional experience in civil and commercial practice. He specialises in legal issues related to surrogacy and assisted reproductive technology in India. His firm, Surrogacy Laws India, based in New Delhi, provides services in the area of surrogacy law in India. He and his team have assisted parents from other jurisdictions with surrogacy arrangements in India.

Kate Galloway is a Senior Lecturer and Director of Teaching and Learning at the School of Law at James Cook University in Queensland, Australia. She was previously a practising solicitor in property law, commercial law and native title. Her research interests lie in property law, feminist legal theory and social justice. She has a particular interest in theorising the legal conceptualisation of the human body – as property or otherwise – and the consequences that flow from this, especially for women.

Paula Gerber is an Associate Professor in the Faculty of Law at Monash University, Melbourne, Australia and a Deputy Director of the Castan Centre for Human Rights Law. She is an expert in the law pertaining to children's rights, which she both teaches and researches. She has published numerous peer-reviewed journal articles, edited collections and monographs in the human rights field, including most recently Paula Gerber and Melissa Castan (eds), *Contemporary Perspectives on Human Rights Law in Australia* (2013, Thomson Reuters); Paula Gerber, *Understanding Human Rights: Educational Challenges for the Future* (2013, Edward Elgar); and Paula Gerber and Adiva Sifris (eds), *Current Trends in the Regulation of Same-sex Relationships* (2010, Federation Press).

Alexandra Harland is a judge of the Federal Circuit Court of Australia. Before being appointed to the Bench she practised in family law for 16 years in private practice and with Legal Aid New South Wales. She has taught family law at the University of Sydney. She is the lead author of the family law text book *Family Law Principles* (Thomson Reuters, 2011). She has published several peer-reviewed journal articles and written and presented numerous papers on a variety of family law topics, including surrogacy issues. She is undertaking a Masters of Law at UTS researching international surrogacy. She is currently working on the second edition of *Family Law Principles.*

Tammy Johnson is an Assistant Professor at Bond University in Queensland, Australia. A sole practitioner for a number of years, Tammy eventually sold her practice to pursue her academic interests. Tammy practised in the areas of property law, commercial law and succession and estate administration. In 2008, Tammy received her Master of Laws (Corporate and Commercial Law) and she is now close to completing her PhD at Queensland University of Technology, Australia on the topic of commercial surrogacy in Australia.

Cressida Limon is a Lecturer at the School of Law, University of Western Sydney, Australia. She was previously a Research Fellow at the University of Melbourne where she worked with the Family Law Council of Australia on its recent inquiry into parentage and the *Family Law Act* 1975 (Cth). Cressida has research expertise in the fields of biological anthropology, science studies and feminist legal theory. Cressida has a particular interest in how concepts of the natural and the technical are constructed in law and legal theory.

Katie O'Byrne is a barrister at Doughty Street Chambers, London, United Kingdom, specialising in human rights, public law and international law. She has previously practised as a solicitor at Freehills and was an associate to Justice Kenneth Hayne AC of the High Court of Australia. She has also been a Lecturer at Melbourne Law School and a Research Assistant at Monash University Law Faculty, Australia. In 2011–12 she was a David M Livingstone Scholar in the LLM at the University of Cambridge, where she completed a thesis examining transgender recognition law. She has published in the areas of refugee law, children's rights and the relationship between law and gender.

Richard F. Storrow is Professor of Law at City University of New York. He brings human rights and social justice perspectives to his comparative research on the regulation of assisted reproduction. His recent articles have explored the legal dimensions of cross-border reproductive care, the use of the proportionality principle by European courts reviewing restrictions on assisted reproduction, and the resurrection of illegitimacy classifications in the regulation of international commercial surrogacy. During the fall of 2010, he was a Fulbright scholar to Spain where he conducted research on the development of the Spanish law of human assisted reproduction.

Anita Stuhmcke has had a long-standing interest in the legal regulation of surrogacy in Australia. She is a Professor in the Law Faculty of the University of Technology Sydney, Australia. Her scholarship in this area explores social exclusion and public access to reproductive services, especially with respect to surrogacy. Anita has contributed to law reform inquiries across several Australian jurisdictions on this issue. The central premise of her research is to conceptualise the ways in which law operates as a continuum of effectiveness, the basic argument being that black-letter law is just one regulatory option available to policy-makers.

Normann Witzleb is an Associate Professor in the Faculty of Law at Monash University, Melbourne, Australia. Prior to joining Monash University in 2008, he worked at the University of Western Australia and the European University Viadrina Frankfurt (Oder), where he also obtained his PhD. Normann is dually qualified in German and Australian law. He has published extensively on the law of obligations and the law of privacy but also maintains an active research interest in comparative family law.

Anthony Wood lives in Melbourne with his partner, Lee Matthews, and their two children. He is a partner at Herbert Smith Freehills, where he is the Section Head of that firm's Employment group. He is a member of the Herbert Smith Freehills Diversity Steering Committee and convenor of the firm's LGBT network. He holds Bachelor of Commerce and Law degrees from the University of Melbourne (1986). Tony and his partner were one of the first Australian couples to successfully pursue international surrogacy and their story was chronicled in the Australian SBS documentaries *Man Made: The Story of Two Men and a Baby* (2003) and *Two Men and Two Babies* (2008).

Foreword

Modern human rights law has typically evolved in response to egregious human rights violations. The 1945 UN Charter followed the Second World War, and recognised that global peace depends on effective human rights protection. The 1948 Universal Declaration of Human Rights then provided the keystone for the subsequent development of treaties on the rights of refugees, civil, political, economic, cultural and social rights, the right to be free from discrimination on the grounds of race, gender and disability and the rights of the child.

These core international agreements now provide a body of law that can inform our approaches to new ethical and legal challenges, including those stimulated by scientific advances.

Surrogacy has emerged as one such contemporary challenge. The human desire to be a parent is fundamental to society and surrogacy offers the opportunity of parenthood to those otherwise unable to bear a child. But surrogacy is also fraught with legal, religious, ethical, regulatory and practical challenges.

In this collection of essays, the editors, Paula Gerber and Katie O'Byrne, bring together international and Australian approaches to surrogacy, viewed through the lens of human rights law and philosophy. It is this human rights perspective that provides an original contribution to the surrogacy debate. Indeed, it is encouraging that human rights law and jurisprudence have evolved over the last nearly 70 years to provide relatively coherent benchmarks against which to consider emerging social issues.

Surrogacy poses many troubling questions. Critically, and as a primary consideration, the rights of the child must be protected under all surrogacy arrangements. Other complex issues arise. How can 'compensated' surrogacy arrangements be developed that protect women against the commodification of their bodies? Especially for women in developing countries, how can abuse of poverty and powerlessness be prevented? Should surrogacy be available to same-sex couples? Is criminalisation of extra-territorial surrogacy under Australian law consistent with the freedom to choose the means of reproduction? How are the often competing rights of children, surrogates and parents to be balanced? What is the role of the state in regulating complex personal matters such as reproduction? Is the free market approach of some jurisdictions in the United States to be preferred to the trend, for example, in Australia, towards more restrictive regulation?

The thesis common to each author in this collection is that some guidance in answering these questions is to be found in human rights law and practice. The *Queensland Investigation into Altruistic Surrogacy* in 2008 recommended the decriminalisation of altruistic surrogacy in that state by recognising the 'liberty of consenting adults to conceive a child and to parent'.[1]

It nonetheless remains true that the law, including human rights law, tends to follow some way behind scientific developments. The editors acknowledge that it is not yet possible to reach unequivocal conclusions about many of the issues raised by surrogacy and that the chapter authors raise more questions than they answer. The value of this collection lies in the objective, research-based reasoning of the various authors.

The Australian Human Rights Commission is considering the legal and policy issues raised by compensated surrogacy and hopes to contribute to the public debate in 2015. The views expressed in this collection will provide an invaluable foundation both for the Commission's analysis of the human rights implications of surrogacy and for the work of all policy-makers, scholars and social activists who seek an approach that respects human rights and dignity.

Professor Gillian Triggs
President, Australian Human Rights Commission

1 Investigation into Altruistic Surrogacy Committee, Report (October 2008), 22.

Chapter 1
Surrogacy and Human Rights: Contemporary, Complex, Contested and Controversial

Katie O'Byrne and Paula Gerber

I. Introduction

At the intersection of science, law, ethics and human rights, surrogacy[1] presents a myriad of legal and moral questions, regulatory challenges and practical problems. Given these flashpoints, the global debate on surrogacy regulation is unsurprisingly both intense and sophisticated, providing a rich source of material for policy- and law-makers to consider. However, one area that has not previously been the subject of sustained and multidimensional analysis in a collection such as this is the relationship between surrogacy and human rights,[2] and how human rights might influence the regulation of surrogacy.

The purpose of this edited collection is to collate and explore a wide range of human rights perspectives on international and domestic surrogacy regulation. In an area that interacts so fundamentally with the most intimate of human needs, the operation of the human body, the exercise of free will, the possibility of exploitation and the generation

1 '[S]urrogacy, *n* ... (The practice of) surrogate motherhood (*Oxford English Dictionary*, Draft Additions 1993). '[S]urrogate, *n* ... A woman whose pregnancy arises from the implantation in her womb of a fertilized egg or embryo from another woman' (*Oxford English Dictionary*). It is accepted in this collection that terminology in this field is contested: see nn. 10–12 below and accompanying text.

2 The term 'human rights' is often used to refer to international human rights law; that is, to the rights enumerated in the International Bill of Human Rights (comprising the *Universal Declaration of Human Rights*, adopted by General Assembly Resolution 217 A(III), 10 December 1948, the *International Covenant on Civil and Political Rights*, 999 UNTS 171, opened for signature by General Assembly Resolution 2200A (XXI), 16 December 1966, entered into force 23 March 1976, and the *International Covenant on Economic, Social and Cultural Rights*, 993 UNTS 3, opened for signature by General Assembly resolution 2200A (XXI), 16 December 1966, entered into force 3 January 1976), and in other international agreements including the *Convention on the Rights of the Child*, 1577 UNTS 3, opened for signature by General Assembly Resolution 44/25, 20 November 1989, entered into force 2 September 1990. However, rather than focusing narrowly on international legal human rights instruments, many of the chapters in this collection utilise a broader understanding of human rights as a foundation for evaluating surrogacy regulation, drawing on the philosophy of natural rights and conceptions of human dignity.

of life itself, using human rights as a framework for analysis can illuminate how best to protect the most important and vulnerable interests of those involved.

While the focus of many of the chapters is on Australian law and regulation, there are also chapters analysing the issue of surrogacy and human rights from an international law standpoint, as well as in the domestic law of other jurisdictions. In order to ensure a rich array of opinions, this collection includes a wide range of views from academics and practitioners around the world who have varied expertise and experience.

II. Themes and Contents

To provide a context for the debate, the collection begins with a personal and practical reflection on surrogacy. Melbourne lawyer Tony Wood shares his real life journey through surrogacy in the US in the early 2000s. Tony and his same-sex partner had a strong desire to experience the joys of parenthood, and so engaged a surrogate, who carried first their son and later their daughter. Tony and his partner built a relationship with the surrogate and provided both financial and emotional support throughout her pregnancies. She is now a special person in the lives of their kids who, Tony assures the reader, are doing just fine. Tony is no casual observer of the surrogacy debate – what he witnessed and experienced prompts him to challenge value judgments about commercial surrogacy and same-sex parenting. Given the often-heated legal and ethical debates that surround these issues, Tony's story is a moving and heart-warming example of how many human lives can be changed positively through one surrogacy experience.

Expanding this exploration of context by adopting a broader theoretical perspective, Kate Galloway's chapter delves into some of the deeper philosophical concepts and ethical justifications underpinning the debate about whether to regulate surrogacy and why. Galloway begins with an analysis of liberal approaches to reproductive and contractual freedom in view of state intervention in surrogacy regulation, before turning to examine feminist critiques. Galloway suggests that the Kantian moral perspective, which prioritises human dignity in order to avoid commodification of the human body, assists in protecting parties with little power – particularly the child and the surrogate. It is from this foundation that a human rights perspective on surrogacy arrangements can be developed.

The remaining academic contributions are presented in three parts. Tammy Johnson's chapter and Anita Stuhmcke's chapter each provide an analysis of the surrogacy regulation landscape in Australia. Johnson focuses on the fragmentation of surrogacy regulation across Australian states and territories, suggesting that this curbs the freedom of individuals to procreate. She proposes a harmonised model for national reform drawn from existing inquiries and research. Her considerations may also be broadly relevant to other federated nations with disparate surrogacy regulation, such as the US.

Stuhmcke observes that Australia is one of only two countries that have laws making it a criminal offence for residents to pursue surrogacy arrangements overseas. She examines the consequences of extraterritorial criminalisation of surrogacy in the Australian Capital Territory, Queensland and New South Wales, and argues for repeal of these provisions in order to promote the liberty of reproductive choice. In support of this position, she notes that there is no evidence that extraterritorial criminalisation serves the purposes of shaping behaviour, promoting transparency or reducing exploitation.

The next three chapters examine the human rights of particular participants in the complex network of relationships that exists in each surrogacy arrangement. First is an examination of the rights of children born via surrogacy arrangements, using the UN Convention on the Rights of the Child ('CRC') as the lens through which to assess whether the practice of surrogacy, and the laws regulating it, are consistent with the best interests of children born via surrogacy. Surrogacy laws and practices are analysed according to:

- the right of the child to freedom from discrimination;
- the best interests of the child;
- the child's rights to identity and to be cared for by his/her parents; and
- the prohibition on the sale of children.

Australia is then used as a case study to measure a selection of domestic laws against the CRC, in particular immigration and citizenship laws, family law and criminal law. The results of this analysis highlight the importance of using a child-centred human rights approach to surrogacy.

In Chapter 7, Sonia Allan explores the human rights ramifications of entering into a surrogacy arrangement from the perspective of the surrogate herself, especially in cases of compensated surrogacy. Allan examines issues including human trafficking, exploitation of inequalities and lack of informed consent. In one of the most contested and controversial areas of surrogacy regulation, Allan argues that the risks of compensated surrogacy to the human rights of the surrogate render it an unacceptable practice. Surrogacy regulation in the form of minimum legal standards in domestic law could be made more consistent in order to protect the rights and interests of the people involved.

Next, Federal Circuit Court Judge Alexandra Harland and academic Cressida Limon collaborate in analysing the human rights of the intended parents. These authors examine the ways in which parentage is recognised in Australian domestic law and its application to overseas commercial surrogacy arrangements. This involves a detailed analysis of Family Court surrogacy cases and exploration of options for federal reform to improve effective legal solutions for families and to reconcile the sometimes competing rights of children, surrogates and intended parents.

The final two chapters present international and comparative examples of the interaction between surrogacy and human rights. Dr Normann Witzleb and Anurag Chawla provide a human rights analysis of surrogacy regulation in India, often touted as a 'global health destination'. To give a sense of context, they trace the early portrayals of surrogacy arrangements in Indian mythology. In recent years, modern medical infrastructure, low costs, permissive regulation and the ready availability of surrogates have meant that commercial surrogacy has become common in India, with around 2,000 children being born via surrogacy each year. While for surrogates the process may be a way to lift themselves and their families out of poverty, they often do not obtain independent advice or counselling and their interests may be surrendered to the control of clinics. Witzleb and Chawla provide a critical overview of Indian surrogacy regulation, including the *National Guidelines for Accreditation, Supervision and Regulation of ART Clinics in India 2005*, court decisions and passport laws. They illustrate the uncertainty inherent in this framework in their discussion of the *Baby Manji*[3] and *Balaz Twins*[4] cases. Some of these issues may be improved in the future with the introduction of proposed legislation, but compensated surrogacy will continue to form part of a wider debate on the appropriate relationship between private health services and public health in India.

Professor Richard Storrow provides an overview of surrogacy regulation in the United States. To the outside observer, the US appears unique amongst developed nations in the extent to which it has embraced commercial surrogacy, representing the pinnacle of laissez-faire regulation. The real picture, Storrow explains, is more complex. Like Australia, surrogacy in the US is regulated at the state level, and the range of prohibitive to permissive regimes across the country reflects a diversity of attitudes about the clinical, ethical and legal aspects of the debate. These range from criminalisation of surrogacy in Oklahoma to an adoption model in Florida, to prohibition of compensation in Kentucky and liberal legislation in California. While efforts to create uniform legislation have so far been unsuccessful, the overall trend is towards more rather than less regulation. Storrow also notes that there is no uniform treatment in legislation and case law of parentage entitlements in different types of surrogacy arrangements, meaning that cross-border issues can arise within the US when the parties are from different states. Storrow concludes that the outsider's impression of the US as an unconstrained free market in commercial surrogacy is misplaced.

Weaving through the various contributions are themes of human dignity, choice and vulnerability, law and ethics, and the rights and responsibilities of individuals and governments. Intentionally, it is difficult, if not impossible, to draw firm conclusions from the chapters presented in this collection. In many ways, they raise more questions than they answer.

3 *Baby Manji Yamada v Union of India and Anor* (2008) INSC 1656 (Supreme Court of India).

4 *Balaz v Anand Municipality*, LPA 2151/2009 (Gujarat High Court).

III. Other Pieces of the Jigsaw

In a collection of this size, it is not possible to include all aspects of the relationship between surrogacy and human rights, and there are several issues that have not been covered in detail.

For example, there is no in-depth analysis of the concept of so-called 'reproductive tourism' insofar as it relates to surrogacy and human rights, though Stuhmcke touches on how use of the term 'tourism' connotes a casual choice made from a position of power and based on an assumption of exploitation. The concept, referring to both interstate and international travel for the purpose of reproductive care, has been studied and interrogated extensively elsewhere.[5] A number of commentators critique its legal pitfalls,[6] or explicitly disavow the term 'tourism' as inapt to reflect the realities of travel undertaken by intended parents for reproductive purposes.[7]

This contestation of terms is symptomatic of a wider theme, which underlies all of the contributions but merits further emphasis here; that is, the unresolved use of labels, definitions and language in the context of surrogacy and surrogacy arrangements. Language has long been a topic of debate in the field,[8] which is appropriate in light of the diversity of perspectives on surrogacy. While much of the controversy has centred on the terms 'surrogate', 'mother' and 'parent', the advent of surrogacy may be said to have contributed to a fundamental redefinition of motherhood, parentage and the family itself[9] – for better or for worse, depending

---

5 See, for example, Eric Blyth and Abigail Farrand, 'Reproductive Tourism – A Price Worth Paying for Reproductive Autonomy?' (2005) 25 *Critical Social Policy* 91; Jean Cohen, 'Procreative Tourism and Reproductive Freedom' (2006) 13 *Reproductive Biomedicine Online* 145; Zeynep B. Gürtin and Marcia C. Inhorn, 'Introduction: Travelling for Conception and the Global Assisted Reproduction Market' (2011) 23 *Reproductive Biomedicine Online* 535.

6 Richard Storrow, 'Assisted Reproduction on Treacherous Terrain: The Legal Hazards of Cross-Border Reproductive Travel' (2011) 23 *Reproductive Biomedicine Online* 538.

7 Jenni Millbank, 'Rethinking "Commercial" Surrogacy' (2014) *Journal of Bioethical Inquiry* DOI 10.1007/s11673-014-9557-9, advance access; Marcia C. Inhorn and Pasquale Patrizio, 'Rethinking Reproductive "Tourism" as Reproductive "Exile"' (2009) 92 *Fertility and Sterility* 904.

8 For early discussions see Rita Arditti, Renate Duelli Klein and Shelley Minden (eds), *Test-tube Women: What Future for Motherhood?* (London and Boston, MA: Pandora Press, 1984); Barbara Katz Rothman, *The Tentative Pregnancy: Prenatal Diagnosis and the Future of Motherhood* (New York: Viking, 1986); Michelle Stanworth (ed.), *Reproductive Technologies: Gender, Motherhood, and Medicine* (Minneapolis, MN: University of Minneapolis Press, 1987); Marilyn Strathern, 'Still Giving Nature a Helping Hand? Surrogacy: A Debate about Technology and Society' (2002) 319 *Journal of Molecular Biology* 985.

9 See, for example, Elly Teman, 'Fragmentation and Women's Empowerment: Surrogate Motherhood in Israel' (2001) 29 *Women's Studies Quarterly* 11; Bryn Williams-Jones, 'Commercial Surrogacy and the Redefinition of Motherhood' (2002) 2 *Journal of*

on the perspective adopted. As a further example, while it appears to be accepted in most of the jurisdictions canvassed that gestational surrogacy is preferable to traditional surrogacy, the question of how to characterise 'payment for services rendered' in terms of contracts or compensation is still vexed,[10] prompting a spectrum of responses. These are not mere boundary disputes but go to the core of a human rights approach, at both an individual and state level.

Debate also exists around the use of the term 'commercial' to describe arrangements where a surrogate is compensated. The term 'commercial' suggests a crude business transaction that commodifies all those involved. It is perhaps more accurate, and less emotive, to refer to arrangements where there is payment over and above reasonable expenses, as 'compensated' surrogacy.

This book does not purport to provide a complete examination of all jurisdictions where surrogacy takes place, or even all the places that people frequently travel to for the purposes of surrogacy. While comprehensive data on surrogacy regulation around the world would be very difficult to compile,[11] especially given variations from state to state in federal jurisdictions such as Australia and the US, existing research shows that global trends in surrogacy regulation remain in flux.[12] Domestic regulatory models range from criminalisation to non-regulation, and from pre-approval for altruistic surrogacy to compensated surrogacy. Consistent with this ad hoc approach to surrogacy at the domestic level, there is no accord about how surrogacy should be regulated at the international level.[13] The only certainty is that a human rights perspective is an indispensable component in both international and domestic discussions about the future of surrogacy regulation.

IV. Conclusion

Though not without historical precedents and context, the interaction of surrogacy with human rights is a truly contemporary issue. As revealed by the chapters in this collection, surrogacy presents particularly complex questions for human

Philosophy, Science and Law, available at http://www6.miami.edu/ethics/jpsl/archives/papers/comsur_williamsjones.html#_ednref12.

10 See, for example, Jennifer L. Watson, 'Growing a Baby for Sale or Merely Renting a Womb: Should Surrogate Mothers Be Compensated for their Services?' (2007) 6 *Whittier Journal of Child and Family Advocacy* 529.

11 But see International Federation of Fertility Societies, 'IFFS Surveillance 2010' (2010), available at https://c.ymcdn.com/sites/iffs.site-ym.com/resource/resmgr/newsletters/iffs_surveillance_2010.pdf.

12 See, for example, Katarina Trimmings and Paul Beaumont (eds), *International Surrogacy Arrangements* (2013), especially Pt 1 which contains National Reports on domestic approaches to surrogacy from a wide range of countries.

13 See, for example, the survey conducted in Permanent Bureau of The Hague Conference of International Law, 'A Preliminary Report on the Issues arising from International Surrogacy Arrangements' (March 2012), Pt III.

rights law. Alongside its technical and ethical facets, each surrogacy arrangement engages intimately with the human rights of a number of different participants, impacting the human rights of each participant in different ways. It is an area where, as is often typical, the law lags some way behind the moving frontier of scientific advancement. In Australia, and around the world, rapid regulatory development has occurred in recent years and continues to occur as this book goes to print.

Therefore, surrogacy is not at a stage where there is any conclusive consensus about what it means and how the law should respond. Part of the challenge for cohesive regulation lies in the reality that many of the facets and boundaries of the surrogacy issue remain controversial and, indeed, that the terminology itself is frequently contested.

For all these reasons, this book endeavours to present a rich diversity of reflection and analysis about the human rights dimensions of surrogacy, with the aim of adding value to the processes of debate, reform and regulation.

Chapter 2
Surrogacy: A Personal Perspective

Anthony Wood*

Surrogacy stories – or other stories about gay parenting, sex selection, multiple pregnancies, selective reduction or, more generally, IVF advances – evoke interest. Every other week it seems there are stories about various aspects of surrogacy. In particular, curiosity tends to pique in relation to offshore commercial surrogacy. There have been countless stories about Indian and Thai surrogacy – perhaps because it seems to highlight some community concerns about outsourcing ('where will it stop?') and exploitation. Or for some, perhaps some moralising dressed up in more objective clothing. When the 'news' of my surrogacy experiences broke a decade ago, the Sydney *Sun-Herald* published a full-page banner promoting their story: REVEALED: THE BABY WITH TWO GAY DADS.[1] As I prepared this chapter, the Australian media reported the story[2] of Justice Ryan of the Family Court, requiring an Australian couple who had applied for parental recognition, to travel back to India to prove that their twins' surrogate mother, an illiterate Indian woman, was competent to provide an informed consent to the surrogacy arrangements entered into in that country. The media reported that the Hindi-speaking woman, who cannot read and does not understand English, used a thumb print to sign a 29-page contract written in English. Who doesn't react with curiosity when alerted to facts like that? Or feel uneasy about the baby Gammy story which highlighted numerous concerns about the ethics of Thai surrogacy and the Australians who fuel the demand for international surrogacy.

When my partner and I commenced our journey in 2000, commercial surrogacy was a fledgling industry in the United States only. There were no local trailblazers for us to follow and the Australian legal framework was either barren or mostly

---

* Anthony Wood is a partner at a large international law firm. He and his partner reside in Melbourne, Australia. Their story has been featured in two documentaries broadcast on the Australian SBS TV network: *Man Made: The Story of Two Men and a Baby* (2003) and *Two Men & Two Babies* (2008).

1 The accompanying article was C. Sutton and L. Schwartz, 'Gay dads want their son to grow up straight', *The Sun-Herald* (14 September 2003), available at www.smh.com.au/articles/2003/09/13/1063341818025.html, accessed 15 June 2014.

2 B. Hills, 'A couple who hired an illiterate Indian woman to be surrogate of their twins ordered to prove she wasn't exploited', *The Sunday Telegraph* (30 June 2013), available at www.dailytelegraph.com.au/news/nsw/a-couple-who-hired-an-illiterate-indian-woman-to-be-surrogate-of-their-twins-ordered-to-prove-she-wasn8217t-exploited/story-fni0cx12–1226672063788, accessed 15 June 2014.

untested. Although as a gay couple we were suitable to be entrusted with fostering local special-needs kids, we were not eligible for adoption of local or overseas children. Remember, this was more than a decade ago. Permitting same-sex couples to marry was barely on the horizon as a political issue. Our local member of state Parliament couldn't shunt us out of his office quickly enough when we wanted to discuss adoption reform for gay couples. He seemed to think we'd be happy that the Government considered us as fit for foster care.

The desire or trigger for parenting strikes people in different ways. Approaching 40, I had watched most of my school and university friends get married and have kids. My partner, Lee, and I were missing out. Sure, we had friends and family, but we wanted to make a difference. And I suppose we were just the same as most couples: we wanted the joys and love of becoming parents. We were drawn to the United States. In California, a surrogacy 'industry' had developed, supported by a sympathetic legal framework which recognised the legal rights of the intended parents (or IPs). Contracts governed by Californian law were recognised as binding throughout the nation, although some US states still continued to outlaw commercial surrogacy.

We engaged a US agency, 'Growing Generations', which was run by a lesbian and a gay man who had felt shut out of the industry and had established their own agency to cater for prospective gay IPs. Soon, Growing Generations became the largest surrogacy agency in the US. The deal was fairly simple. The agency engaged surrogates and egg donors and matched them with IPs: sort of like matchmaking. The agency also coordinated physicians and IVF specialists to facilitate the process, as well as brokering any necessary insurance arrangements. Because we were international clients, the immigration and legal advice was fairly crude at the time, but effective nonetheless. In short, any child born in the US is automatically a US citizen and eligible for a US passport. But a child with at least one Australian parent is also eligible for Australian citizenship by descent. (The question that arose before the Family Court in *Re Mark*,[3] as to whether an Australian sperm donor in an international surrogacy arrangement was a 'parent', had not yet arisen.)

Selecting a surrogate or egg donor is not easy. The two processes are quite distinct and 'traditional surrogacy' (where the surrogate is also the egg donor) is extremely rare. We were informed by our agency that they required surrogates to be at least 25 years old and to have already given birth to their own children before being considered for the process. For egg donors, on the other hand – fertility and youth are entwined: college students are the preferred source. And if you want an Ivy League student, be prepared to pay a premium.

We interviewed three potential egg donors before we eventually chose Monica. Selecting a donor sounds easy, until you are burdened with a portfolio full of height and weight statistics, genetic and family medical history, SAT scores and psychological profiling. Looking back, I can't believe we spent time fretting over whether a balding maternal or paternal grandfather was important. But of all the

3 [2003] FamCA 822.

criteria, the most important to us was that the donor would not be anonymous. We knew we wanted our kids to understand their genetic heritage. And anyway, it's pretty hard for two gay dads to lie to their kids about where they came from.

Choosing the surrogate is actually the more fraught process, despite the lack of genetic connection. If egg donation creates a fleeting interaction, your surrogate – the woman who carries your babies – can't be taken for granted. At least in the US model of surrogacy, the surrogate is the queen. To be adored and feted. They get paid for doing this, of course, but I have met many surrogates, and not one did it 'just' for the money. In my experience, these are intelligent women who are driven by a variety of personal and altruistic motives. I cannot attest to the role of surrogates from, say India or Thailand, save that our western values are challenged by some of the stories of surrogacy in those countries. Some Indian surrogates never meet the IPs and many do not enjoy an ongoing relationship or bond with the IPs and their children. It's unsurprising that legislators in those countries have significantly tightened access to international commercial surrogacy. Nor is it surprising that new 'markets' have opened up. Mexico and Nepal are now apparently the new favoured destinations. We interviewed three wonderful surrogates from as far afield as Boston, Denver and Iowa. One was a military mom, the wife of a sniper in Desert Storm. Another was a suburban mom of three kids, working full time. And Junoa, from Iowa, who was only 25 when she met us. We also met many other surrogates through friends and acquaintances as we conducted our due diligence about the process.

Junoa had married her college sweetheart when she was very young and they had two kids while building their own home near Cedar Rapids. When we first met her in Los Angeles, Junoa had never previously travelled further than a few hours' drive from her home. She'd never dipped her toes in the ocean until our meeting at Santa Monica. After the initial tentative steps, we bonded and agreed to work together. Junoa told us that she had wanted to be a surrogate ever since, as a teenager, she watched a tele-movie about a surrogate. We signed contracts, as we did with our chosen egg donor. The contracts were all regulated by the laws of the state of California. At the time, Lee and I were living between Sydney and Melbourne. Fortunately, the New South Wales laws[4] that now render it unlawful for residents to pursue offshore commercial surrogacy, had not yet been enacted.

Junoa underwent the normal IVF process while, at the same time, our donor was stimulated to produce egg follicles to coincide with the planned retrieval and embryo transfer processes. Our first two transfers failed. Everyone was forlorn. This wasn't meant to happen. More trips from Australia to LA followed. So many, in fact, that we eventually even understood the freeways and neighbourhoods. But these were testing times. The Aussie dollar was as low as 0.49 to the greenback. We were compensating our surrogate throughout the process for her availability, even though she was employed full-time. Health care and fertility services in the US are expensive and were not covered by our insurance. We thought about giving up. Our

4 See *Surrogacy Act 2010* (NSW), ss 8, 9, 11.

third transfer with Junoa was a success. She sent us an email with a scanned image of the faint blue line on the home pregnancy test. We dialled in from Melbourne as Junoa first had her blood tests confirming the pregnancy, and then underwent the first ultrasound. Whether it was joy or relief, or both, we all cried. Overjoyed.

For the next nine months, we called each other weekly. And emailed almost daily. How we must have suffocated Junoa! We subscribed to those weekly pregnancy alerts, telling us as our embryo turned from a walnut into a foetus and then into various shapes of fruits over 40 weeks. Impertinently, we tried to convert Junoa's American diet of bad coffee and burgers to grilled fish and folate supplements. And we gradually adjusted to dealing with the hormonal mood swings of a pregnant woman on another continent. If we needed any reminding, Junoa was in charge throughout this process. Junoa certainly deserved the money we paid her. Putting aside the physical exertions of pregnancy, just putting up with us deserved a premium. But seriously, why shouldn't someone be fairly compensated for such a commitment? At 16 weeks, Junoa flew out with her family to Melbourne. She'd never had a passport before. We attended the ultrasound and were told we were expecting a boy. More tears.

Our son was born in Cedar Rapids in December 2002. Our daughter, also carried by Junoa, was born two and a half years later. We were present at both births. We cut the umbilical cords. We cried tears of happiness. The hospital gave us the suite next to Junoa's and our kids slept with us from the day of their births. We have been back to the US twice since they were born and have kept up constant contact with Junoa. She and her family have also visited us twice in Australia. We share stories with Junoa's kids – now teenagers – about who was the fattest/skinniest/funniest baby. Our kids, now 12 and 9, have two dads and no mum. Their school friends, teachers and others surrounding them all understand this. The kids send Junoa emails and cards for Christmas and birthdays, just as she does for us. But, she's not their mother. At law, in the US, Junoa relinquished her parental rights pursuant to a court order made shortly after each birth. But more importantly, in life, Junoa is a special person in our kids' lives.

Where does one start to analyse the effects of all this? Our kids play footy and basketball and do gymnastics. They're in the dance competitions and the choir at school. They're angels and monsters in the same week. I think that makes them pretty normal. I'm no casual observer of the commercial surrogacy debate. And how can I be objective? I've witnessed the benefits of the regulated commercial surrogacy practices in the US. I've seen so many lives changed, all positively, as a result. I've also seen the families excluded from participating in surrogacy because of the financial impediments imposed by having to travel offshore. And for those able to afford it, I've met couples now excluded by state laws here which criminalise their pursuit of parenthood. People who would make amazing parents. And women who would willingly be wonderful surrogates, but are forbidden from doing so. It's hard to sit back and listen to uninformed critics making moral judgments, frequently based on 'religious' grounds, or the 'best interests of the child'. Trust me, the kids are OK.

Chapter 3

Theoretical Approaches to Human Dignity, Human Rights and Surrogacy

Kate Galloway

I. Introduction

Legal regulation of transactions in the human body is in one sense a new phenomenon. Traditionally, in seeking to delineate between what is human and what is not, the common law has sought to exclude the human body from its conceptualisation of transactions as involving commodities.[1] This approach theoretically avoids the potential for a human to become the very antithesis of personhood: namely property. From this perspective, bodily transactions that are now routine, including organ transplants, assisted reproduction and surrogacy, present a challenge for the law.

On the other hand, property itself is a construct of its time and the society in which it exists.[2] The exclusion of humans and their bodies from regulatory frameworks has depended upon who is within the law and who is *homo sacer*[3] (outside the law), and how social custom perceives the body from time to time.[4] For example, at one end of a spectrum of bodily transactions, slavery was actively practised in England until the late eighteenth century. Slavery is now completely prohibited within an international human rights framework.[5] Far more recently, the bodies of children and women have been under the control of the head of the household, the *pater familias*, and the paternalistic state.[6]

---

1 In what Maneesha Deckha refers to as 'commodification' in 'Holding onto Humanity: Animals, Dignity, and Anxiety in Canada's Assisted Human Reproduction Act' (2009) 5 *Unbound* 21.

2 Margaret Davies, *Property: Meanings, Histories, Theories* (New York: Routledge-Cavendish, 2007).

3 Georgio Agamben, *Homo Sacer: Sovereign Power and Bare Life*, trans. Daniel Heller-Roazen (Stanford, CA: Stanford University Press, 1998).

4 Leon R. Kass, 'Organs for Sale? Propriety, Property, and the Price of Progress' (1992) 107 *The Public Interest* 65.

5 *Slavery Convention* (signed 25 September 1926, entered into force 9 March 1927).

6 Susan Moller Okin, *Justice, Gender and the Family* (New York: Basic Books, 1989).

This perhaps reflects a duality in the law – protecting what is described as the inherent dignity of humanity,[7] while simultaneously accepting a 'natural order' of bodily submission of women and children to their father or husband[8] and also to regulation by the state. It is part of the Enlightenment project[9] that freedom and power are properties of the human individual: that '[e]very man is naturally the proprietor of his own person, that natural right is derived from property in one's own person'.[10] While this philosophy is central to the modern democratic state, the use of the word 'man' to describe the human individual is not without significance.

In spite of this apparent freedom, the law is uncertain about supporting an unfettered reproductive liberty. Abortion for example remains a contested legal and policy space, and assisted reproduction has been restricted on a number of bases including marital status[11] (and therefore also on sexuality). This uneasy relationship is spelled out in the law's approach to surrogacy arrangements – arguably the most complex form of assisted reproduction fusing as it does gamete donation[12] which may or may not involve assisted reproductive technologies (ART) such as IVF, and parentage issues, including adoption.[13] In theoretical terms, surrogacy operates within a complex matrix of:

> devotion to scientific and medical progress for the relief of man's [*sic*] estate; private property, commerce, and free enterprise; and the primacy of personal autonomy and choice, including freedom of contract. [Yet they collide] with certain other notions of decency and propriety, pre-modern and quasi-religious, such as the sanctity of man's [*sic*] bodily integrity ...[14]

This chapter explores the theoretical arguments relating to justification of the legality and regulation of surrogacy. In particular, it looks at whether surrogacy

---

7 See, for example, R. James Fyfe, 'Dignity as Theory: Competing Conceptions of Human Dignity at the Supreme Court of Canada' (2007) *Saskatchewan Law Review* 1.

8 Ratna Kapur, 'Human Rights in the 21st Century: Take a Walk on the Dark Side' (2006) 28(4) *Sydney Law Review* 665.

9 Represented through the writing of political philosophers such as John Hobbes, *Leviathan* (1651); John Locke, *Second Treatise of Government* (1690); Jean Jacques Rousseau, *On the Social Contract* (1762); and Immanuel Kant, *Critique of Pure Reason* (1781).

10 Elizabeth Kingdom, 'Body Politics & Rights', in Jo Bridgeman and Susan Millns (eds), *Law and Body Politics: Regulating the Female Body* (Aldershot: Dartmouth Publishing, 1995), 1, 4.

11 *McBain v Victoria* [2000] FCA 1009 (28 July 2000).

12 'Gamete donation' may occur from the birth mother to the intended parents, from the intended mother to the birth mother, or from a third party man or woman.

13 Melissa Lane, 'Ethical Issues in Surrogacy Arrangements', in Rachael Leigh Cook, Shelley Day Sclater and Felicity Kaganas (eds), *Surrogate Motherhood: International Perspectives* (Oxford: Hart Publishing, 2003) 121, 124.

14 Leon R. Kass, above n. 4, 68.

should be regulated and why, using examples, primarily from Australia, to illustrate the issues. It considers the tensions within the theoretical justifications of surrogacy, starting with the liberal rights discourse that encompasses freedom of contract and personal choice. Such freedoms though occur not within a disembodied individualist framework but also within a particular social context and to this extent can be challenged based on women's long-standing structural disadvantage and deep-seated beliefs about women and motherhood. This is a strong theme in feminist critiques of surrogacy, which identify surrogacy as a touchstone feminist issue lying at the juncture of social constructions of women and individual autonomy.[15] All of these arguments, however, raise questions of Kantian morality, and the justification of humans as means rather than as ends in themselves. Accordingly, this chapter suggests a way to navigate these tensions through the application of a human rights based approach founded on the principle of dignity.

II. Reproduction and Freedom

For intending parents, starting a family is a freedom expected as a matter of course. Indeed for a coital conception, there is no question that for consenting adults the law will not interfere with this freedom. Even in terms of the regulation of surrogacy, Australian governments, for example, have recently assumed a principle of limited governmental intrusion into private lives.[16] To the extent that surrogacy arrangements raise a variety of concerns, however, this freedom is potentially challenged. As an example of profound government intervention, until 2010 in Queensland, surrogacy of any sort was criminalised.[17] In most jurisdictions internationally, surrogacy is regulated in one way or another. Supporters of surrogacy therefore face the task of elucidating what are the freedoms and rights of intending parents, and how they can be given legitimate expression in light of competing elements of parenthood – genetic, gestational and social[18] – and the interests of the child.

An individualist rights based approach to reproduction justifies surrogacy along with other reproductive transactions. It founds an argument in favour of

---

15 See, for example, Janice G. Raymond, *Women as Wombs: Reproductive Technologies and the Battle over Women's Freedom* (Melbourne: Spinifex Press, 1993); Natalie Fixmer-Oraiz, 'Speaking of Solidarity: Transnational Gestational Surrogacy and the Rhetorics of Reproductive (In)Justice' (2013) 34(3) *Frontiers: A Journal of Women Studies* 126.

16 Standing Committee of Attorneys-General Joint Working Group, *A Proposal for a National Model to Harmonise Regulation of Surrogacy* (2009).

17 *Surrogacy Parenthood Act* 1988 (Qld) s 3, repealed by the *Surrogacy Act* 2010 (Qld).

18 Enohumah Kingsley Osagie, 'Surrogacy: Whose Child Is It?' (2010) 1(11) *Journal of Medicine and Medical Sciences* 505.

recognition of reproductive rights based on the autonomy and self-determination of women and men to beget and rear children[19] – whether genetically related to them, or not.[20] Robertson, for example, finds that married couples have a right to procreate within a sexual relationship, and extrapolates from this to posit that other types of reproductive transaction designed to achieve the same end (that is, reproduction) are equally protected. While he is less certain about such rights for unmarried people, he gives qualified support here also.[21]

As might be expected, in jurisdictions such as US and Canada where there is constitutional recognition of personal rights and liberties, the case for reproductive rights and liberty is a lot stronger than in those jurisdictions such as the UK and Australia where there are no such protections.[22] Indeed it is difficult to say whether a 'procreative right' would, or could, be protected by the courts in Australia. The concept of rights or freedom to choose to have a child or not (including through surrogacy) did, however, shape the recommendation of the Queensland Parliamentary Committee on Surrogacy to decriminalise altruistic surrogacy[23] in Queensland.[24] In the Queensland case, the principle of liberty found its expression in the 'liberty of consenting adults to conceive a child and to parent'.[25] While the Queensland and other Australian legislation does not itself provide for a positive right of reproductive freedom, the regulatory framework surrounding altruistic surrogacy implicitly recognises this freedom.

Even within an approach that supports such freedom, state intervention might be justified through the application of the harm principle:[26] intervention in an otherwise private freedom, say through regulation, is justified to protect others – particularly the child and the birth mother – from ensuing harm. This approach can be seen in the 2009 Queensland amendments, where significant legislative change

19 John A. Robertson, 'Liberalism and the Limits of Procreative Liberty: A Response to My Critics' (1995) 52(1) *Washington and Lee Law Review* 233.

20 John A. Robertson, 'Embryos, Families and Procreative Liberty: The Legal Structure of the New Reproduction' (1986) 59 *Southern California Law Review* 939.

21 Ibid., 959–65.

22 Athena Liu, *Artificial Reproduction and Reproductive Rights* (Aldershot: Dartmouth Publishing, 1991), 34.

23 An altruistic surrogacy arrangement is one other than a commercial surrogacy arrangement, which is defined, for example, as one in which 'a person does not receive a reward or other material benefit or advantage (other than the reimbursement of the birth mother's surrogacy costs)' *Surrogacy Act* 2010 (Qld), s10.

24 Investigation into Altruistic Surrogacy Committee, Queensland Parliament, *Report* (2008), 18, 20. The Committee had been established to 'investigate and report to the Parliament on the possible decriminalisation and regulation of altruistic surrogacy in Queensland'. The recommendations resulted in the enactment of the *Surrogacy Act* 2010 (Qld).

25 Ibid., 22.

26 John Stuart Mill, 'On Liberty', in Alan Ryan (ed.), *On Liberty and the Subjection of Women* (London: Penguin, 2006; first published 1859), 16.

sought to '[balance] the prevention of harm and the protection of personal liberty in the creation of families through altruistic surrogacy'.[27]

Freedom to procreate is as much a tenet of liberalism as the concomitant freedom of contract. A foundational principle of classical contract theory and a pillar of the common law, freedom of contract supports the rights of both intended parents and the birth mother to enter into and enforce a surrogacy agreement. Robertson, for example, is of the view that contracts for surrogacy should not only be lawful, but should be upheld by the courts in favour of the intending parents whose liberty is otherwise at stake.[28]

In moving from reproductive freedom to freedom of contract, a range of additional rights potentially come into play and it is arguably this aspect of the justification for surrogacy that is most problematic. While contract is designed to facilitate the competition of the market, it is not generally equipped to balance power relations in an intimate dealing such as surrogacy. Additionally, such an arrangement brings into being a third party – the child – by definition not a party to negotiations. The question therefore becomes how the law navigates contractual rights and the fundamental principle of the dignity of the parties and their child.

The basis of Robertson's justification of surrogacy contracts was not applied in the judgement of the Supreme Court of New Jersey in the *Baby M*[29] case, where the surrogacy contract was struck down for breaching statutory prohibitions on adoption transactions involving money – in other words, the sale of children. In one sense however, the procreative liberty of the father (and by extension the intending parents) was protected, as guardianship of the child was granted to the genetic father in preference to the birth mother, on the grounds of the 'best interests of the child'.

The court in that case did not have to consider issues associated with the contract as between the parties, framing the issue instead as one concerning the illegality of the subject matter of the contract. Robertson's framework validates both the subject matter of the contract and the relationship of the parties as representing free expression of procreative liberty. He mentions the contracting parties' relationship only in passing. If, however, the transaction is examined instead based upon the parties' own freedom to contract, there are other issues that arise that centre around the meaning of the exercise of free choice. It is these issues – including the 'coercion of contract' involving taking advantage of a woman's need for money or an unwanted pregnancy[30] – that inform broader notions of reproductive justice.

In a more nuanced approach, London outlines some human rights dimensions of reproductive rights, identifying four inter-related principles:

---

27 Investigation into Altruistic Surrogacy Committee, above n. 23, foreword, 26. This reflects also the focus of the Standing Committee of Attorneys-General commitment to consistent regulation of altruistic surrogacy, above n. 14.

28 Robertson, above n. 20, 1013.

29 *In re Baby M*, 109 NJ 396 (1988).

30 Ibid., 422, 438–9.

1. choice (that is, women must have a choice about whether and when to bear a child);
2. privacy (that is, personal decisions about sexual intimacy and childbearing are private);
3. freedom from governmental interference (that is, the government should not interfere with a medical decision that is made by an individual in consultation with her physician); and
4. personal autonomy (that is, the freedom to make decisions about one's body is an essential component of autonomy).[31]

She differentiates reproductive rights from reproductive justice, arguing that such rights are necessary but not sufficient to achieve reproductive justice. In shifting from a legal to a political approach, reproductive justice has the capacity to consider the effect of power relations and differential resources, as well as 'barriers to enjoying those rights, such as racism, sexism, economic injustice, and immigration policies'.[32]

This explicit human rights based approach helps identify the shortcomings of Robertson's articulation of liberty. Robertson's argument canvasses the impacts of surrogacy arrangements on foetuses, on sperm and egg donors and on birth mothers, and he finds that none of the inconveniences or possible outcomes for these collaborators, or the resulting child, outweigh the procreative liberty of the intending parents. This of course fails to take into consideration anything but the paramountcy of individual rights – notably, those of the intending parents – and omits the social and emotional context of reproduction.

A critique of the parties' 'freedom' of contract arguably has two elements representing the dual nature of reproduction as individual and social.[33] First are the personal circumstances of the birth mother in relation to the intending parents. Poverty or the need for greater income may put a potential birth mother at a significant disadvantage vis-à-vis the intending parents. While payment for a surrogacy transaction raises the spectre of selling babies with all its attendant moral concerns, it also raises other issues including just how free the birth mother was to enter into the transaction. It is for this reason that in most Australian jurisdictions, only altruistic surrogacy is permitted.[34] The focus on altruism seeks to avoid the potential of a power imbalance in favour of the intending parents, on the assumption that a woman

31 Sarah London, 'Reproductive Justice: Developing a Lawyering Model' (2011) 13 *Berkeley Journal of African American Law and Policy* 71, 76.

32 Ibid., 77.

33 Rosalind Pollack Petchesky, 'Reproductive Freedom: Beyond "a Woman's Right to Choose"' (1980) 5(4) *Signs* 661.

34 *Surrogacy Act* 2010 (Qld); *Parentage Act* 2004 (ACT); *Surrogacy Act* 2010 (NSW); *Assisted Reproductive Treatment Act* 2008 (Vic) and *Status of Children Act* 1974 (Vic); *Family Relationships Act* 1975 (SA); *Surrogacy Act* 2008 (WA).

will genuinely give free consent to be a birth mother, as a true expression of her reproductive liberty, when not pursuing a financial motive.

Second, as highlighted in the approach of reproductive justice, are the broader social and economic conditions surrounding a woman's decision to become a surrogate. This is intrinsically a gender issue as it is women alone who are biologically capable of gestation. That women, to a greater extent than men, tend to suffer economic disadvantage highlights the economic vulnerability of potential gestational mothers.[35] It is of note also that becoming a gestational mother is becoming increasingly attractive to women from developing countries such as India and Thailand.[36] In the US context, it has been noted that African American women have historically been preferred as gestational mothers.[37] These examples indicate that racial and social background of gestational mothers is also a relevant context, one that is particularly pronounced in the cross-cultural context of international surrogacy.[38] Through the lens of contract law, social conditions such as these that embody a significant power imbalance become irrelevant once a contract becomes binding, opening the potential for exploitation by the powerful parties with the law on their side. Contract law assumes a free 'market', whereas, in fact, systemic disadvantage skews the 'market' in favour of the commissioning parents. Such a view puts surrogacy at the heart of the ongoing issue of women's equality in employment opportunity and wages: to the extent that (commercial) surrogacy may be undertaken for financial reasons,[39] if women were to have equal opportunity in work and conditions, there would be no need to resort to surrogacy as a means of financial support.

This second issue of the structural inequality of women in general has implications for reproductive liberty and power relations within surrogacy

---

35 Australian Council of Social Service, *Poverty in Australia* (ACOSS Paper 194 (2012)). It has been noted, however, (in the US context) that it is not the poorest women who enter into surrogacy arrangements. See Jennifer Damelio and Kelly Sorensen, 'Enhancing Autonomy in Paid Surrogacy' (2008) 22(5) *Bioethics* 269, 274.

36 Stanford University, *Surrogate Motherhood in India: Understanding and Evaluating the Effects of Gestational Surrogacy on Women's Health and Rights* http://www.stanford.edu/group/womenscourage/Surrogacy/economics.html, accessed 6 February 2015; Alison Bailey, 'Reconceiving Surrogacy: Toward a Reproductive Justice Account of Indian Surrogacy' (2011) 26(4) *Hypatia* 715. See also in this volume Norman Witzleb and Anurag Chawla, 'Surrogacy in India: A Globalised Demand meets (a lack of) local laws'.

37 Damien Riggs and Clemence Due, 'Gay Men, Race Privilege and Surrogacy in India' (2010) 22 *Outskirts: Feminisms along the Edge* http://www.outskirts.arts.uwa.edu.au/volumes/volume-22/riggs, accessed 20 June, 2014.

38 See, for example, Nadimpally Sarojini, 'Globalisation of Birth Markets: A Case Study of Assisted Reproductive Technologies in India' (2011) 7 *Globalization and Health* 27; Centre for Social Research, 'Surrogate Motherhood: Ethical or Commercial' (March 2012) *India Women in Leadership* http://womenleadership.in/Csr/SurrogacyReport.pdf, accessed 6 February 2015.

39 See, for example, Stanford University, above n. 36.

arrangements in particular – and therefore for the so-called 'freedoms' of the liberal justification of surrogacy.

III. Structural Inequality of Women

Structural inequality of women is a long-standing feature of society.[40] In the Western liberal tradition, in spite of the Enlightenment project and its focus on individual rights and freedoms, women remain constructed in ways that disadvantage them politically,[41] economically,[42] in the workplace[43] and within the family.[44]

By and large women, including at law, remain constrained by their identification with sexuality and procreation.[45] Such attitudes reflect an essentialist notion of what it means to be a woman, including so-called 'biological truths' about women as nurturers and natural child-rearers.[46] These attitudes perpetuate gender stereotypes, including heteronormative hierarchies that harm all people.

While economic disadvantage is a measurable outcome of systemic discrimination, what is less tangible is the deep cultural expectations of womanhood – in particular of motherhood as the ultimate expression of womanhood. By men and women internalising the elevated status of motherhood, women may be oppressed into believing that personal success, fulfilment and happiness will only happen through motherhood. Such a universal stereotype results in discrimination against

---

40 See, for example, Shulamith Firestone, *The Dialectic of Sex: The Case for Feminist Revolution* (London: Paladin, 1972); Okin, above n. 6; Carol Smart, *Feminism and the Power of Law* (London: Routledge, 1989); Raymond, above n. 15.

41 In spite of being 50.2 per cent of the Australian population, women have an overall level of representation in Australian parliaments at only 30 per cent (Joy McCann and Janet Wilson, *Representation of Women in Australian Parliaments* (Parliamentary Library Background Note (7 March 2012)).

42 On average, Australian women working full-time earn 17.4 per cent less than men working full-time (Australian Bureau of Statistics, Cat 6302.0, *Average Weekly Earnings – Trend* (February 2012)) and female graduates in Australia in 2012 earned $5,000 per annum less than male graduates on entering the workforce (Graduate Careers Australia, *Employment and Salary Outcomes of Recent Higher Education Graduates* (December 2012)).

43 In Australia, women constitute 70.0 per cent of all part-time employees, 35.3 per cent of all full-time employees (Australian Bureau of Statistics, Cat 6202.0, Labour Force, Australia, Status by Sex – Trend Table 1, (June 2012)) and 55.1 per cent of all casual employees (Australian Bureau of Statistics, Cat 6359.0, Forms of Employment (November 2012)).

44 Belinda Hewitt et al., Men's Engagement in Shared Care and Domestic Work in Australia (Office for Women, Department of Families, Housing, Community Services and Indigenous Affairs (2011)).

45 Okin, above n. 6.

46 Belinda Bennett, 'Reproductive Technology, Public Policy and Single Motherhood' (2000) 22(4) *Sydney Law Review* 625.

women who do not have children and reduces women who do, to the essentialist role of child-rearing.[47] In the cross-cultural context, Western cultural expectations of womanhood intersect with the construction of race and the implications of poverty.[48] Thus, some critics of the growing 'globalised fertility market' find it implicitly exploitative.[49]

If the cultural connotation of motherhood is indeed part of women's oppression, the question might be asked whether surrogacy can be justified – for intended mothers, genetic mothers or birth mothers. Raymond, for example, suggests that allowing surrogacy at all simply upholds essentialist notions of what it is to be a woman and that even an altruistic surrogacy arrangement between family members plays on social expectations of sisterly love to give freely what might be considered the greatest gift of all.[50] On this basis, she argues, it should be opposed.

Radin, on the other hand, points out the inherent tension within such a feminist critique as it denies the possibility of motherhood (or surrogacy) as an expression of a woman's autonomy and her individualism.[51] Constraining the way in which women engage with their world is not simply because systemic discrimination exists. In contrast to Raymond's approach, this opens the possibility for motherhood as part of the fabric of women's experiences. It allows for women to be mothers – gestational, genetic or birth – as an expression of their own view of womanhood and of altruisim. It also allows for an economic basis for motherhood, in terms of commercial surrogacy.

In addition, there is an increasing literature into the experience of gestational mothers which demonstrates that, overall, most have a positive surrogacy experience.[52] Indeed many act as a gestational mother more than once. This supports the idea that the arrangement need not be exploitative, and can in fact be

47 Elizabeth S. Scott, 'Surrogacy and the Politics of Commodification' (2009) 72 *Law and Contemporary Problems* 109.

48 The educational and employment backgrounds of Indian gestational mothers surveyed by the Centre for Social Research revealed a largely uneducated and poor cohort, most of whom became surrogates because of poverty. Above n. 38.

49 Jyotsna Agnihotri Gupta, 'Reproductive Biocrossings: Indian Egg Donors and Surrogates in the Globalized Fertility Market' (2012) 5(1) *International Journal of Feminist Approaches to Bioethics* 25. See also discussions in Alison Bailey, 'Reconceiving Surrogacy: Toward a Reproductive Justice Account of Indian Surrogacy' (2011) 26(4) *Hypatia*, 715; Mary Keyes, 'Cross-Border Surrogacy Agreements' (2012) 26 *Australian Journal of Family Law* 28.

50 Raymond, above n. 15.

51 Margaret Jane Radin, 'What, If Anything, Is Wrong with Baby Selling?' (1995) 26 *Pacific Law Journal* 135.

52 Vasanti Jadva et al., 'Surrogacy: The Experiences of Surrogate Mothers' (2003) 18(10) *Human Reproduction* 2196; Helena Ragone, 'Chasing the Blood Tie: Surrogate Mothers, Adoptive Mothers and Fathers' (1996) 23(2) *American Ethnologist* 352; Elly Teman, *Birthing a Mother: The Surrogate Body and Pregnant Self* (California: University of California Press, 2010); Karen Busby and Delaney Vun, 'Revisiting the Handmaid's

a form of self-expression. Likewise, overseas gestational mothers are reported to gain a sense of economic empowerment through their own surrogacy experience. The benefits of this are very real to those who otherwise experience poverty.[53]

In the face of these experiences, and in contrast with anachronistic beliefs concerning a woman's place in society and the family, contemporary laws in the West appear at first glance to represent a more enlightened and egalitarian view towards gender – though as Fixmer-Oraiz argues, not necessarily in the transnational context.[54] In Australia the *Sex Discrimination Act* 1984 (Cth),[55] for example, seeks to give effect to the *Convention on the Elimination of All Forms of Discrimination Against Women*.[56] In doing so, it proscribes discrimination based on grounds of sex, marital status, pregnancy or potential pregnancy or breastfeeding, and promotes recognition and acceptance within the community of the principle of the equality of men and women.[57]

Yet the *McBain*[58] case, in 2000, highlights the extent to which women remain constructed by law and how the law impacts upon their identity in terms of reproduction.[59] In that case, Victorian legislation precluded single women from accessing ART services and the doctor providing such services sought clarification as to whether the state law required him to refuse to treat Ms Meldrum, a single woman not living in a de facto relationship, or whether he was instead bound by the Commonwealth *Sex Discrimination Act* that required him *not* to refuse service to a woman based on her marital status.

While the matter was decided in favour of the Commonwealth legislation, the fact that the issue arose at all, is telling of ongoing attitudes concerning women and their bodies vis-à-vis reproduction. Indeed similar issues were predicted to arise in Queensland in relation to surrogacy following a 2012 announcement by the Queensland Government that the *Surrogacy Act* 2010 (Qld) would be amended so as to criminalise surrogacy for single women, same-sex couples and women in a de facto relationship of less than two years' standing.[60]

Tale: Feminist Theory Meets Empirical Research on Surrogate Motherhood' (2010) 26 *Canadian Journal of Family Law* 13.

53 See, for example, Stanford University, above n. 36.

54 Fixmer-Oraiz, above n. 15.

55 These principles are now part of the Human Rights and Anti-Discrimination Bill 2012 (Cth) which, if enacted, will replace the *Sex Discrimination Act* 1984 (Cth).

56 *Convention on the Elimination of All Forms of Discrimination against Women*, 1249 UNTS 13 (opened for signature 18 December 1979, entered into force 3 September 1981).

57 *Sex Discrimination Act* 1984 (Cth), ss3(b), (d).

58 *McBain v Victoria* [2000] FCA 1009 (28 July 2000).

59 Bennett, above n. 46.

60 Queensland, *Parliamentary Debates* (21 June 2012), 993 (Jarrod Bleijie), 994; Pip Trowse and Malcolm K. Smith, 'Surrogacy Laws in Queensland: One Step Forward and Two Steps Back?' (2012) 32 *The Queensland Lawyer* 123. The Queensland government has since withdrawn this proposal.

Regardless of whether this proposal ever becomes law, the fact of its pronouncement is sufficient to call into question the way in which women's bodies remain politicised and subject to sanction and control by the law. It is widely accepted that women and their sexuality (and those of diverse sexualities) have moved beyond the concept of *homo sacer*; and are now 'equal to men' in terms of international human rights instruments and national legislation, having the same dignity the law purports to afford all humans. Yet if this is the case, how can it be that there are serious and legitimate calls for the subjugation of women and the exclusion of the other through control of their bodies and constriction of their liberties? This argument would include control over surrogacy as well as access to ART.

The law's ostensible foundation of dignity for the person is represented, for example, through its condemnation of slavery as a form of property in a human or human body. The principle of dignity finds expression elsewhere in the law relating to the human body – for example in the criminal offence of interfering with a corpse. In contrast, regulatory constraints on surrogacy reflect the long-standing tendency of the law to regulate and control women's bodies. Originally the property of her father or husband, control over women's bodies now manifests through regulation of reproductive autonomy – notably abortion, ART and surrogacy. Lying at the heart of this is the social construction of woman as mother within a heteronormative nuclear family context. As mother, particularly when pregnant, a woman loses her individual identity and instead becomes two people – mother and child – each capable of being imbued with attendant rights – if not human rights, then rights in some other guise.[61] For a pregnant woman, her rights are often deferred to considerations about her foetus.

Robertson's approach to procreative freedom in one sense allows for the perspective of the birth mother – he acknowledges that restricting surrogacy may limit the rights of women who wish only to gestate. However, where his argument focuses on the procreative freedom of the intending parents, his view implicitly adopts a disembodied and individualistic approach to the surrogacy transaction. Consequently and reflecting the wider context of the treatment of women before the law, the birth mother as a person is all but invisible, thus denying her presence as an active participant in the process. The subject matter of the contract is the child and the claims of the intending parents on that person exclude the embodied reality of the child's birth mother.

In formulating the terms of a surrogacy contract, the potential for provisions constraining the activities and freedom – in fact the bodily autonomy – of the birth mother is real. To the extent that such provisions would be enforceable, the

61 Anne Morris and Susan Nott, 'The Law's Engagement with Pregnancy', in Bridgeman and Millns, above n. 10, 53. See, for example, Crimes Amendment (Zoe's Law) Bill 2013 (No 2) NSW that seeks to create the specific crime of harm to or destruction of a 'foetus of a pregnant woman'. Its passage through the upper house was delayed because of concerns of the impact of such a law on the rights of the mother.

mother's rights and her very physical being are again subordinated not only to the foetus she carries, but to the procreative liberties of the intending parents.

On the other side of bodily autonomy, one has to ask about the procreative liberty of the birth mother. It is certainly important to recognise personal and systemic inequality that might challenge the assumptions of a free association between the parties to a surrogacy arrangement. However, it is surely possible that the birth mother may indeed seek to exercise her own procreative liberty through bearing a child that she will not rear. It would be wrong to suggest that her agency is necessarily compromised in making this choice.

In this way, both a liberal conception of surrogacy and a feminist critique fall short of giving full expression to the embodied experience of the birth mother who need not be considered a victim within the matrix of surrogacy relationships. The question then becomes one of determining a concept capable of mediating two objectives: on the one hand, the best of liberal freedoms for all parties to the surrogacy arrangement and, on the other, the important and legitimate feminist critique of surrogacy as another means of restricting women's bodily autonomy. Herein lies the potential for a human rights based approach grounded in dignity.

IV. Human Dignity

The common law's encounter with bodily transactions has generally sought to uphold the dignity of the person. This has been expressed traditionally in terms of the rule that there is no property in the human body[62] (albeit this rule is not absolute).[63] The law's overarching aim to uphold the dignity of the person aligns with Kant's essential moral premise that humans are ends in themselves, and the corollary that treatment of humans as means to ends is immoral and cannot be justified.[64]

Dignity has likewise formed the foundation of the primacy of the individual at law and the contours of attendant human rights. Locke's views on property, selfhood and the individual[65] and Mill's arguments for constraining the exercise

62 *Exelby v Handyside* (1749) 2 East PC 652; *R v Sharpe* (1857) Dears & Bell 160, 163; *Williams v Williams* (1882) 20 Ch. D. 659, 664; *Moore v Regents of California*, 793 P 2d 479 (1990); *Colavito v New York Organ Donor Network Inc*, 8 NY 3d 43 (2006).

63 See, for example, *Doodeward v Spence* (1908) 6 CLR 406; *Re the estate of the late Mark Edwards* [2011] NSWSC 478.

64 Immanuel Kant, *Fundamental Principles of the Metaphysic of Morals* (trans. Thomas Kingsmill Abbott) (University Park, PA: Pennsylvania State University Press, 2010; first published 1785).

65 John Locke, 'Second Treatise on Government', in Peter Laslett (ed.), *Two Treatises of Government* (Cambridge: Cambridge University Press, 1963; first published 1690).

of power against citizens,[66] and against the subjugation of women,[67] are but two examples of Enlightenment thinking that is recognised as informing the rights discourse evident in the common law. These ideas are embodied in common law principles of autonomy and self-determination of the person and their body, corresponding with a Kantian interpretation of what dignity entails.[68]

In a contemporary context, dignity underpins the human rights framework – of which the *Universal Declaration of Human Rights*[69] ('UDHR') remains the fulcrum – and justifies protection of human interests.[70] While Article 16 of the UDHR provides specifically for a right to family, the focus here is instead on the application of the principle of dignity – and its concomitant expressions of autonomy and self-determination – as a means to navigate the tensions within the different theoretical positions supporting or against surrogacy.

The first challenge is to clarify the issues. In terms of an analysis based on the role of parties to a surrogacy transaction as means to an end or ends in themselves, the outcome will depend on how the transaction is framed. On the one hand, the surrogacy arrangement can be understood as having as its end the creation of a new life – the child(ren). On this interpretation, those who participate genetically and gestationally might be considered means to this end.

On the other hand, the arrangement may be regarded as furthering the end of generating a new family: recognising the social aspect of parentage. In another vein, it could be suggested that the end for some surrogate mothers might be financial gain. In these characterisations, both the child itself, and the body of the gestational mother, could be considered the means.

However, there seems no reason why the arrangement should not be framed more broadly, particularly as moral objections centre on all three elements of the 'deconstructed' role of parent.

In respect of the children of surrogacy, there is no clear reason why wishing to raise a child of itself renders the child simply a means to the intended parents' end. Any planned pregnancy could be charged with the same intent, as of course would adoption. In her analysis of Kant's formula for humanity, Papadaki points out the problems with Kant's dichotomy between rational beings with absolute intrinsic value and mere objects with contingent value.[71] It is difficult to situate a foetus in either of these categories: as either a fully agentic being or a mere thing. In any event, it seems acceptable to generate the potential for a new life as an end in itself. The fact that this might occur within the context of surrogacy does not

---

66 John Stuart Mill, 'On Liberty', in Alan Ryan (ed.), *On Liberty and the Subjection of Women* (London: Penguin, 2006; first published 1859), 1.

67 Ibid., 132.

68 Kant, above n. 64.

69 UNGA Res. 217A (III), UN Doc. A/810 (10 December 1948).

70 Fyfe, above n. 7, 7.

71 Lina Papadaki, 'Abortion and Kant's Formula of Humanity' (2012) 22 *Humana Mente Journal of Philosophical Studies* 145.

detract from that life having come into being and therefore being accorded dignity through its very existence as a human.

In all jurisdictions, the best interests of the child is a fundamental tenet of surrogacy regulation and this appears to embody the understanding of the importance of upholding the dignity of the child. In Australia, for example, the national harmonisation principles formulated in 2009 recite the protection of children as the primary norm,[72] and this is reflected in Australian statutes.[73] Likewise, US courts have been vocal in their support of the principle of the dignity of the child in considering surrogacy arrangements. The court in the *Baby M* case canvassed New Jersey statutes that vested decisions for child custody in the state based on the child's best interests,[74] as well as public policy that 'the child's best interests shall determine custody'.[75]

While the court in the *Baby M* case differentiated between cases of adoption and surrogacy, the underlying principle seems the same: that neither transaction is intrinsically contrary to the dignity of the child, provided safeguards are in place to ensure that the child's best interests are paramount. The moral status of other means of starting a family is not called into question as it is with surrogacy. Parentage of children as a means of upholding the dignity of the child has long been effectively regulated by the state in other contexts.

What is perceived as more complex, and what was discussed at length in the *Baby M* case, is the payment of money for surrogacy. This raises further issues concerning commodification of the child and the attendant concerns that this converts the baby into property[76] thus interfering with its intrinsic worth as a human. On the other hand, as was argued in the *Baby M* case, payment for surrogacy can be framed instead in terms of payment for services of the gestational mother rather than for the purchase of a human child.

Whilst a difficult issue to determine, the fact of payment need not invalidate arguments in support of surrogacy per se. Indeed if the involved parties' human rights are protected, the fact of payment is just one factor. Alternatively, payment may become relevant in terms of the scope of surrogacy regulation. This has occurred in the Australian context where recent debate has presumed altruistic surrogacy as the sole framework for consideration.[77] On this model, surrogacy itself remains lawful, though constrained.

The commercialisation debate does, however, raise issues concerning the dignity of the birth mother. She may simply be a means to the ends of the intended parents, thus rendering the arrangement immoral on a Kantian basis. Or, in exercising her

---

72 Standing Committee of Attorneys-General Joint Working Group, above n. 16.

73 See, for example, *Surrogacy Act* 2010 (Qld), s22(2)(a).

74 *In re Baby M*, 109 NJ 396 (1988), 426.

75 *In re Baby M*, 109 NJ 396 (1988), 434.

76 Radin, above n. 51; Scott, above n. 47.

77 Jenni Millbank, 'The New Surrogacy Parentage Laws in Australia: Cautious Regulation or "25 Brick Walls"?' (2011) 35 *Melbourne University Law Review* 1.

procreative capacity she may simply be providing a service – whether paid or not – thus existing wholly within her own sense of self. Analysis of the birth mother's position occurs at the intersection of the liberal rights arguments in support of freedom to enter surrogacy arrangements,[78] and those of radical feminists who argue against surrogacy in all its forms, as an inherently exploitative practice.[79]

In terms of reproductive freedom, the birth mother is entitled to enter into a surrogacy arrangement as an expression of her reproductive choice and personal autonomy.[80] What this rights discourse lacks, however, is both the embodiment of the birth mother and the social context of motherhood.

Liberal rights, grounded in Enlightenment thinking, focus on rational, agentic, disembodied (male) decision-makers in the public sphere. As Pateman argues, 'liberal principles have not been universalised to extend to women in the public sphere without raising the acute problem of the patriarchal structure of private life'.[81] She points out that 'women's personal circumstances are structured by public factors such as rape, abortion, the status of wives, child care policies and welfare allowances, sexual division of labour in the home and in the workplace'.[82] It is these factors that together impact upon a woman's decision to have a baby – including whether to enter a surrogacy arrangement.

Feldman points out that 'to develop agency, a person must be able to assent to, or refuse, sex and pregnancy, before and after the fact'.[83] Assent and refusal are preconditions for agency that are otherwise assumed by Kant in his analysis of dignity. If women, owing to structural discrimination and disadvantage, are not in an agentic position, then the concept of surrogacy cannot be upheld on a Kantian basis. It results, as the court in the *Baby M* case found, in exploitation of the birth mother.

Part of structural discrimination and the alienation of women from Enlightenment conceptualisation of the agentic individual relates to the objectification of women's bodies, reducing them to goods. On this reading, through a surrogacy contract, a woman 'transforms her uterus into an "empty vessel" and alienates "the unique physiological, emotional and creative capacity of her body, that is to say, of *herself as a woman*"'.[84] The implications of this are an absence of dignity.

---

78 Such as Robertson, above n. 20.

79 Such as Raymond, above n. 15.

80 London, above n. 31, 76.

81 Carole Pateman, *The Disorder of Women* (Cambridge: Polity Press, 1989), 129.

82 Ibid., 131.

83 S. Feldman, 'From Occupied Bodies to Pregnant Persons: How Kantian Ethics Should Treat Pregnancy and Abortion', in Jane Kneller and Sidney Axinn (eds), *Autonomy and Community: Readings in Contemporary Kantian Social Philosophy* (New York: State University of New York Press, 1998), 265, 275.

84 Rosalind Pollack Petchesky, 'The Body as Property: A Feminist Re-Vision', in Faye Ginsberg and Rayna Rapp (eds), *Conceiving the New World Order: The Global Politics of Reproduction* (Berkeley, CA: University of California Press, 1995), 395.

While the liberal arguments seem to omit the social aspects of a full consideration of the dignity of the birth mother, so too do these feminist arguments omit the individual considerations of autonomy and self-determination. As with considerations about the child, none of these arguments necessarily preclude the surrogacy arrangement per se. Instead, through the lens of dignity, the surrogacy transaction can meet the objections of the radical feminist critique.

Structural disadvantage and the social nature of pregnancy and motherhood, as well as the individual circumstances of the birth mother, are central to upholding her autonomy in entering into a surrogacy arrangement. This requires not freedom of contract in an absolute sense, but a well-regulated approach that considers the genuine desires of the birth mother and upholds her bodily integrity. Apart from the best interests of the child, it is the autonomy and self-determination of the birth mother that must be paramount. This combination of desires and self-determination are implicit in the concept of dignity and justify it as a measure of a just arrangement.

The risks borne by the birth mother – physical, potentially emotional and economic – on any measure outweigh the investment of the intending parents. While the latter may indeed have their own reproductive liberty at stake through contribution of a gamete or DNA, the personal cost to the birth mother still puts her at a disadvantage in the transaction overall. The justice of such a situation must be, in the event of a conflict, to uphold the rights of the party with the least power. This would in the first instance be the child – without the means to speak for itself. While the 'best interests of the child' is the foundation of existing regulatory frameworks,[85] dispute tends to occur around the rights of the intending parents and birth mother. In this scenario, the party with the least power and, on this analysis the most to lose including in terms of dignity, is the birth mother. These rights are derived from the principle of maintaining her dignity.

V. Conclusion

The legal discourse surrounding surrogacy traverses considerable ground in forming arguments for and against its legality and its regulation. Fears about commodifying humans – either babies or their birth mothers – informs much of the debate, stemming from the common law's long-standing characterisation of the essentiality of humanity as other than property and its wrestle with the desirability of enforcing transactions involving personal service. In philosophical terms, Kant's code, requiring honour of humans as ends in themselves, supports this view and the view of an underlying dignity in the human that is, or should, remain inviolable.

---

85 Although this foundation has its own problems, as discussed in Deborah Dempsey, 'Donor, Father or Parent' (2004) 18(1) *International Journal of Law Policy and the Family* 76.

In light of the transactional nature of surrogacy, however, the law of contract has intervened and the question has become one of what framework should be adopted to support or deny the legality of a contract to procreate. While the human rights framework may take the debate so far, it is hard to justify a prioritisation of rights within a contractual framework, where that omits the autonomy of the birth mother. This is particularly so in light of feminist concerns about the objectification of women and their social construction as mothers, against a background of systemic discrimination leaving women as a whole at an economic and social disadvantage.

In light of the issues at stake in a surrogacy arrangement against the background of the possible social or economic inequality of the birth mother, the challenge then becomes how to accommodate parties' interests in a way that ensures their dignity. The answer lies in effective regulation of surrogacy to address the individual circumstances of the child and the birth mother, while also respecting the intending parents.

There seems no theoretical basis for an outright prohibition on surrogacy itself that cannot be overcome without due concern for the individual and social circumstances of the parties. However, without such concern, the transaction runs the risk of undermining key principles of autonomy and dignity – cornerstones of human rights.

Chapter 4

Through the Looking-Glass: A Proposal for National Reform of Australia's Surrogacy Legislation

Tammy Johnson*

I. Introduction

Surrogacy has been the subject of intermittent academic investigation and law reform since the early 1980s.[1] Notwithstanding these reforms, Australian

---

* Assistant Professor, Bond University, PhD candidate, Queensland University of Technology. This chapter has benefited greatly from the comments of Associate Professor Paula Gerber, Monash University Law Faculty; Ms Katie O'Byrne, Doughty Street Chambers; Assistant Professor Louise Parsons, Bond University and the two anonymous reviewers. The author also thanks her research assistant, Lesley Brown, for her endless support and assistance.

1 See, for example, New South Wales Law Reform Commission, *Artificial Conception: Surrogate Motherhood: Australian Public Opinion*, Research Report No 2 (1987); New South Wales Law Reform Commission, *Review of the Adoption of Children Act* 1965 *(NSW)*, Report No 81 (1997); New South Wales Law Reform Commission, *Artificial Conception: Surrogate Motherhood*, Report LRC 60 (1988); Special Committee, Queensland Government, *Report of the Special Committee Appointed by the Queensland Government to Enquire into the Laws Relating to Artificial Insemination, In Vitro Fertilization and Other Related Matters* Volumes I and II (March 1984); Investigation into Altruistic Surrogacy Committee, Queensland Parliament, *Report* (October 2008); ACT Law Reform Commission, *Substitute Parentage Agreements*, Report No 20 (2003); South Australia Legislative Council, Parliament of South Australia, *Report of the Working Party on In Vitro Fertilisation and Artificial Insemination by Donor*, Report (1984); South Australia Legislative Council, Parliament of South Australia, *Select Committee on Artificial Insemination by Donor, In-Vitro Fertilization and Embryo Transfer procedures and related matters in South Australia*, Report (1987); South Australia Legislative Council, Social Development Committee, Parliament of South Australia, *Inquiry into Gestational Surrogacy*, Report 26 (2007); Victorian Law Reform Commission Report, *Assisted Reproductive Technology & Adoption: Final Report* (2007); Western Australia, Parliament, *Report of the Committee Appointed by the Western Australian Government to Enquire into the Social, Legal and Ethical Issues relating to In Vitro Fertilisation and its Supervision* (1986); Standing Committee on Legislation, Parliament of Western Australia, *Report* 12 *in Relation to the Surrogacy Bill* 2007 (2008).

surrogacy laws remain inconsistent. Surrogacy persists as 'an issue with which our community continues to struggle'[2] and Australia has a 'fragmented, illogical and dysfunctional'[3] surrogacy regime. For parties seeking surrogacy intrastate, interstate or internationally, the applicable legislation is often hard to identify, obscure and difficult to navigate. While there may be constitutional hurdles to overcome,[4] the aim of a national model would be to bridge the legislative gaps whilst still respecting the autonomy and minimising the risk of harm for all parties involved.

The purpose of this chapter is twofold: to demonstrate that the existing surrogacy regime in Australia is in need of reform and to provide a framework for a national model. Certain key aspects of current surrogacy legislation in Australia are examined in order to illustrate inconsistencies between states and territories. The chapter then develops recommendations for the framework of a national model for reform.

II. A Chequerboard of Regulation: Australia's Surrogacy Legislation

> Alice stood without speaking, looking out in all directions over the country – and a most curious country it was … 'I declare it's marked out just like a large chess-board!' Alice said at last.[5]
>
> *Through the Looking-Glass and What Alice Found There*

Australia's approach to the regulation of surrogacy is fragmented. The separate regimes in the states and territories create a chequerboard of regulation in which the families involved in surrogacy are reduced to little more than pawns in the game of procreative chess. Aside from an almost[6] uniform prohibition of commercial surrogacy, there is little, if any, consistency between the states and territories. These differing approaches provide only a warped reflection of each other; a reflection that does not fit with reality.

Eligibility to engage in surrogacy varies significantly between jurisdictions and there are even provisions which make it illegal for Australian residents to enter

2 Lindy Willmott, 'Surrogacy: Ill-Conceived Rights' (2002) 10(2) *Journal of Law and Medicine* 198.

3 Lindy Willmott, 'Surrogacy: ART's Forgotten Child' (2006) 29(2) *UNSW Law Journal* 229.

4 In *Lowe & Barry and Anor* [2011] FamCA 625 (5 August 2011), [20] Benjamin J noted that the Commonwealth Government lacks the constitutional power to enact national legislation regulating surrogacy. Therefore referral of power by the states or agreement to enact consistent legislation would be essential in order to implement a national surrogacy framework.

5 Lewis Carroll, *The Complete Illustrated Lewis Carroll* (Ware: Wordsworth Editions, 1998), 150.

6 The Northern Territory is silent on both altruistic and commercial surrogacy.

into surrogacy agreements interstate or overseas.[7] The following brief account of the current legislative regimes provides insight into the disparity of approaches.

A. Smoke and Mirrors: Key Aspects of Australia's Surrogacy Legislation

The following key issues in surrogacy regulation have been selected for detailed consideration in each jurisdiction:[8]

- enforceability of surrogacy agreements;
- eligibility of parties to enter into surrogacy agreements;
- territorial restraint;
- offences; and
- parentage.

For convenience, two tables appear at the end of this chapter. Table 4.1 provides a synopsis of the current surrogacy legislation across Australia, while Table 4.2 contains a summary of the current parentage legislation in Australia. This discussion of Australian surrogacy legislation serves to highlight the inconsistencies between jurisdictions and to create the backdrop for the proposed national model. Millbank notes that in the 'new era of openness to surrogacy, the twin themes of 'altruism' and 'national harmony' dominated'.[9] On the theme of national harmony it has been established that inconsistent regulation fails to provide the 'greatest net benefit to the community',[10] which in turn undermines society's capacity to achieve desirable social and economic goals.[11] In order to achieve the greatest net benefit to the community, legislation should be clear, concise and consistent. The national model outlined in this chapter strives to achieve these objectives while not being unduly prescriptive on those it seeks to regulate.[12]

---

7 For an analysis of these criminal law provisions, see Anita Stuhmcke's Chapter 5 in this volume.

8 The Northern Territory has been excluded from this analysis because it is silent on the issue of surrogacy.

9 Jenni Millbank, 'The New Surrogacy Parentage Laws in Australia: Caution Regulation or "25 Brick Walls"?' (2011) 35(1) *Melbourne University Law Review* 165, 176.

10 Gary Banks, Chairman, Productivity Commission, 'Challenges for Australia in Regulatory Reform' (Paper presented at the Conference on Regulation Reform Management and Scrutiny of Legislation, NSW State Parliament, Sydney, 10 July 2001), 2.

11 Ibid., 1.

12 Ibid., 2.

1. Enforceability of surrogacy agreements

Unlike in some countries such as South Africa,[13] Georgia[14] and the Ukraine,[15] where surrogacy agreements are legally enforceable, the Australian legislation deems all agreements to be unenforceable, save for payment of the surrogate's reasonable[16] or actual[17] expenses.

New South Wales, Queensland and Tasmania each place conditions on these payments. While New South Wales permits parties to enter into either pre-conception or post-conception surrogacy agreements,[18] the legislation only allows claims for payment or reimbursement of the surrogate's expenses where the agreement was entered into prior to conception.[19] In Queensland the agreement must also be entered into prior to conception,[20] but recovery of the surrogate's reasonable expenses is also contingent upon the surrogate relinquishing the child to the intended parents[21] and consenting to transfer of parentage.[22] Similarly, Tasmania permits only pre-conception agreements[23] and the surrogate's right to reimbursement of expenses is contingent upon the consent of her and her partner (if any) to the transfer of parentage.[24]

In the 2012 case of *LWV & another v LMH*,[25] the Queensland Children's Court had an opportunity to examine the issue of conception in the context of a surrogacy agreement. As the Queensland legislation only permits pre-conception surrogacy agreements, but does not provide a definition of 'conception', the court was required to define conception and establish when it had occurred. On the facts of *LWV*, an embryo was created in 2008, a surrogacy agreement entered into in April 2011, and the embryo implanted into the surrogate in July 2011. The resulting child was born on 22 March 2012. In considering whether it was

13 *Children's Act* 2005 (South Africa), s 297 provides that the surrogate has no parental rights or right of contact in relation to the child born and that the surrogate is 'obliged' to surrender the child to the intended parents as soon as reasonably possible after the birth.

14 *Law of Georgia on Health Protection* (Georgia) Article 143 provides that the surrogate retains no parental rights in respect of the child.

15 *Family Code of Ukraine* (VVR), 2002, # 21-2 (Ukraine) Article 123(2) recognises the intended parents as the legal parents of the child from the time of conception.

16 See *Surrogacy Act* 2010 (NSW), s 7(1); *Surrogacy Act* 2010 (Qld), s 11(1); *Parentage Act* 2004 (ACT), s 26(3)(d); *Surrogacy Act* 2008 (WA), s 6.

17 *Assisted Reproductive Treatment Act* 2008 (Vic), s 44(2).

18 *Surrogacy Act* 2010 (NSW), s 5(1)(b) permits a woman who is already pregnant to enter into a surrogacy agreement. This type of arrangement is defined as a 'post-conception surrogacy agreement'.

19 Ibid., s 6(2).

20 *Surrogacy Act* 2010 (Qld), ss 7(1)(a), (22)(2)(e)(iv).

21 Ibid., s 15(2)(b)(i).

22 Ibid., s 15(2)(b)(ii).

23 *Surrogacy Act* 2012 (Tas), s 5.

24 Ibid., s 10(2)(c).

25 [2012] QChC 26.

appropriate to grant parentage orders, Judge Clare SC had to be satisfied that *all*[26] the requirements of section 22 of the *Surrogacy Act* 2010 (Qld) had been complied with. The only apparent impediment to the granting of the orders was whether the surrogacy agreement had been entered into prior to the conception[27] of the child (given that the embryo from which the child resulted was created in 2008).

Her Honour found that the answer seemed 'straightforward'[28] regardless of the method of statutory interpretation employed, and that conception occurred at 'the commencement of the pregnancy, which involves an active process within a woman's body'.[29] Her Honour reasoned that the commonly used phrase 'conceived a child'[30] refers to an actual (as opposed to a possible) pregnancy. Expert evidence was led that the 2008 creation of the embryo was 'an act of fertilisation'[31] which is 'a step on the path way to conception'.[32]

Ultimately, Judge Clare SC determined that the surrogacy agreement had been entered into before conception, thereby satisfying the legislative requirements. Parentage orders were granted to the intended parents and the case cemented its place in surrogacy (and potentially even ART)[33] history by providing a world-first[34] ruling that conception occurs with pregnancy, not fertilisation. In the absence of any other judicial discussion on this topic, this decision is the first step in putting to rest any uncertainty that may have previously existed about when conception occurs in a surrogacy or ART context and can be relied upon to satisfy the legislative provisions that require surrogacy agreements to be entered into prior to conception. Further, by demonstrating that the parties have complied with all legislative requirements regarding formation and performance of the agreement, the surrogate's entitlement to reimbursement of her expenses is preserved.

2. Eligibility to enter into surrogacy agreements

To be eligible for surrogacy, intended parents must usually satisfy the requirement that the surrogacy agreement arises in response to either a medical or a social

---

26 *Surrogacy Act* 2010 (Qld), s 22(2) requires that the court be satisfied that *all* of the matters listed in that section have been complied with (emphasis added).

27 Ibid., s 22(2)(e)(iv).

28 *LWV & another v LMH* [2012] QChC 26 [7].

29 Ibid.

30 Ibid., [8].

31 Ibid., [13].

32 Ibid.

33 Assisted Reproductive Technology.

34 *LWV & another v LMH* [2012] QChC 26 [14]. At the time of the hearing, there was only one other case in the world that had considered the notion of conception, that of *R (John Smeaton on Behalf of the Society for the Protection of Unborn Children) v the Secretary of State for Health* 5 [2002] EWHC 610 (Admin) which centred on the legality of the morning after pill and contemplated conception in the 'context of sexual intercourse rather than scientific intervention' and which concluded that there are two biological stages following intercourse; fertilisation and implantation.

need. The specifics of eligibility in each jurisdiction are discussed below, but the requirements are largely designed to prevent fertile intended parents from accessing surrogacy purely for reasons of convenience. For medical eligibility, the threshold requires the intended mother to be unable or unlikely to conceive, carry a pregnancy or give birth or to have some other significant medical or genetic risk associated with pregnancy. A social need occurs in the context of singles and same-sex couples[35] where natural procreation is physically impossible, even in the absence of any medical infertility.

Victoria requires surrogacy agreements necessitating ART to be assessed by, and receive approval from, the Patient Review Panel.[36] The Panel's assessment criteria is aimed at protecting the welfare of children born through surrogacy,[37] as well as that of the surrogate, by ensuring that the surrogate has attained 'a sufficient level of maturity to be able to understand the implications of entering into the arrangement'[38] including the legal and personal consequences of the arrangement not proceeding as anticipated.

Similarly in Western Australia, in order to 'minimise the risk of harm to the parties involved',[39] pre-conception[40] surrogacy agreements require the consent of the Reproductive Technology Council,[41] which necessitates an independent review of the proposed agreement. From a practical perspective, requiring an independent body to approve the surrogacy agreement creates a record which is then available to a child who may wish to gain information about their conception and birth at a later date.[42]

---

35 Particularly male same-sex couples because in a lesbian relationship it may be possible to satisfy the medical eligibility criteria if the intended mother(s) is infertile. Single men are identified as having a social need because a single woman, if she is infertile, would be able to satisfy the medical eligibility criteria.

36 *Assisted Reproductive Treatment Act* 2008, ss 39–40. The Panel must be satisfied that the parties meet certain criteria before it provides its approval. The assessment criteria includes the infertility of the intended parents, the age of the surrogate and that she has previously given birth to a live child and that the surrogate is not providing her own genetic material to achieve the surrogate pregnancy. Further criteria include the parties receiving legal advice and counselling and being able to make informed decisions about proceeding with the agreement and understanding the legal and personal consequences of the arrangement, including the consequences associated with the agreement not proceeding as intended where either the surrogate refuses to relinquish the child or the intended parents refuse to accept the child.

37 Victorian Law Reform Commission, above n. 1, 176.

38 Ibid., 177.

39 Standing Committee on Legislation, Parliament of Western Australia, above n. 1, 47.

40 *Surrogacy Act* 2008 (WA), s 17(e).

41 Ibid., s 17.

42 Similarly, *Surrogacy Act* 2008 (WA), ss 37(2), 38(1) permits a child born through surrogacy to obtain access to any parentage orders and birth records made in relation to them.

Access to records is important because Western Australia, in particular, permits the use of donor material in surrogacy arrangements. In cases where donor material is used, the donor is deemed to be a party to the arrangement and is required to sign the surrogacy agreement.[43] The importance of keeping proper records of donated genetic material has recently been highlighted in Denmark where a sperm donor carrying the rare genetic condition Neurofibromatosis type 1 (Von Recklinghausen's disease)[44] is believed to have fathered 43 children in 10 countries, passing that condition onto at least five of those children.[45] Efforts must now be made to contact the parents of those children to inform them of the possibility of transmission of the disease.

For eligibility based on marital status or sexual orientation, New South Wales, Victoria, Tasmania and the ACT all permit singles and same-sex couples to undertake surrogacy. At the time of writing, Queensland also permits singles and same-sex couples to enter into surrogacy agreements. However, following a change in state government, a potential amendment of the eligibility criteria was flagged by the government, with the possibility that singles and same-sex couples may in the future be ineligible for surrogacy.[46]

Western Australia limits eligibility to single women and heterosexual couples who satisfy the definition of an 'eligible person'[47] or 'eligible couple'.[48] These definitions have the effect of excluding single men and gay couples from accessing surrogacy in that state. For lesbian couples, it is foreseeable that one of the partners may be able to satisfy the definition of 'eligible person' and could thereby make the

---

43 *Surrogacy Act* 2008 (WA), s 17(b)(iii).

44 Neurofibramatosis type 1 is a genetic disease characterised by tumours which grow on the organs and tissues of the body.

45 Ayesha Ahmad, 'Danish sperm donation law tightened after donor passes on rare genetic disease' (2012) *BioNews* 675, http://www.bionews.org.uk/page_186913.asp?dinfo=EybV4Ks4Z9SF0XkDhtjlqfhd&PPID=186913.

46 See, for example, Daniel Hurst, 'Queensland LNP to Ban Same-Sex Surrogacy Amid Civil Union Changes', *Brisbane Times* (online), 22 June 2012, accessed 17 June 2014, available at http://www.brisbanetimes.com.au/queensland/gays-face-surrogacy-ban-as-lnp-pushes-civil-union-changes-20120621-20q9j.html, Matt Wordsworth, 'No more surrogacy for same-sex couples in Qld' ABC News, 22 June 2012, accessed 17 June 2014, available at http://www.abc.net.au/news/2012-06-22/no-more-surrogacy-for-same-sex-couples-in-qld/4086064.

47 *Surrogacy Act* 2008 (WA), s 19(2) defines *eligible person* as a woman who 'is unable to conceive a child due to medical reasons … or although able to conceive a child, would be likely to conceive a child affected by a genetic abnormality or a disease … or although able to conceive a child, is unable for medical reasons to give birth to a child'.

48 *Surrogacy Act* 2008 (WA), s 19(2) defines *eligible couple* as '2 people of opposite sexes who are married to, or in a de facto relationship with, each other and who, as a couple – (a) are unable to conceive a child due to medical reasons not excluded by subsection (3); or (b) although able to conceive a child, would be likely to conceive a child affected by a genetic abnormality or a disease'.

application as an individual. While this is obviously not an ideal situation, it is the only mode by which a lesbian couple can circumvent the Act's eligibility provisions.

Even more restrictively, South Australia renders *all* singles and same-sex couples ineligible for surrogacy. The provisions of the South Australian legislation permit only legally married[49] or heterosexual de facto couples[50] to undertake surrogacy. These provisions were enacted notwithstanding the 2007 report of the South Australian Parliament Social Development Committee which 'heard no evidence to suggest that either marital status or sexual preference can predict whether or not an individual will be a good parent'.[51] Additionally, in referring to the decisions in *Pearce v South Australian Health Commission*[52] and *McBain v State of Victoria*[53] which both found that prohibiting single women from accessing ART was inconsistent with the *Commonwealth Sex Discrimination Act* 1984, the Committee expressly declared that it 'does not support the restriction on surrogacy based on discriminatory criteria'.[54]

The eligibility provisions of the South Australian and Western Australian legislation may eventually be subject to a *Pearce-* or *McBain*-type challenge and if (or when) that happens, it is likely to lead to a decision in favour of non-discriminatory access to ART for the purpose of surrogacy.

3. Territorial restraint

Anita Stuhmcke's Chapter 5 in this volume provides a comprehensive coverage of this topic, and therefore this section is brief. There are three Australian jurisdictions that impose territorial restraint on surrogacy: Queensland, New South Wales and the ACT. The Queensland legislation extends its application beyond state borders by declaring it to be an offence for a resident of Queensland to advertise for surrogacy, enter into a commercial surrogacy agreement or provide technical, professional or medical services for a commercial surrogacy agreement, regardless of whether or not the act was done in Queensland.[55]

The New South Wales surrogacy legislation extends the scope of its offence provisions by establishing a link[56] with the *Crimes Act* 1900 (NSW),[57] creating a geographical nexus when an offence is committed outside New South Wales but has effect within that state. Therefore commercial surrogacy undertaken outside New South Wales but which has an effect in that state is prohibited. This provision

---

49 *Family Relationships Act* 1975 (SA), s 10HA(2)(b)(iii)(A).

50 Ibid., s 10HA(2)(b)(iii)(B).

51 South Australia Legislative Council, Social Development Committee, Parliament of South Australia, *Inquiry into Gestational Surrogacy*, Report 26 (2007) 64.

52 (1996) SASR 486.

53 (2000) 99 FCR 116.

54 South Australia Legislative Council, above n. 51, 64.

55 *Surrogacy Act* 2010 (Qld), ss 54–8.

56 *Surrogacy Act* 2010 (NSW), s 11.

57 *Crimes Act* 1900 (NSW), s 10C.

is particularly relevant in terms of the recent trend towards what has been labelled 'reproductive tourism' or 'fertility tourism' in jurisdictions where commercial surrogacy is permitted, such as (until recently) India, Mexico and the United States. Any person participating in a commercial surrogacy agreement outside Australia with the intention of bringing the child to New South Wales commits an offence.

In *Johnson and Anor & Chompunut*[58] Watts J discussed this newly created geographical nexus, noting that those people 'resident and/or domiciled in New South Wales *do* commit an offence if they enter into a commercial surrogacy agreement whether within New South Wales or anywhere outside New South Wales'.[59] Notwithstanding the court's acknowledgement of this offence, to date there have been no reported prosecutions under these provisions.

The other jurisdiction to impose a territorial restriction on surrogacy is the ACT. The *Parentage Act* 2004 (ACT) expressly acknowledges the operation of section 64(2) of the *Criminal Code* 2002 (ACT) which creates a geographical nexus for offences committed within the ACT, whether or not they have any effect in the ACT, and offences committed outside the ACT but that have an effect in the ACT. This operates in the same manner, and has the same effect, as its counter-part in New South Wales.

These territorial restraint provisions, Millbank posits, 'will not prevent Australians from engaging in paid surrogacy overseas, nor do anything to render that practice less risky for any of those involved'.[60] Criminalisation, she argues, 'may inhibit constructive discussion about how domestic surrogacy could be expanded or international surrogacy made safer'.[61] Stuhmcke's Chapter 5 in this volume discusses these criminal offence provisions and she argues that, in the absence of demonstrable harm, the government should not apply moralistic legislation which has the effect of restraining a person's procreative liberty.

4. Offence provisions

While offences under the various Acts are similar, all containing restrictions on advertising and an express prohibition of commercial surrogacy, Queensland, Western Australia and the ACT also prohibit the provision of any technical or professional services for commercial surrogacy.[62]

In terms of advertising restrictions, Queensland prohibits advertising a willingness to enter into a surrogacy agreement[63] or advertising in a manner that is designed to induce entry into a surrogacy agreement.[64] The South Australian

58 [2011] FamCA 505.

59 *Johnson and Anor & Chompunut* [2011] FamCA 505 at [13] (emphasis added).

60 Millbank, above n. 9, 197.

61 Ibid., 198.

62 See *Surrogacy Act* 2010 (Qld), s 58; *Surrogacy Act* 2008 (WA), s 11; *Parentage Act* 2004 (ACT), s 44.

63 *Surrogacy Act* 2010 (Qld), s 55.

64 Ibid.

legislation contains similar provisions while in the ACT it is an offence to enter into, procure[65] or advertise with the intention of inducing someone to enter into a commercial surrogacy agreement.[66] New South Wales prohibits advertising or soliciting for participants in commercial surrogacy agreements.[67] In Western Australia it is also an offence to receive payment for introducing parties to a surrogacy agreement (whether or not the arrangement itself is commercial)[68] and to advertise a willingness to make a commercial surrogacy agreement.[69] Tasmania prohibits the commercial brokerage or advertising of surrogacy agreements[70] and also declares that it is an offence to publish particulars of any application for parentage or other orders where publication may lead to the identity of the parties being revealed.[71] Finally, Victoria's offence provisions state that it is an offence to advertise a willingness to be a surrogate, enter into or procure a person to enter into a surrogacy agreement, seek a participant in or be willing to arrange a surrogacy agreement or accept a benefit under a surrogacy agreement.[72]

These offence provisions appear to have been incorporated into the surrogacy legislation as a matter of public policy to minimise the potential for harm to occur in surrogacy transactions and to safeguard against the commercialisation of the practice. Commercialisation in this regard refers not to commercial surrogacy (where the surrogate receives payment for her services) but rather to profit-making surrogacy agencies as often seen in the United States. By prohibiting third parties advertising for, inducing or introducing parties to a surrogacy agreement, the legislative provisions represent a proactive approach to protecting parties to a surrogacy agreement from the risks of commodification and exploitation.

5. Parentage

All Australian jurisdictions presume the birth mother to be the legal mother of a child born through surrogacy, but there are different presumptions relating to legal fatherhood (or parenthood in the case of a same-sex partner).[73] Similarly, there are variations on the mechanisms for transferring legal parentage of any child born through surrogacy.

---

65 Except where the person procuring the agreement intends to be a party to the surrogacy agreement.

66 *Parentage Act* 2004 (ACT), ss 40–43.

67 *Surrogacy Act* 2010 (NSW), s 10(1).

68 *Surrogacy Act* 2008 (WA), s 9.

69 Ibid., s 10.

70 *Surrogacy Act* 2012 (Tas), s 41.

71 Ibid., s 42.

72 *Assisted Reproductive Treatment Act* 2008 (Vic), s 45(1).

73 Table 4.2 provides a convenient synopsis of the Australian parentage legislation, current as at the date of submission for publication.

Before any court grants an order transferring legal parentage, irrespective of jurisdiction, it must be satisfied that doing so is in the best interests of the child.[74] This principle, enshrined in the United Nations Convention on the Rights of the Child,[75] is reflected in domestic legislation[76] which requires that in all decisions regarding children, their parenting or welfare, the child's best interests are paramount.[77] Similarly, in all applications for transfer of legal parentage, unless there are legitimate reasons for not doing so (such as death, disappearance or loss of capacity), the surrogate and her partner (if any) must consent to the orders being sought by the intended parents.

The various legislation provides differing mechanisms and timing for the transfer of legal parentage; vesting power in their Magistrates',[78] Children's,[79] Supreme,[80] County,[81] Youth[82] or Family[83] Courts to decide these matters. While all Acts require applications to be made no later than six months after the child's birth, the earliest time for the lodgement of an application for the transfer of legal parentage varies between 28 days,[84] 30 days[85] and six weeks[86] after the child's

74 For a comprehensive analysis of parentage orders see Alexandra Harland and Cressida Limon's Chapter 8 in this volume and for a discussion of the best interests of children born via surrogacy arrangements, see Paula Gerber and Katie O'Byrne's Chapter 6 in this volume.

75 Adopted by the UN General Assembly on 20 November 1989, 1577 UNTS 3 (entered into force on 2 September 1990).

76 See, for example, *Adoption Act* 1993(ACT), s 6; *Surrogacy Act* 2010 (NSW), s 22; *Adoption Act* 2000 (NSW), s 8; *Adoption Act* 2009 (Qld), s 6; *Surrogacy Act* 2010 (Qld), s 6; *Adoption Act* 1988 (SA), s 7; *Assisted Reproductive Treatment Act* 2008 (Vic), s 5.

77 Although Article 3 of the Convention requires that 'the best interests of the child shall be a primary consideration' the domestic legislation referred to in n. 76 above extends the scope of the best interests principle by requiring that the best interests of the child are paramount.

78 *Surrogacy Act* 2012 (Tas), s 4.

79 *Surrogacy Act* 2010 (Qld), s 13.

80 See, for example, *Surrogacy Act* 2010 (NSW), s 4(1); *Parentage Act* 2004 (ACT), s 26(1).

81 *Status of Children Act* 1974 (Vic), s 18.

82 *Family Relationships Act* 1975 (SA), s 10HB(3). The Youth Court of South Australia is a specialised court that deals with, amongst other things, applications for the adoption of children.

83 *Surrogacy Act* 2008 (WA), s 14.

84 See, for example, *Surrogacy Act* 2010 (Qld), s 21(1); *Status of Children Act* 1974 (Vic), s 20(2); *Family Relationships Act* 1975 (SA), s 10HB(5); *Surrogacy Act* 2008 (WA), s 20(2).

85 *Surrogacy Act* 2010 (NSW), s 16(1); *Surrogacy Act* 2012 (Tas), s 15(1)(a).

86 *Parentage Act* 2004 (ACT), s 25(3).

birth. Further, the South Australian[87] and Western Australian[88] Acts preclude same-sex couples from seeking parentage orders.

B. Where to from Here?

> 'Would you tell me, please, which way I ought to go from here?'
>
> 'That depends a good deal on where you want to get to', said the Cat.[89]
>
> (Alice and the Cheshire Cat, *Alice's Adventures in Wonderland*)

It is evident from the above examination of Australia's surrogacy legislation that, while there are elements of consistency, there is also significant disparity between the various jurisdictions. If Australia is to effectively regulate surrogacy, consensus must be reached between the states and territories as to an appropriate legislative framework. Although, in Australia, most steps towards harmonisation of laws have occurred in the sphere of commercial law,[90] there are signs that this is changing with moves underway to harmonise occupational health and safety laws.[91] Surrogacy is an issue that is in urgent need of a nationally uniform approach, whether through consistent state and territory enacted legislation or by referral of power to the Commonwealth. Indeed, this view is reflected in the 2009 Standing Committee of Attorneys-Generals' *A Proposal for a National Model to Harmonise Regulation of Surrogacy* (the SCAG Proposal)[92] considered below.

III. Through the Looking-Glass: National Reform

> To venture an opinion is like moving a piece at chess: it may be taken, but it forms the beginning of a game that is won.[93]

87 *Family Relationships Act* 1975 (SA), s 10HB.

88 *Surrogacy Act* 2008 (WA), s 19.

89 Lewis Carroll, *The Complete Illustrated Lewis Carroll* (Ware: Wordsworth Editions, 1998), 64.

90 See for example, *Corporations Act* 2001 (Cth); *Competition and Consumer Act* 2010 (Cth); *Personal Property Securities Act* 2009 (Cth).

91 See http://www.safeworkaustralia.gov.au/sites/swa/model-whs-laws/background/pages/background, accessed 27 February 2015.

92 Attorney-General for Australia, Standing Committee of Attorneys-General Australian Health Ministers' Conference Community and Disability Services Ministers' Conference, Joint Working Group, *A Proposal for a National Model to Harmonise Regulation of Surrogacy* (January 2009).

93 Johann Wolfgang von Goethe, *The Maxims and Reflections of Goethe*, trans. Bailey Saunders (New York: Macmillan & Co, 1906), 83.

For some time commentators have called for national reform of surrogacy legislation. In particular, Willmott believes that 'failure to support this form of assisted reproduction by putting in place an appropriate legislative and regulatory framework to the same extent as exists for other forms of ART cannot be justified'.[94] She emphasises that 'surrogacy agreements are not isolated occurrences'[95] and as a result, 'there is a need for uniform legislation'.[96] Notwithstanding this need, as recently as 2011, the difficulties of undertaking national surrogacy reform were highlighted. In *Lowe & Barry and Anor*,[97] which dealt with an application for orders for parental responsibility following a traditional altruistic surrogacy agreement between family members, Benjamin J observed that:

> The law in Australia in relation to surrogacy is complex. There is no uniform legislation between the States and Territories governing surrogacy. The Commonwealth Government lacks the constitutional power to enact effective national legislation.[98]

Referring in that judgment to another surrogacy case, *Dudley and Anor & Chedi*,[99] His Honour continued:

> However, there is some indication of policy development. Watts J observed:
>
> In very recent times Australia has been moving towards a uniform position in relation to the legality of surrogacy agreements and all places in Australia, except Tasmania and the Northern Territory, now have laws about surrogacy agreements.[100]

In the absence of constitutional power to enact uniform surrogacy legislation, it will be incumbent upon each of the states and territories to either refer legislative power to the Commonwealth under 51 (xxxvii) of the *Constitution*, or agree to each enact consistent legislation. The division between the law-making powers of the

94 Willmott, 'Surrogacy: ART's Forgotten Child', above n. 3, 232.

95 Willmott, 'Surrogacy: Ill-Conceived Rights', above n. 2, 202.

96 Ibid.

97 [2011] FamCA 625 (5 August 2011), [20].

98 *Lowe & Barry and Anor* [2011] FamCA 625 (5 August 2011), [20].

99 [2011] FamCA 502, [13]. This case involved a commercial surrogacy agreement which took place in Thailand in 2009. The intended parents resided in Queensland at the time of the surrogacy agreement and the agreement was illegal pursuant to the provisions of the *Surrogate Parenthood Act 1988* (Qld). In granting parentage orders in favour of the intended parents Watts J ordered that a copy of the judgment be provided 'to the Office of the Director of Public Prosecutions, Queensland for consideration of whether a prosecution should be instituted against the applicants'. Research reveals that no action has been taken to prosecute the intended parents for their breach of the Act.

100 *Lowe & Barry and Anor* [2011] FamCA 625 (5 August 2011), [21].

Commonwealth and the states and territories is founded on the general principle that 'private rights were regarded as more appropriately a matter for the states than for the Commonwealth'.[101] Therefore, from a practical perspective, referral of power to the Commonwealth is unlikely. Even though there have been instances of referral of powers in relation to matters concerning the welfare of children (for example, to encompass coverage of ex-nuptial children),[102] states and territories are generally loath to surrender their law-making autonomy. Therefore, if national reform is to occur, attention should focus on encouraging the states and territories to reach consensus as to an acceptable national surrogacy model that considers not only the mechanics of the surrogacy agreement itself, but also broader policy considerations including respect for autonomy, harm minimisation and the privacy of the parties.

Scholars, including Stuhmcke[103] and Willmott,[104] have discussed the possibility of a national regime, with Stuhmcke noting in 2004, that 'in Australia, incremental legal change is now occurring to allow surrogacy without national debate'.[105] At the national level, the Standing Committee of Attorneys-General (SCAG) undertook an investigation into altruistic surrogacy, and in 2009, the Joint Working Group submitted the SCAG Proposal which discussed a national model for the regulation of altruistic surrogacy across Australia. While steps have yet to be taken to implement the SCAG Proposal, it provides further hope that national reform can soon begin. Founded on elements of the Victorian, ACT and Western Australian surrogacy legislation, the aim of the SCAG Proposal was to ensure that intended parents are formally 'recognised throughout Australia as the legal parents of the child in place of the birth parent(s)'.[106] Accompanying this aim, the following principles underpin the SCAG Proposal:

- Parentage orders should only be made if they are in the best interests of the child.

---

101 Lisa Young and Geoff Monahan, *Family Law in Australia* (Chatswood, NSW: LexisNexis Butterworths, 7th edn, 2009), [3.6].

102 Between 1986 and 1990, all states (except Western Australia) referred state powers to the Commonwealth with respect to 'guardianship, custody, maintenance and access' in relation to ex-nuptial children. In 1983 there was an attempt to expand the categories of children covered by the *Family Law Act* 1975 ('Family Law Act') but in *Re Cormick* (1984) 156 CLR 170 it was held that the marriage power could not extend to ex-nuptial children. As the attempt to expand the coverage of the Family Law Act was held to be constitutionally invalid, referral of power to the Commonwealth became necessary.

103 Anita Stuhmcke, 'National surrogacy system would clarify parents' rights: Expert', *AAP* (Sydney), 7 November 2006.

104 Willmott, 'Surrogacy: ART's Forgotten Child', above n. 3, 232.

105 Anita Stuhmcke, 'Looking Backwards, Looking Forwards: Judicial and Legislative Trends in the Regulation of Surrogate Motherhood in the UK and Australia' (2004) 18 *Australian Journal of Family Law* 1, 28.

106 Ibid., 2.

- The privacy of the parties to the surrogacy agreement is paramount and any legal intervention should be kept to a minimum.
- Legal disputes between the intending parents and the birth parent(s) should be avoided.[107]

The national model proposed in this chapter supports these principles and acknowledges the liberal beliefs entrenched in Australian society that 'governments should not prohibit private activity unless that activity does harm to others'.[108] As such, in the absence of significant demonstrable harm, people should be at liberty to make decisions regarding the conduct of their lives, including decisions regarding their procreative choices. Writing in support of the liberty of private citizens, John Stuart Mill stated that 'the only part of the conduct of anyone, for which he is amenable to society, is that which concerns others … over his own body and mind, the individual is sovereign'.[109]

A. The Proposed Model

1. Scope

The national model would widen the scope of existing legislation so that both altruistic and commercial surrogacy are regulated. In relation to commercial surrogacy, academic debate exists on the issue of whether or not its prohibition in Australia is justified. Since as early as 1996,[110] Stuhmcke has called for law reform in this area, asserting that the 'continued application of criminal penalties to commercial surrogacy requires review'.[111] The proposed national model would regulate commercial surrogacy rather than criminalising it. This proposal may be controversial, but it is not radical. It is consistent with academic thought over time, and justified because governments should not intervene unnecessarily in the

107 Ibid.

108 Willmott, 'Surrogacy: ART's Forgotten Child', above n. 3, 230.

109 Jeremy Bentham and John Stuart Mill, *The Utilitarians: An Introduction to the Principles of Morals and Legislation* (New York: Doubleday, 1961), 484. It is acknowledged that some may argue that the Harm Principle does not contemplate the child that is created as a result of the surrogacy arrangement because that child cannot be said to be an autonomous person that is capable of exercising free choice about the arrangement. That may well be a legitimate argument, but philosophical arguments about whether it is better to be born through surrogacy than never to be born at all are deserving of consideration in a separate paper. The scope of this chapter is limited to a contemplation of the accepted liberal principles so far as they relate to the autonomy of the parties to the surrogacy arrangement; the surrogate and the intended parent(s).

110 Anita Stuhmcke, 'For Love or Money: The Legal Regulation of Surrogate Motherhood' (1996) 3(1) *eLaw Journal: Murdoch University Electronic Journal of Law* 1, http://www.murdoch.edu.au/elaw/issues/v3n1/stuhmck1.html, accessed 14 June 2014.

111 Anita Stuhmcke, 'The Criminal Act of Commercial Surrogacy in Australia: A Call for Review' (2011) 18 *Journal of Law and Medicine* 601, 601.

lives of private citizens, except when there is concern that one citizen's actions can result in significant harm to another.[112] Scott concludes that a 'contemporary pragmatic approach to regulating surrogacy'[113] should be adopted over absolute prohibition. She advocates that 'well-designed regulation can greatly mitigate most of the potential *tangible* harms of surrogacy, and this would seem to be the appropriate function of law in a liberal society in response to an issue on which no societal consensus exists'.[114]

For the child, these tangible harms can include 'attachment disorders, post-traumatic stress disorder, psychosomatic symptoms and mental health problems'.[115] However studies on the cognitive and social development of children born through ART conducted from infancy to adolescence, reveal 'comparative cognitive functioning to other children and in some cases … higher in social and communication skills'.[116] But, irrespective of how alternative families[117] are formed, Beckett et al. identify that 'one additional role unique to substitute parenting is the need to explain to the child their origins and to help them to make sense of their beginnings',[118] and parents need to appreciate that 'open communication appears to be … positively associated with self-esteem'.[119] Through appropriate regulation of commercial surrogacy such safeguards (including requiring pre-approval of surrogacy agreements, ensuring the availability of information regarding the child's conception and providing access to counselling for the resulting child) can be introduced to minimise the risk of harm occurring.

Turning to the surrogate, Appleton suggests that 'while surrogacy opens a window of opportunity to many childless couples it is also open to abuse'.[120] It

---

112 Bentham and Mill, above n. 110, 484.

113 Elizabeth S. Scott, 'Surrogacy and the Politics of Commodification' (2009) 72(3) *Law and Contemporary Problems* 109, 146.

114 Ibid., emphasis in original.

115 Judy Barker and Deborah Hodes, *The Child in Mind: A Child Protection Handbook* (Abingdon and New York: Routledge, 3rd edn, 2002), 19.

116 Janice C. Ciccarelli and Linda J. Beckman, 'Navigating Rough Waters: An Overview of Psychological Aspects of Surrogacy' (2005) 61(1) *Journal of Social Issues* 21, 37 citing C.A. McMahon et al., 'Psychosocial Outcomes for Parents and Children after in Vitro Fertilization: A Review' (1995) 13 *Journal of Reproductive and Infant Psychology* 1; and F. Van Balen, 'Development of IVF children' (1998) 18 *Developmental Review* 30.

117 The term 'alternative families' is used to refer to families formed through adoption, ART and surrogacy.

118 Celia Beckett et al., 'The Experience of Adoption (2): The Association between Communicative Openness and Self-esteem in Adoption' (2008) 32(1) *Adoption & Fostering* 29 citing Harold D. Grotevant, Yvette V. Perry and Ruth G. McRoy, 'Openness in Adoption: Outcomes for Adolescents within their Adoptive Kinship Networks', in David Brodzinsky and Jesus Palacios (eds), *Psychological Issues in Adoption Research and Practice* (Westport, CT: Praeger, 2005).

119 Beckett et al., above n. 118, 38.

120 T. Appleton, 'Surrogacy' (2001) 11(4) *Current Obstetrics & Gynaecology* 256.

is therefore imperative to protect surrogates from exploitation which occurs when a person's wrongful behaviour violates 'the moral norm of protecting the vulnerable'.[121] Interestingly though, van den Akker's research reveals that notwithstanding a tendency for surrogates to have a lower level of education and come from a lower socio-economic class than the intended parents, rather than feeling exploited, surrogates believe that they made an informed choice when they decided to bear a child for another.[122]

There is undoubtedly scope for commercial surrogacy to be harmful; but the same could also be said for altruistic surrogacy which is now considered to be an acceptable practice in Australia.[123] Without appropriate regulation, *any* form of surrogacy can be harmful. The SCAG Proposal confined its recommendations to altruistic surrogacy and failed to give appropriate consideration to whether the risk of harm occurring in commercial surrogacy is so significant that prohibition is the appropriate regulatory response. In the absence of demonstrable significant harm, rather than criminalising commercial surrogacy, governments should take the steps necessary to introduce appropriate levels of regulation in order to minimise the risk of harm occurring. It is appropriate, and preferable, for the distinction between altruistic and commercial surrogacy to be dissolved, and to regulate both in a similar manner.

2. Enforceability and parentage

The national model would strive to provide certainty regarding surrogacy agreements by presuming that a child born through gestational surrogacy is the legal child of the intended parent(s).[124] This recommendation represents an epic

---

121 Robert E. Goodin, *Reasons for Welfare: The Political Theory of the Welfare State* (Princeton, NJ: Princeton University Press, 1988), 147.

122 Olga B.A. van den Akker, 'Genetic and Gestational Surrogate Mothers' Experience of Surrogacy' (2003) 21(2) *Journal of Reproductive and Infant Psychology* 145, 146.

123 It could be argued that altruistic surrogates are potentially at even greater risk of emotional exploitation than commercial surrogates. Altruistic surrogates are usually close relatives or friends of the intended parents and therefore may succumb to emotional pressure to act as a surrogate for those close to them. Conversely, commercial surrogates are paid to provide a service to the intended parents. Whilst there is scope for economic exploitation to occur, if the parties undertake a voluntary arms-length commercial arrangement having obtained appropriate legal advice and psychological counselling before entering into the arrangement, the risk of emotional exploitation is minimal.

124 There are a number of states in the United States of America that permit the issuance of pre-birth parentage orders including California, Colorado, Connecticut, Kansas, Maine, Alaska, Maryland, Mississippi, North Carolina, Oklahoma, Pennsylvania, Rohde Island, and South Dakota, Massachusetts and New Jersey. See Steven H. Snyder and Mary Patricia Byrn, 'The Use of Prebirth Parentage Orders in Surrogacy Proceedings' (2005) 39(3) *Family Law Quarterly* 633, and Victorian Law Reform Commission: Occasional Paper by John Seymor and Sonia Magri, ART, *Surrogacy and Legal Parentage: A Comparative*

shift in the established presumptions as to parentage,[125] but there are two provisos, namely that: (i) only gestational surrogacy is permitted under the proposed model and (ii) the presumption is rebuttable by the surrogate. If the surrogate is unwilling to relinquish the child, she may bring an application to rebut the presumptions and seek legal parentage. In deciding matters of parentage, courts must, at all times, give paramount consideration to the best interests of the child.[126]

This proposed new presumption as to parentage would result in partial enforceability of surrogacy agreements; subject to the surrogate's ability (as the birth mother of the child) to bring an application rebutting the presumption. While space precludes a full debate of the policy issues that this recommendation raises, it is premised on the assertion that the subject matter of the surrogacy agreement is not the sale of a baby but, rather, the supply of the surrogate's gestational services. Surrogacy agreements 'are transactions in which custody of a child is transferred from one person to another, whereas the sale of a baby implies the transferral of property rights in a human being as a variation on slavery'.[127] A properly regulated regime for pre-conception gestational surrogacy agreements would not involve 'the purchase of transferable rights or imply a right to resell a child'.[128] Instead, the intended parent(s) should be regarded as 'purchasing the reproductive labour of a birth mother so as to acquire the privilege of being responsible for the long-term care of the child'.[129]

As such, in the language of contract (and as mentioned above), the subject matter of the surrogacy agreement is not the sale of a child; it is the gestational services of the surrogate, and relinquishment of the child would usually be a condition precedent to the payment of fees. This condition precedent is mirrored

---

Legislative Review (2004). Further, *Gestational Surrogacy Act* 2004 (Illinois), s 47/15(b)(1) recognises that the intended parents are the legal parents of the child 'immediately upon the birth of the child'. The effect of this provision is to establish a presumption of parentage in favour of the intended parents in a gestational surrogacy agreement.

125 See, for example, *Status of Children Act* 1978 (Qld), ss 19(2), 23(2); *Status of Children Act* 1996 (NSW), s 14; *Status of Children Act* 1974 (Vic), ss 5, 10E(2); *Family Relationships Act* 1975 (SA), ss 8, 10C; *Artificial Conception Act* 1985 (WA), s 5; *Parentage Act* 2004 (ACT), ss 7, 11(2).

126 This would result in matters regarding parentage being decided in the same manner as they are under the current regime where the surrogate is presumed to be the mother and the intended parents apply for legal parentage of the child.

127 Carmel Shalev, *Birth Power* (New Haven, CT: Yale University Press, 1989), 157. See also Katherine Drabiak et al., 'Ethics, Law, and Commercial Surrogacy: A Call for Uniformity', (2007) 35(2) *Journal of Law, Medicine & Ethics* 300, 301; and Emily Gelmann, '"I'm just the Oven, It's Totally Their Bun": The Power and Necessity of the Federal Government to Regulate Commercial Gestational Surrogacy Arrangements and Protect the Legal Rights of Intended Parents' (2010) 32 *Women's Rights Law Report* 159, 160.

128 Ibid.

129 Ibid.

in the Queensland legislation,[130] which provides that the payment of fees is be contingent upon a child being born and the surrogate relinquishing that child to the intended parent(s) immediately following the birth. The payments permitted by a surrogacy agreement should be properly defined and should comprise, in addition to a capped surrogacy fee (in a commercial agreement),[131] the surrogate's expenses which would include reasonable legal and counselling expenses, medical expenses not provided for by Medicare, private health insurance premiums and lost income (not otherwise provided for through paid maternity leave).

The proposed national model would provide certainty for the parties by recognising the intended parent(s)[132] as the legal parent(s) and making payment of the surrogacy fees contingent upon the successful gestation, birth and relinquishment of the child. The national model would also uphold the principle of

---

130 *Surrogacy Act* 2010 (Qld), s 15(2).

131 While ultimately any statutory cap would be set by Parliament and would be subject to regular review, it is proposed that $26,500.00 is a reasonable commercial surrogacy fee (exclusive of expenses). The North American Surrogacy Center advertises a minimum surrogacy fee of $25,000.00 (exclusive of any other fees such as medical, psychological or legal fees), http://northamericansurrogacycenter.com/fees.php accessed 17 June 2014. Other American Centres advertise surrogacy fees up to $35,000.00, http://www.creatingfamilies.com/IP/IP_Info.aspx?Type=42 accessed 17 June 2014. When considering an appropriate cap, it is appropriate to also consider the national minimum wage rates available from the Australian Government Department of Employment website, https://employment.gov.au/news/fair-work-commission-annual-wage-review-increases-national-minimum-wage accessed 5 March 2015 which reported Australia's minimum wage in 2015 to be $640.90 per week. This is also similar to the amount payable under the Australian Government's 18 weeks Paid Maternity Leave Scheme which, in 2015, is $622.10 per week, http://www.ncoa.gov.au/report/phase-one/part-b/7-6-paid-parental-leave-and-child-care.html accessed 5 March 2015. The suggested cap has been calculated by multiplying the minimum wage by 41 weeks (40 weeks gestation + 1 week recovery after birth) which equals $26,276.90. For convenience, this amount has been rounded up to nearest $500.00. As this amount is equivalent to the legal minimum wage, it should be considered a reasonable amount of remuneration for the surrogate considering that, excluding any medical conditions arising, she would normally be able to continue her usual employment while pregnant until shortly before the child's due date. Further, capping surrogacy fees at a level equivalent to the legal minimum wage will go some way towards acting as a counter-measure to claims that surrogates are victims of financial exploitation by ensuring that they are appropriately remunerated for their services. In order to ensure that the surrogacy fee does not become an inducement that influences the surrogate's capacity to make a free and fully informed choice, it is recommended later in this chapter that any national model will require all parties to undergo pre-agreement psychological counselling and obtain independent legal advice. This will ensure that the integrity of the surrogate's decision-making capacity is respected and that she is put in the position of being able to make a voluntary and fully informed decision whether to enter into the surrogacy agreement.

132 If there is more than one intended parent, at least one of them must also be a genetic parent.

ensuring that the best interests of the child are of paramount consideration because in the event of any dispute over parental responsibility or parentage of the child, the best interests of the child test must be applied by the court.[133]

The intended parent(s) would be limited to recovering money already paid to the surrogate in the event that, due to the surrogate's actions, there is no resulting child[134] or in circumstances where the surrogate successfully rebuts the presumption of parentage and is granted parental responsibility for the child. Of course, the parties would have the freedom to incorporate into their agreement provision for some payment to be made to the surrogate in the event that, through no fault of her own, there is no resulting child.[135]

The rationale for these particular recommendations is threefold: to accurately reflect the intentions of the parties and provide certainty of contract, to ensure that the best interests of the child are paramount and to ease the burden on the judicial system. By modifying the presumptions as to parentage, the child's birth certificate could be recorded with the names of the intended parent(s) in the first instance. The significance of accurate parentage being reflected on a child's birth certificate was discussed in the 2011 case, *AA v Registrar of Births Deaths and Marriages and BB*,[136] where the court had regard to the historical purposes of documenting births. Walmsley SC noted that the purpose of birth certificates has evolved to 'fulfil the needs of real property and succession in establishing title'.[137] Recording the names of the intended parent(s) on the birth certificate in the first instance would, in addition to being in the child's best interests, protect the child's legitimate legal interests.

If the surrogate sought to rebut the presumption of parentage, she would be permitted to make an application to the Family Court within 28 days[138] of the

133 For an in-depth analysis of the application of the best interests of the child principle to children born via surrogacy, see Paula Gerber and Katie O'Byrne's Chapter 6 in this volume.

134 For example, the surrogate unilaterally terminated the pregnancy against the wishes of the intended parent(s).

135 For example, the surrogate could still receive part or full payment of the surrogacy fee in instances where she miscarries, the child is stillborn or the pregnancy is terminated because tests reveal that the foetus has (or is likely to be born with) a significant genetic condition or defect.

136 [2011] NSWDC 100 (17 August 2011).

137 *AA v Registrar of Births Deaths and Marriages and BB* [2011] NSWDC 100 (17 August 2011), [35] quoting *The Laws of Australia* (Lawbook) volume 20.10 at [8].

138 The 28 day time limit is consistent with the lower limit of the minimum time for an application for parentage orders to be made as prescribed in the current state surrogacy legislation and would give the surrogate sufficient time to make her application while ensuring that the matter is heard without undue delay. Regard should be had to the emotional upheaval that such an application would cause to all of the parties involved and it is imperative that the application be brought without delay to ensure that the best interests of the child remain paramount. For time limits regarding applications for transfer of legal parentage. See, for

child's birth seeking a transfer of legal parentage. Obviously, to put this proposal in place, the relevant state and territory Acts dealing with the status of children would require amendment; but this is not an insurmountable hurdle. Amendment of these Acts has already been undertaken in a number of jurisdictions to reflect both partners in a same-sex relationship as parents.[139]

Finally, implementing this proposal would alleviate the judicial burden by reducing the volume of parentage applications requiring consideration. Currently the surrogate is always presumed to be the legal parent thereby requiring the intended parent(s) to seek formal recognition as the child's legal parent(s). Such applications not only create a burden on the judicial system but necessitate significant expenditure by the intended parent(s); expenditure which is wholly avoidable in most instances as demonstrated by evidence showing that less than one-tenth of one per cent of surrogacy agreements result in disputes.[140] Given these statistics, it is anticipated that under the proposed model, judicial consideration of surrogacy agreements would become a rarity.

3. Eligibility

Reflecting the provisions of the existing legislation,[141] the national model would determine eligibility by reference to a legitimate medical or social need. As foreshadowed by the Warnock Report,[142] it is 'ethically unacceptable'[143] to permit healthy, fertile women to enter into surrogacy agreements purely as a matter of convenience. In this regard, 'that people should treat others as a means to their own ends, however desirable the consequences, must always be liable to moral objection'.[144] Singles and same-sex couples would be recognised as having a social need, thereby allowing them to undertake surrogacy. This recommendation is consistent with Millbank's view that 'discriminatory requirements, such as

---

example, *Surrogacy Act* 2010 (Qld), s 21(1), *Surrogacy Act* 2010 (NSW), s 16(1), *Parentage Act* 2004 (ACT), s 25(3), *Assisted Reproductive Treatment Act* 2008 (Vic), s 20(2), *Surrogacy Act* 2008 (WA), s 20(3), *Family Relationships Act* 1975 (SA), s 10HB(5).

139 See, for example, *Status of Children Act* 1974 (Vic), s 13; *Status of Children Act* 1996 (NSW), s 14.

140 See, for example, Elly Teman, 'The Social Construction of Surrogacy Research: An Anthropological Critique of the Psychosocial Scholarship on Surrogate Motherhood', (2008) 67 *Social Science and Medicine* 1104 citing Judy Keen, 'Surrogate relishes unique role', *USA Today* (online), 22 January 2007, accessed 17 June 2014, available at http://www.usatoday.com/news/health/2007–01–22-surrogate-role_x.htm; Lori B. Andrews, 'Beyond Doctrinal Boundaries: A Legal Framework for Surrogate Motherhood' (1995) 81 *Virginia Law Review* 2351.

141 See, for example, *Surrogacy Act* 2010 (Qld), s 22(2); *Surrogacy Act* 2010 (NSW), s 30; *Surrogacy Act* 2012 (Tas), s 7.

142 Department of Health and Social Services (UK), *Report of the Committee of Inquiry into Human Fertilisation and Embryology* (Dame Mary Warnock, chairperson, 1984).

143 Ibid., 8.17.

144 Ibid.

those concerning marital status and sexual orientation ought to be removed' and that requirements regarding marital status are 'inconsistent with the modern approach to Australian family and relationship laws, which largely includes same-sex couples and parents on an equal footing with heterosexual families'.[145]

Significant empirical research demonstrating that children and adolescents of single or lesbian-parents are not disadvantaged by the circumstances in which they are raised to adulthood lends support to this recommendation.[146] Bos et al. report that there 'are no empirical data supporting the normative claim that there are associations between the availability of ... role models and the children's ... psychological adjustment'.[147] Indeed Golombok and Badger's comparative research on 19-year-olds born into single mother and lesbian-parent families in the UK revealed that the children of single 'heterosexual mothers or lesbian mothers from infancy continue to function well as they enter adulthood'.[148] Further, in respect of the psychological well-being of the young adults surveyed, the results revealed that:

> those from female-headed households showed lower levels of anxiety, depression, hostility and problematic alcohol use than their counter-parts from traditional families, and higher levels of self-esteem, indicating more positive psychological adjustment among young adults who had grown up in solo and lesbian mother homes.[149]

4. Territorial restraint

Unlike the provisions in Queensland, New South Wales and the ACT, under the proposed national model there would be no jurisdictional restraint on surrogacy. This would allow Australian citizens to enter into interstate or international altruistic or commercial surrogacy agreements and, as long as all immigration requirements applicable to bringing the child into the country are satisfied, to raise their child in Australia.

---

145 Millbank, above n. 9, 207.

146 See, for example, Cynthia J. Telingator and Charlotte Patterson, 'Children and Adolescents of Lesbian and Gay Parents' (2008) 4(12) *Journal of the American Academy of Child and Adolescent Psychiatry* 1364; Henny Bos et al., 'Adolescents of the U.S. National Longitudinal Lesbian Family Study: Male Role Models, Gender Role Traits, and Psychological Adjustment', (2012) 26(4) *Gender & Society* 603; Timothy J. Biblarz and Evren Savci, 'Lesbian, Gay, Bisexual, and Transgender Families' (2010) 72(3) *Journal of Marriage and Family* 480.

147 Bos et al., above n. 146, 604–5.

148 Susan Golombok and Shirlene Badger, 'Children Raised in Mother-headed Families from Infancy: A Follow-up of Children of Lesbian and Single Heterosexual Mothers, at Early Adulthood' (2010) 72(3) *Human Reproduction* 154. In the study, the children of 27 single heterosexual mothers and 20 lesbian families were compared with those of 36 two-parent heterosexual families.

149 Ibid., 156.

Anita Stuhmcke's Chapter 5 in this volume provides a detailed discussion of the undesirability of maintaining a jurisdictional restraint on surrogacy. She emphasises that imposing jurisdictional restrictions on surrogacy will result in the practice being driven underground. If this occurs it will thwart the objective of ensuring that children born through surrogacy have access to information regarding their conception and birth[150] and that appropriate measures are undertaken to minimise harm and prevent the exploitation of surrogates.

5. The agreement: formalities and conditions precedent

The proposed national model would require that all surrogacy agreements be evidenced in writing and signed by all parties to the agreement including the surrogate's partner (if any). This is consistent with existing legislative requirements and is advocated both to ensure that the rights and obligations of the parties are properly protected throughout the transaction and to minimise the risk of disputes occurring through misunderstanding or miscommunication of intentions. While the parties' freedom to contract must be respected, the minimum thresholds for the agreement are expounded below.

(a) Autonomy The parties to a surrogacy agreement may elect to include provisions that, in the best interests of the child to be born and for the duration of the pregnancy, have a limited moderate impact on the surrogate's autonomy. An example of such provisions include abstaining from smoking, consuming alcohol and drugs, a requirement that the surrogate take pregnancy vitamins or other medications as prescribed or recommended by the medical practitioner overseeing the pregnancy, eating a balanced diet, undertaking regular recommended exercise and undergoing certain pre-natal screening or procedures. Notwithstanding these agreed temporary modifications to the surrogate's lifestyle, the intended parent(s) would not be permitted to influence the surrogate's preferences for giving birth or to significantly restrain or manipulate the surrogate's other lifestyle choices before, during, or after the pregnancy. As expressed by Damelio and Sorensen:[151]

> When the ... surrogate signs the contract, she makes an agreement to perform certain specific duties, but ... the couple cannot use the surrogate's body in any

150 This matter was discussed by the Victorian Law Reform Commission in its 2007 report in the context of donor-conceived children. See Victorian Law Reform Commission, above n. 1. The Commission was of the view that 'donor conceived people deserve to know about their genetic origins' and that 'secrecy about a child's genetic origins, once revealed, can cause feelings of betrayal, mistrust and grief within the family': at 8. Recommendations were made that 'children born as a result of the use of donated gametes have a right to information about their genetic parents': at 9[1] and that a register be maintained to include identifying information about the surrogate mother which can be accessed by the child: at 16 [129].

151 Jennifer Damelio and Kelly Sorensen, 'Enhancing Autonomy in Paid Surrogacy', (2008) 22(5) *Bioethics* 269, 272.

way they please; they can only expect that she carry out the specific expectations set forth in the contract.

(b) Pre-conception The proposed national model would require all surrogacy agreements to be entered into prior to conception.[152] This requirement supports the principle of safeguarding against the risk of harm by ensuring that all parties receive adequate legal advice, counselling and approval of the agreement *before* they take any steps towards achieving a pregnancy.

(c) Legal advice Consistent with current legislative requirements, the proposed national model would require all parties to a surrogacy agreement to receive independent legal advice before entering into the formal agreement. In order to ensure that the parties make a fully informed and voluntary decision to enter into the agreement the legal advice should, at a minimum, include verbal and written advice regarding:

- the nature and effect of the agreement;
- the legal consequences of entering into the agreement;
- the parties' expectations, so far as can be established in the agreement, as to whether (or in what circumstances) the surrogate will undergo pre-natal screening, selective embryo reduction, abortion or other necessary or desirable testing or treatment during the pregnancy;
- the nature of payments permitted by the agreement, the calculation of amounts payable and the timing of amounts payable;
- the parties' rights regarding termination of the agreement before and after birth of the child; and
- the legal presumptions as to parentage of the child born and the process for challenging legal parentage.

The legal practitioner would be required to provide the client with written confirmation of the advice given and attach a Certificate of Independent Legal Advice[153] to the agreement, thereby providing rebuttable evidence to any allegation that the agreement was entered into after conception or that the parties did not provide their informed and voluntary consent to the agreement.

152 See the discussion in Part II of this chapter on when conception occurs.

153 Certificates of Legal Advice are regularly used in commercial transactions such as mortgages or guarantees to provide evidence that the parties entering into the agreement have received legal advice and are aware of the legal implications of entering into the transaction. Therefore, the suggested use of such a Certificate in the surrogacy context is merely an extension of the range of agreements for which parties may require evidence of informed consent.

(d) Counselling The proposed national model would acknowledge the desirability of preserving the legislative status quo[154] in relation to counselling. Therefore the national model would, as a prerequisite to entering into a surrogacy agreement, require all parties to undertake independent counselling as to the nature of the proposed arrangement and the potential social and psychological implications of entering into such an arrangement. The surrogate and her partner (if any) would be counselled as to the ongoing social and psychological consequences that may be associated with the relinquishment of the child to the intended parent(s). Similarly, the intended parent(s) would be counselled and assessed in the same manner as the surrogate with the additional requirement that they be assessed as to whether, in the counsellor's expert opinion, they are fit and proper persons to assume the role of parent(s) of the intended child.

The proposed national model would require the counsellor to be appropriately qualified to counsel and assess the parties and to produce a report as to their fitness to enter into the agreement. The counsellor's written report would be attached to the agreement, as a safeguard against assertions that the parties did not fully understand the nature or implications of the surrogacy arrangement. By taking steps to ensure that the parties to the agreement are fully cognisant of the legal, medical and social risks associated with surrogacy, the potential for harm is minimised and positive steps are taken to ensure that the best interests of the child to be born are given paramount consideration.

(e) Conditions precedent to the surrogacy agreement While it is essential to ensure that any statutory intrusion into the liberty of private citizens is minimised, it would be irresponsible for governments to enact surrogacy legislation which failed to impose some conditions precedent to the formation of each surrogacy agreement. A laissez-faire approach resulting in a legislative 'free for all' would almost certainly result in ill-conceived agreements being entered into by parties who have not received counselling or legal advice and thus, are potentially unable to provide their fully informed voluntary consent. Also, a lack of appropriate regulation may ultimately result in the number of surrogacy disputes increasing and the best interests of the intended child being given subsidiary, rather than paramount, consideration. In order to avoid such a situation eventuating, in addition

154 While the specifics of the requirements vary between jurisdictions, all existing Australian surrogacy legislation requires that the parties receive independent counselling prior to entering into the surrogacy agreement. See *Parentage Act* 2004 (ACT), s 26(3); *Surrogacy Act* 2010 (NSW), s 35; *Surrogacy Act* 2010 (Qld), s 22(2); *Family Relationships Act* 1975 (SA), s 10HA(2); *Assisted Reproductive Treatment Act* 2008 (Vic), s 43; *Surrogacy Act* 2008 (WA), s 17; *Surrogacy Act* 2012 (Tas), s 16(2)(f).

to the requirements for legal advice and counselling, the proposed national model would require the following conditions precedent to the surrogacy agreement:

- All parties to the agreement must be at least 25 years old. This mimics the requirement of the current provisions in Queensland,[155] New South Wales,[156] Tasmania,[157] and Victoria.[158] In support of the 25-year minimum age requirement, the Victorian Law Reform Commission resolved that 'becoming a surrogate should not be seen as the mere exercise of a legal right attained on turning 18, but rather a decision that requires a level of maturity that most people have not developed until [the] age [of 25]'.[159]
- The surrogate should have previously borne at least one child. Experiencing pregnancy and childbirth previously will ensure that the surrogate is 'able to give informed consent as to the task she proposes to undertake'.[160]
- All parties must undergo criminal history and child protection order checks. This supports the more interventionist approach of the Victorian legislation,[161] which was also supported in the SCAG Proposal. This approach proposes that, as a precondition to obtaining counselling, the counselling clinic arranges criminal history and child protection checks of the parties. This recommendation is made as a further mechanism for ensuring that the best interests of the child to be born are given paramount consideration.[162]
- The surrogate and the surrogate's partner (if any) must not be a genetic parent of the child. The rationale for this proposal is discussed below.
- If there is more than one intending parent, at least one of the intending parents must be a genetic parent of the child.
- The child was conceived via an ART procedure.
- The agreement must be approved by a Surrogacy Review Panel, which would be an independent body similar to Victoria's Patient Review Panel or Western Australia's Reproductive Technology Council whose purpose it is to ensure that all legislative requirements have been complied with. Requiring approval by an independent body will assist in safeguarding against the risk of harm by enabling any potential 'red flags'[163] to be

155 *Surrogacy Act* 2010 (Qld), s 23(2)(f).

156 *Surrogacy Act* 2010 (NSW), s 27(1).

157 *Surrogacy Act* 2012 (Tas), s 16(2)(c).

158 *Assisted Reproductive Treatment Act* 2008 (Vic), s 40(1)(b).

159 Victorian Law Reform Commission, above n. 1, 177.

160 Ibid., quoting Submissions PP3 18 (Fertility Society of Australia) and PP3 56 (Melbourne IVF Counselling Service).

161 *Assisted Reproductive Treatment Act* 2008 (Vic), s 42.

162 Attorney-General for Australia, above n. 92, 19.

163 For example, a criminal history or psychological condition as occurred in the case of Amy Kehoe, an intended parent who suffered from paranoid schizophrenia and whose condition was not discovered until after the birth of the resulting twins. See Louisa Ghevaert, 'What happens when surrogacy goes wrong: The recent Indiana surrogacy case

raised before steps are taken to facilitate pregnancy and to ensure that the agreement is not detrimental to the interests of any of the parties. The agreement will be allowed to proceed only if the legislative requirements are satisfied and the parties are fully cognisant of the potential psychological and social effects of surrogacy as well as the agreement's legal effect.

The proposed national model would permit only gestational[164] surrogacy agreements. The rationale for this limitation is to minimise the risk of psychological harm by discouraging circumstances where the surrogate might be more inclined to bond with the child during pregnancy and then find herself unwilling to relinquish the child to the intended parent(s) after the birth. Such restraint is not uncommon in surrogacy legislation and similar provisions appear in the Western Australia,[165] ACT[166] and Victorian[167] Acts. Internationally, as early as 1996, in order to satisfy Halachic law,[168] Israel permitted gestational but prohibited traditional surrogacy agreements,[169] and studies conducted by Van den Akker reveal that the gestational surrogates surveyed 'did not believe they could relinquish a genetically related baby as easily as a non-genetically related gestated baby'.[170] Likewise, evidence from gestational surrogates was positive when compared to that of traditional surrogates who sometimes experienced regret.[171]

The 1998 Australian case of *Re Evelyn*,[172] highlights the difficulties sometimes associated with traditional surrogacy and the bond formed between the surrogate and the child she is carrying.[173] Trowse suggests that a traditional surrogate's 'job

---

in wider context', (2010) *BioNews*, available at http://www.bionews.org.uk/page_54415.asp, accessed 9 February 2015.

164 In gestational surrogacy, the surrogate has no genetic relationship to the child she is gestating. The genetic material often used in gestational surrogacy comes from the intended parents or donor(s). Gestational surrogacy is sometimes referred to as full or non-genetic surrogacy. In the other type of surrogacy, traditional surrogacy, the surrogate uses her own egg to become pregnant and is both the birth mother and the biological mother of the child. Traditional surrogacy is sometimes referred to as partial or genetic surrogacy.

165 *Surrogacy Act* 2008 (WA), s 21(4).

166 *Parentage Act* 2004 (ACT), s 24.

167 *Assisted Reproductive Treatment Act* 1008 (Vic), s 40.

168 Halachic law refers to the body of Jewish laws, derived from both the written and oral Torah.

169 Elly Teman, 'The Birth of Surrogacy in Israel (review)' (2006) 2(3) *Journal of Middle East Women's Studies* 114.

170 Olga B.A. van den Akker, 'Psychosocial Aspects of Surrogate Motherhood' (2007) 13(1) *Human Reproduction Update* 53, 56.

171 Van den Akker, 'Genetic and Gestational Surrogate Mothers' Experience of Surrogacy', above n. 122, 157.

172 (1998) 23 Fam LR 53.

173 This case involved a traditional surrogacy agreement where the surrogate, after initially relinquishing the child to the intended parents, struggled with her decision and later

is more difficult' as she has 'two hurdles to overcome ... that of her biological attachment and her role as the delivering mother'.[174] She states that:

> [t]he process of cognitive restructuring suggests that the genetic surrogate is placed in a more vulnerable position than the gestational surrogate. The gestational surrogate makes a single contribution to motherhood and that is to carry the child to the point of delivery, after which she should surrender the child to the commissioning parents. By focusing on the two aspects of pregnancy she lacks – a genetic connection and the prospect of being the social mother – she can detach herself from the child, thereby making relinquishment easier.[175]

6. Offences

While the proposed national model would provide a regime under which commercial surrogacy is legal, it should be noted that any form of surrogacy is still potentially harmful. Therefore, it is essential to take all steps necessary, and to act responsibly, to minimise the potential for such harms to occur. While the national model would permit commercial surrogacy, it is unacceptable for society to allow a person who is not essential to the agreement to profit from it. Arneson highlights the limits of acceptable behaviour in liberal society when he notes that Mill 'countenanced the possibility that a due regard for the value of individual liberty might lead a society to permit fornication and gambling but prohibit pimping and the keeping of gambling houses'.[176]

The proposed national model would therefore continue the current prohibition on advertising by third parties, but would permit advertising on one's own behalf as a legitimate means of finding willing parties to conclude a surrogacy agreement. An inability to advertise on one's own behalf would create unnecessary barriers to surrogacy by making it virtually impossible for intended parents and surrogates to find one another.

Specifically, to ensure that those not connected with surrogacy arrangements are unable to profit from them, the proposed national model would prohibit the publication by any agency or third party of material that is likely to induce or source a person to become a surrogate. Similar provisions are contained in the Queensland, New South Wales, Tasmanian and Western Australian legislation, lending support to this recommendation. The offence provisions in the Victorian and ACT legislation are somewhat more restrictive, making it an offence for *any*

---

sought to reclaim custody. The genetic connection between the surrogate and the child was an important consideration for the court which ultimately awarded custody of the child to the surrogate.

174 Pip Trowse, 'Surrogacy: Is it Harder to Relinquish Genes?" (2011) 18 *Journal of Law and Medicine* 617.

175 Ibid.

176 Richard J. Arneson, 'Commodification and Commercial Surrogacy' (1992) 21(2) *Philosophy and Public Affairs* 132, 133.

person to advertise in relation to surrogacy.[177] The proposed model would favour a more liberal approach, making it an offence only for a person who does not intend to become a party to the surrogacy agreement to advertise in respect of one.

IV. Conclusion

> It would be so nice if something would make sense for a change.[178]
>
> (Alice, *Alice in Wonderland*)

This chapter has provided some insight into the fragmentation of the current surrogacy legislation in Australia, highlighting the need for reform that strikes a balance between these various regimes. In response to this need, the foundation for a national surrogacy model has been proposed.

In what is anticipated to be a rather controversial proposal, this chapter contends that commercial surrogacy should be legitimised in Australia, subject to appropriate measures to minimise the risk of harm that might flow from the practice. Also somewhat controversially, the notion that the birth mother should *always* be presumed to be the parent of a child is challenged and it is recommended that there be a presumption in favour of the intended parent(s) in gestational surrogacy arrangements.

The matters considered in the proposed national model draw in part from the existing surrogacy legislation in Australia and the SCAG Proposal with the objective of striking a balance and, dare it be hoped, achieving a consensus among the states and territories. States and territories could use this model to finally take steps to either enact consistent legislation or refer power to the Commonwealth so that surrogacy can be regulated at the federal level.

177 See *Assisted Reproductive Treatment Act* 2008 (Vic), s 45; *Parentage Act* 2004 (ACT), s 43.

178 *Alice in Wonderland* (Disney, 1951).

Table 4.1 Australian Surrogacy Legislation[179]

	QLD	**NSW**	**ACT**	**VIC**	**SA**	**TAS**	**WA**	**NT**
Legislation	*Surrogacy Act* 2010 *(Qld)*	*Surrogacy Act* 2010 *(NSW)*	*Parentage Act* 2004 *(ACT)*	*Assisted Reproductive Treatment Act* 2008 *(Vic)*	*Family Relationships Act* 1975 *(SA)*	*Surrogacy Act* 2012 *(Tas)*	*Surrogacy Act* 2008 *(WA)*	NIL
Altruistic surrogacy	Permitted	Permitted	Permitted	Permitted	Permitted	Permitted	Permitted	Silent
Commercial surrogacy	Prohibited	Prohibited	Prohibited	Prohibited	Prohibited	Prohibited	Prohibited	Silent
Enforceability of agreements	Unenforceable except for recovery of surrogate's reasonable expenses	Unenforceable except for recovery of surrogate's reasonable expenses	Silent, but definition of 'commercial substitute parent agreement' permits payment of surrogate's expenses	Unenforceable except for recovery of surrogate's actual expenses	Silent, but definition of 'recognised surrogacy agreement' allows payment of surrogate's expenses	Unenforceable except for recovery of surrogate's reasonable expenses	Unenforceable except for recovery of surrogate's reasonable expenses	Silent

179 Current at the time of submission for publication.

	QLD	NSW	ACT	VIC	SA	TAS	WA	NT
Eligibility of same-sex couples	Permitted but both female same-sex partners must be infertile	Permitted but both female same-sex partners must be infertile	Permitted	Permitted but for female same-sex couples at least one must be infertile	Not eligible	Permitted but both female same-sex partners must be infertile	Female same-sex couples eligible but one must be infertile. Male couples ineligible	Silent but adoption not permitted by same-sex couples
Territorial restraint	Yes	Yes	Yes	No	No	No	No	Silent
Offences	Advertising a willingness to enter into a surrogacy agreement or advertising in a manner designed to induce entry into a surrogacy agreement, providing technical or professional services for commercial surrogacy	Advertising or soliciting for participants in commercial surrogacy arrangements	Advertising, providing technical or professional services for commercial surrogacy	Advertising a willingness to be a surrogate, accept a benefit, enter into or procure someone to enter into a surrogacy agreement, seek a participant in or be willing to arrange a surrogacy arrangement	Advertising a willingness to enter into a surrogacy agreement or advertising in a manner designed to induce entry into a surrogacy agreement, providing technical or professional services for commercial surrogacy	Commercial brokerage or advertising of surrogacy, reporting of applications for parentage or other orders	Advertising, providing technical or professional services for commercial surrogacy, receiving payment for introducing parties to a surrogacy agreement	Silent

continued

Table 4.1 *continued*

	QLD	**NSW**	**ACT**	**VIC**	**SA**	**TAS**	**WA**	**NT**
Transfer of Parentage	Parentage Orders through Children's Court	Parentage Orders through Supreme Court	Parentage Orders through Supreme Court	Parentage Orders through Supreme or County Court	Parentage Orders through the Youth Court	Parentage Orders through Magistrates Court (Children's Division)	Parentage Orders through Family Court	Adoption

Table 4.2 Australian Parentage Legislation[180]

	QLD	NSW	ACT	VIC	SA	TAS	WA	NT
Legislation	*Status of Children Act* 1978 *(Qld)*	*Status of Children Act* 1996 *(NSW)*	*Parentage Act* 2004 *(ACT)*	*Status of Children Act* 1974 *(VIC)*	*Family Relationships Act* 1975 *(SA)*	*Status of Children Act* 1974 *(TAS)*	*Artificial Conception Act* 1985 *(WA)*	*Status of Children Act* 1978 *(NT)*
Presumption as to mother	Birth mother	Birth mother	Birth mother	Birth mother	Birth mother	Birth mother	Birth mother	Birth mother
Presumption as to father	Birth mother's husband or male de facto	Birth mother's husband or male de facto	Birth mother's husband or civil or domestic partner	Birth mother's husband or male de facto	Birth mother's husband or ex-husband if the birth occurs within 10 months of the marriage being dissolved or the death of the husband	Birth mother's husband or male partner	Birth mother's husband or male de facto	Birth mother's husband or male de facto
Presumption as to parent in same-sex relationship	Same-sex partners not recognised as parents	Female same-sex partners recognised	Recognised under definitions of 'civil partner' and 'domestic partner'	Female same-sex partners recognised	Same-sex partners not recognised as parents	Same-sex partners recognised under definition of 'significant relationship'	Female same-sex partners recognised	Female same-sex partners recognised

180 Current at the time of submission for publication.

Chapter 5
Extra-Territoriality and Surrogacy: The Problem of State and Territory Moral Sovereignty

Anita Stuhmcke*

I. Introduction

Crime and reproduction are areas of citizen activity that have historically been local or personal phenomena. Traditionally the regulation of such activities has been territorial in the sense that it has been applied within a particular geographical territory. Today, however, the application of extraterritorial criminal provisions to international reproductive practice is increasingly common. This accretion of jurisdiction by a (nation) state over conduct occurring outside its borders has been attributed to the rise of globalisation as '[c]heap travel, advances in technology and telecommunications and the anonymity of the internet have created rapid expansion of transnational crimes such as child sex tourism, terrorism, and human rights abuse'.[1] McSherry and Bronitt frame the emergence of a more flexible approach to jurisdiction and a move away from territoriality as being related to the 'globalisation of crime', observing that:

> Crimes of international jurisdiction are those that international law regards as so 'grave and heinous' that every nation is entitled to try them irrespective of where the conduct occurred. There is disagreement over what crimes fall within this category. It is commonly agreed that war crimes, piracy and slavery fall within it.[2]

Internationally, extraterritorial offences apply to a small number of areas that impinge upon private sexual or reproductive practice. Commercial surrogacy

---

* Professor of Law, University of Technology, Sydney. This chapter was supported by Discovery Project Grant DP0986213 from the Australian Research Council and from funding by the Faculty of Law, University of Technology, Sydney. Many thanks to Jenni Millbank, Isabel Karpin and Eloise Chandler for their comments.

1 Danielle Ireland-Piper, 'Extraterritoriality and the Sexual Conduct of Australians Overseas' (2010) 22(2) *Bond Law Review* 16, 32.

2 Simon Bronitt and Bernadette McSherry, *Principles of Criminal Law* (Pyrmont, NSW: Lawbook Co., 3rd edn, 2010), 950.

thus joins this relatively small list of private-life offences, which includes female genital cutting and child sex.[3]

In March 2010, Turkey became the first country to legislate against its citizens seeking third-party reproductive assistance overseas through donor gametes or surrogacy.[4] In doing so, Turkey joined the Australian jurisdictions of the Australian Capital Territory and Queensland, which introduced similar legislative provisions in 1994 (ACT) and 1988/2010 (Qld) respectively. In 2011, New South Wales became the third Australian jurisdiction to apply extraterritorial criminal laws to residents pursuing surrogacy overseas.

It is remarkable that three of the four jurisdictions worldwide which currently impose extraterritorial prohibitions on commercial surrogacy are Australian states and territories. Indeed, given the first extraterritorial commercial surrogacy law was introduced in Queensland almost 30 years ago, Australia has, without fanfare, become a world leader in both quantity and longevity of extraterritorial criminal legislation regulating cross-border assisted reproduction.

This chapter examines the cause, effect and validity of the ACT, NSW and Queensland extraterritorial laws.[5] It questions the justifications offered for the restrictive extraterritorial regulation of commercial surrogacy, and refers to empirical research as to Australian usage of Thai reproductive services,[6] media analysis as to the numbers of Australians who engage in cross-border commercial surrogacy[7] and commentary as to the establishment of Australian owned and operated assisted reproduction clinics in Thailand.[8] Such research reveals no evidence of harm and it is argued that criminal law should not apply to surrogacy in the absence of evidence as to harm[9] and, as authors such as Storrow[10] and Van

3 Wannes Van Hoof and Guido Pennings, 'Extraterritoriality for Cross-Border Reproductive Care: Should States Act against Citizens Travelling Abroad for Illegal Infertility Treatment?' (2011) 23 *Reproductive Biomedicine Online* 546.

4 Zeynep B. Gürtin, 'Banning Reproductive Travel: Turkey's ART Legislation and Third-Party Assisted Reproduction' (2011) 23 *Reproductive Biomedicine Online* 555.

5 See also Mary Keyes, 'Cross-border Surrogacy Agreements' (2012) 26 *Australian Journal of Family Law* 28; Pip Trowse, 'Surrogacy: Competing Interests or a Tangled Web?' (2013) 33(3) *The Queensland Lawyer* 199, Jenni Millbank, 'Rethinking "Commercial" Surogacy in Australia" (2014) *Bioethical Inquiry*, Published Online 12 July 2014.

6 Andrea M. Whittaker, 'Reproduction Opportunists in the New Global Sex Trade: PGD and Non-Medical Sex Selection' (2011) 23 *Reproductive Biomedicine Online* 609.

7 Jenni Millbank, 'The New Surrogacy Parentage Laws in Australia: Cautious Regulation or "25 Brick Walls"?' (2011) 35 *Melbourne University Law Review* 165.

8 Andrea Whittaker, 'Cross-border Assisted Reproduction Care in Asia: Implications for Access, Equity and Regulations' (2011) 19(37) *Reproductive Health Matters* 108.

9 Anita Stuhmcke, 'The Criminal Act of Commercial Surrogacy in Australia: A Call for Review' (2010) 18 *Journal of Law and Medicine* 601.

10 Richard F. Storrow, 'Assisted Reproduction on Treacherous Terrain: The Legal Hazards of Cross-Border Reproductive Travel' (2011) 23 *Reproductive Biomedicine Online* 538.

Hoof and Pennings[11] argue, it is unjustifiable to impose an extraterritorial criminal law in areas of contested morality such as commercial surrogacy.

II. Overview of the Operation of Australian Extraterritorial Surrogacy Legislation

In Australia, as in the United States, there is a 'state-by-state patchwork quilt of reproductive autonomy'.[12] As there is both a lack of constitutional power and political will on the part of the Australian federal government to make laws in relation to surrogacy, regulation has been left to the states and territories. The result has been described as 'medicine by postcode',[13] where ineligible parents travel interstate for treatment with fertility services in restricted states actively facilitating such travel.[14]

This regulatory dissensus is exemplified by the fact that while almost all Australian jurisdictions (with the exception of the Northern Territory) render commercial surrogacy illegal, only three Australian jurisdictions have passed extraterritorial criminal provisions. Implicit extraterritorial regulatory measures such as geographical nexus requirements and parentage orders,[15] which exist to indirectly restrict access to surrogacy, are not discussed in this chapter as they are discussed in-depth elsewhere in this volume. It is worth briefly noting that any intending parents who have entered into international surrogacy arrangements will have to request parentage orders and apply for visas for their children. A child (subclass 101) visa[16] will enable a child born of a surrogacy arrangement overseas to enter, and reside permanently in, Australia. To obtain that visa, the child must satisfy certain requirements relating to age, biology, custody, health, character and

---

11 Van Hoof and Pennings, above n. 3.

12 Seth F. Kreimer, 'The Law of Choice and Choice of Law: Abortion, the Right to Travel, and Extraterritorial Regulation in American Federalism' (1992) 67 *New York University Law Review* 451, 453.

13 Social Development Committee, Parliament of South Australia, *Inquiry into Gestational Surrogacy* (2007), 51 (Dr Christine Kirby).

14 Kerry Petersen, H.W.G Baker, Marian Pitts and Rachel Thorpe, 'Assisted Reproductive Technologies: Professional and Legal Restrictions in Australian Clinics' (2005) 12 *Journal of Law and Medicine* 373.

15 Jenni Millbank, 'Resolving the Dilemma of Legal Parentage for Australians Engaged in International Surrogacy' (2013) 27(2) *Australian Journal of Family Law* 135; Keyes, above n. 5.

16 See Department of Immigration and Citizenship, Australian Government, *Visas, Immigration and Refugees: Family Members: Child Visa (Subclass* 101*)* (2012), available at http://www.immi.gov.au/migrants/family/child/101, accessed 9 February 2015.

sponsorship.[17] If a visa is granted and the child enters Australia, they may then be able to apply for Australian citizenship by conferral.

While there is a general presumption that offences in state legislation do not have extraterritorial effect,[18] it is now well established that state legislatures are nonetheless competent to make laws that operate extraterritorially by express provision in the relevant statute, as long as there is a sufficient nexus between the legislating state and the prohibited act.[19] Following is a brief summary of the three Australian jurisdictions that have operational extraterritoriality provisions to prohibit their residents engaging in international commercial surrogacy.

A. Australian Capital Territory

The provisions with respect to extraterritorial application were first introduced in 1994 in the *Substitute Parent Agreements Act* 1994 (ACT). The aim of the legislation was to prevent people who are normally residents of the ACT from 'procuring the services of a person for the purposes of a substitute parent agreement, or advertising for a birth mother in another State or country'.[20]

The *Substitute Parent Agreements Act* 1994 (ACT) has since been replaced by the *Parentage Act* 2004 (ACT), section 45 of which provides the extraterritorial prohibition for all offences under Part 4 of the Act. The offences under Part 4 include: intentionally entering into (s 41), procuring someone for (s 42), advertising for (s 43) and facilitating pregnancy for (s 44) a commercial surrogacy arrangement.

The exact wording of s 45, titled 'Geographical nexus for offences', is:

1. A geographical nexus exists between the ACT and an offence against this part if, when the offence is committed, the person who commits the offence is ordinarily resident in the ACT.
2. This section is additional to, and does not limit, the Criminal Code, section 64(2) (Extension of offences if required geographical nexus exists).

In the ACT, the penalty for breaching these provisions is up to one year's imprisonment and/or a $11,000 fine.

---

17 Requirements include that the child must be: a natural (biological) child of the Australian parent; or an adopted child or a step-child of the Australian parent within the meaning of the *Migration Act* 1958; or a child conceived through an artificial conception procedure; or a child born under surrogacy arrangements, where parentage has been transferred by court order under a prescribed state or territory law. See http://www.immi.gov.au/allforms/pdf/1128.pdf, accessed 16 June 2014.

18 *Morgan v Goodall* (1985) 2 NSWLR 655, 656.

19 *Australia Act* 1986 (UK), s 2(1); *Pearce v Florenca* (1976) 135 CLR 507.

20 Explanatory Memorandum, Substitute Parent Agreements Bill 1994 (ACT), 4.

B. Queensland

In Queensland, section 3 of the *Surrogate Parenthood Act* 1988 (Qld) initially rendered both commercial and altruistic extraterritorial surrogacy a criminal offence. That is, the legislation prohibited a Queensland resident from entering into a surrogacy agreement, regardless of the jurisdiction in which the surrogacy agreement was entered. As of 1 June 2010, the extraterritorial prohibition in the QLD *Surrogacy Act* 2010 is found in s 54, titled 'Territorial application'. The section reads:

> This part applies in relation to:
> a. acts done in Queensland regardless of the whereabouts of the offender at the time the act is done; or
> b. acts done outside Queensland if the offender is ordinarily resident in Queensland at the time the act is done.

The offences listed in Part 1 to which this section applies are: advertising for (s 55), entering (or offering to enter) into (s 56), giving or receiving consideration for (s 57) and assisting professionally, technically or medically (s 58), a commercial surrogacy arrangement.

In Queensland the penalty for breaching these provisions is up to three years' imprisonment and/or a fine of $10,000.[21]

C. New South Wales

Since March 2011, it is an offence to enter a surrogacy agreement whether within or outside NSW as long as there is a geographical nexus with the state. Section 11 of the *Surrogacy Act* 2010 (NSW) is titled 'Geographical nexus for offences' and states:

> 1. This section applies for the purposes of, and without limiting, Part 1A of the *Crimes Act* 1900.
> 2. The necessary geographical nexus exists between the State and an offence against this Division if the offence is committed by a person ordinarily resident or domiciled in the State.
>
> *Note:* Section 10C of the *Crimes Act* 1900 also provides that a geographical nexus exists between the State and an offence if the offence is committed wholly or partly in the State or has an effect in the State.

Section 8 of the *Surrogacy Act* 2010 (NSW) applies a penalty for paid surrogacy of $110,000 (1,000 penalty units) or imprisonment for two years or both for an

---

21 The penalty is 100 penalty units which equates to $10,000. See *Penalties and Sentences Act* 1992 (Qld), s 5(1).

individual. The *Surrogacy Act* 2010 (NSW) also amends the *Assisted Reproductive Technology Act* 2007 (NSW) to prohibit clinics from carrying on business in contravention of the *Surrogacy Act* 2010 (NSW) – meaning that ambiguity now surrounds clinic involvement in facilitating surrogacy overseas such as through the exportation of already generated embryos.

D. Enforcement?

The extraterritorial criminal provisions which apply to commercial surrogacy have never been enforced in any of the three Australian jurisdictions. This remains the case despite the existence of high-profile legal and media cases where residents of the ACT, Queensland and NSW have used international commercial surrogacy agencies. There were only a handful of unsuccessful prosecutions of altruistic surrogacy arrangements in Queensland under the now repealed *Surrogate Parenthood Act* 1988 (Qld). As Brown, Willmott and White outline,[22] there were only three prosecutions under that legislation in Queensland. None of them were extraterritorial in operation. In 1991, two women were charged and the magistrate dismissed them without recording a conviction; similarly in 1993, more women were charged under the Act and the magistrate recommended that the charges against them under the legislation should not proceed. Finally, in 1993, a medical practitioner was fined $2,000 and placed on a good behaviour bond for facilitating altruistic surrogacy.

This lack of appetite to proceed with prosecutions was also seen in a high-profile custody case concerning an altruistic surrogacy arrangement that went without criminal charge. The first case in Australia where the Full Court of the Family Court of Australia determined legal parentage following a dispute over the custody of a child following the breakdown of a surrogacy arrangement concerned a couple from Queensland and a couple from South Australia. In *Re Evelyn*,[23] the court applied the traditional family law test of the child's 'best interests' to place her with the South Australian surrogate mother. There was no prosecution of the Queensland couple under the then-operational s 3 of the *Surrogate Parenthood Act* 1988 (Qld).

More recently, Justice Watts in the Family Court of Australia referred two Queensland surrogacy cases to the Director of Public Prosecutions with respect to contraventions of the extraterritorial provisions of the former *Surrogate Parenthood Act* 1988 (Qld). The first case, *Dudley & Anor v Chedi*,[24] concerned an application for parentage of two boys born in August 2009 through surrogacy in Thailand. The boys were conceived using Mr Dudley's sperm and donated eggs, and were carried

22 Catherine Brown, Lindy Willmott and Ben White, 'Surrogacy in Queensland: Should Altruism Be a Crime?' (2008) 20(1) *Bond Law Review* 1.

23 (1998) 145 FLR 90.

24 [2011] FamCA 502.

to term by a Thai surrogate. The second case, *Findlay & Anor v Punyawong*,[25] was an application to the Family Court by Mr Findlay and Ms Adrei to have equal shared parental responsibility for two children born in Thailand in January 2011, pursuant to a surrogacy arrangement. Like in *Dudley*, the surrogacy arrangement involved Mr Findlay providing his sperm to be used with eggs donated by an egg donor with the resulting embryo carried to term by a Thai surrogate mother. In each case it was reported that the egg donor was unknown and was not a party to the proceedings. Each Thai birth certificate showed the name of the father – Mr Dudley and Mr Findlay as applicable – and the name of the surrogate mother as the parents of the children.

In each case, the applicants applied to the Family Court for orders under the *Family Law Act* 1975 (Cth) for parental responsibility and for the children to live with them at their home in Queensland. The applicants required the said orders to assist them to apply for Australian citizenship for the children. Each surrogate mother consented to the orders being sought by the applicants. In each case, the Court examined whether the orders sought by the applicants were in the children's best interests and made orders for the children to live with the applicants and for the applicants to have equal shared parental responsibility for making decisions about both long-term and day-to-day issues in respect of the children.

In both cases, the Australians travelling to Thailand were Queensland residents and, at the time the children were conceived (prior to 1 June 2010), had committed an illegal act under the *Surrogate Parenthood Act* 1988 then in force. The Court made an additional order that a copy of the judgment be provided to the Office of the Director of Public Prosecutions, Queensland for consideration of whether a prosecution should be instituted against the applicants under section 3 of the *Surrogate Parenthood Act* 1988 (Qld). In the final paragraph in *Dudley* at [32] (and in similar words in *Findlay* at [32]) Justice Watts stated:

> It appears that what the applicants have done in this case is illegal. I would direct the Registrar to send a copy of the judgment to the Office of the Director of Public Prosecutions, Queensland for consideration of whether a prosecution should be instituted against the applicants under s 3 *Surrogate Parenthood Act 1988* (Qld) and if requested, the Registrar is to supply any document on the court file to the Office of the Director of Public Prosecutions.

There have been no resulting prosecutions.

The ongoing absence of any prosecution supports the view that the Australian laws are an exercise in pure symbolism. Of course this observation does not deny that even where laws are symbolic in application, symbolism can cause great

25 [2011] FamCA 503.

harm.[26] For example, symbolism often uses pejorative language,[27] which not only results in immediate frustration and disappointment for those individuals who wish to use commercial surrogacy but casts people who evade the extraterritorial laws through travel as morally degenerate and even a national threat.[28]

In this sense, the fact that the recent referral to the Director of Public Prosecutions was made in a family law case with respect to an act of international commercial surrogacy takes on fresh significance. Today in Australia, extraterritorial reproductive autonomy provisions have created two tiers of citizens with respect to liberty to travel freely – those from states and territories that do not impose extraterritorial regulation on reproduction and those that do. Australian regulation of surrogacy therefore entails a 'moral Balkanization, in which competing moral agendas seek without restraint to conquer foreign territories … a system in which citizens carry home-state law with them as they travel, like escaped prisoners dragging a ball and chain'.[29] The criminal referral with respect to international surrogacy confirms that the moral sovereignty of the Australian state of Queensland no longer ends at its borders. Infringement upon the liberty of NSW, ACT and Queensland residents to avoid the moral prohibition of their home jurisdiction with respect to reproductive choice is complete.

III. The Justifications for the Extraterritorial Laws

The regulatory dissensus that applies to commercial surrogacy throughout Australia is legally justifiable on the basis that the powers of a state to make laws are found in state constitutions. Kirby J outlined the historical view of extraterritoriality in *Mobil Oil Australia Pty Ltd v Victoria*:[30]

> At the time of federation, the prevailing view was that the colonial legislatures were incompetent to enact legislation having an extraterritorial operation. That view was reflected in the early decisions of this court concerning the legislative powers of the states. However, in 1932 this approach was abandoned, so far as the dominions of the Crown were concerned, by the decision of the Privy Council in *Croft v Dunphy* [[1933] AC 156].[31]

---

26 Storrow, above n. 10, 542.

27 Joan C. Callahan (ed.), *Reproduction, Ethics, and the Law: Feminist Perspectives* (Bloomington, IN: Indiana University Press, 1995), 27.

28 Storrow, above n. 10, 542–3. For an example of a Family Court decision concerning international commercial surrogacy which does not address extraterritoriality, see, *Fisher-Oakley & Kittur* [2014] Fam CA 123 at [22].

29 Kreimer, above n. 12, 463.

30 (2002) 211 CLR 1.

31 Ibid., 53.

That 'the legislative powers of the Parliament of each State include full power to make laws for the peace, order and good government of that State that have extra-territorial operation' was later enshrined in s 2(1) of the *Australia Act* 1986 (UK). In *Union Steamship Company of Australia Pty Ltd v King*,[32] the High Court held unanimously that the words 'peace, welfare [or order], and good government' in state constitutions are not to be read as words of limitation.[33] Thus, legislation of a state parliament having extraterritorial effect 'should be held valid if there is any real connexion – even a remote or general connexion – between the subject matter of the legislation and the State'.[34]

While this proposition is regarded as settled law, there is very little constitutional debate as to the extent of any 'territorial limitations upon the legislative powers of the States which arise from the federal structure of which each State is a part'.[35] Kirby J in *Mobil Oil* suggested that state power may be curtailed to 'the extent of any implied limitation derived from the federal Constitution controlling the exercise of that power'.[36]

More fundamentally, the fact that extraterritorial legislation is permissible does not determine whether it is justified in the regulation of any particular subject matter. If, as McSherry and Bronnitt suggest,[37] the option of extending geographical jurisdiction will be 'hard for legislators to resist', it becomes more pressing to examine the reasonableness and desirability of states' expanding their jurisdictions internationally.

Clearly the extension of moral sovereignty over cross-border reproductive travel has proliferated at a state and territory level with respect to commercial surrogacy. Less clear, however, is whether such restrictive Australian extraterritorial legislation is both principled and well thought through. This point is important to consider given the priority placed upon clear justification of an extension of criminal law extraterritorially. For example, as a former Attorney-General noted: 'Naturally, it is intended that extended forms of jurisdiction will only be applied where there is justification for this, having regard to considerations of international law, comity and practice'.[38]

---

32 (1988) 166 CLR 1.

33 Ibid., 10 (Mason CJ, Wilson, Brennan, Deane, Dawson, Toohey and Gaudron JJ).

34 *Pearce v Florenca* (1976) 135 CLR 507, 518 (Gibbs J); *Union Steamship* (1988) 166 CLR 1, 14; *Port MacDonnell Professional Fishermen's Association Inc v South Australia* (1989) 168 CLR 340, 372.

35 *State Authorities Superannuation Board v Commissioner of State Taxation (WA)* (1996) 189 CLR 253, 271 (Brennan CJ, Dawson, Toohey and Gaudron JJ). See also *Port MacDonnell Professional Fishermen's Association Inc v South Australia* (1989) 168 CLR 340, 369–73.

36 (2002) 211 CLR 1, 54.

37 Bronitt and McSherry, above n. 2, 952.

38 Commonwealth, *Parliamentary Debates*, House of Representatives, 24 November 1999, 12 464 (Daryl Williams, Attorney-General).

In contrast to federal attempts to extend jurisdiction according to 'international law, comity and practice', such principles are not readily applicable at the state and territory level to extraterritorial criminal laws on commercial surrogacy. Queensland is the only jurisdiction where the 1988 extraterritorial provisions were debated at any length by parliament. In the ACT and NSW the extraterritorial provisions were introduced with a noticeable absence of comprehensive parliamentary debate as to the import and impact of the extraterritorial restrictions.

In the original 1988 Queensland parliamentary debates, the then Opposition moved a last-minute amendment, which was subsequently defeated, to remove the extraterritorial provisions of the Surrogate Parenthood Bill 1988 (Qld). The amendment was brought by Ms Warner (Member for South Brisbane, who became Minister for Families), who stated: 'The Opposition will be opposing the extraterritorial provision, which is quite outside the scope of the legislation and brings to mind some frightening developments',[39] and went on to explain that:

> The reason the Opposition seeks an amendment is that the second part of the clause attempts to use Queensland law in an extraterritorial sense, that is, to chase the residents of Queensland all over the other Australian States and perhaps all over the world to try to limit their activities according to the norms which apply in this State ... It seems that the Queensland Government has a desire to proclaim almost anybody a Queenslander. The Opposition also has difficulty in accepting the term 'ordinarily resident in Queensland'. What does that term mean? Does it apply to a person who goes away for a week, two weeks, three weeks of a year?[40]

Further on in the debates, Mr Wells (Qld Attorney-General 1988–95) added:

> To give extraterritorial effect to a clause such as that is contrary to the spirit of the common law, contrary to the spirit of the statute law of Queensland and contrary to sound policy, and is a symptom of a degree of legal paternalism that is creeping through this Parliament ... We are dealing with Queenslanders who have every right to make up their minds to be law-abiding citizens in whatever place they choose.[41]

While the Queensland debate was limited, in that the Government offered minimal justification for the extraterritorial provisions (see further below), it provided a wealth of discussion when compared to that in the ACT and NSW. In the 1994 Australian Capital Territory parliamentary debates, the only comment made was by the ACT Attorney-General and Minister for Health, Mr Connolly, that:

39 Queensland, *Parliamentary Debates*, Legislative Assembly, 7 September 1988, 662 (Ms Warner).

40 Ibid., 682 (Ms Warner).

41 Ibid., 683, 686 (Mr Wells).

> There was also no objection in the submissions to the provision that a person may be liable for an offence where the action occurs in the ACT, regardless of the whereabouts of the person at the time, or if the person is normally resident of the ACT, irrespective of where the action occurs.[42]

In NSW, the extraterritorial provision was introduced in a last-minute amendment by Linda Burney, the NSW Community Services Minister. Even then the amendment did not excite much comment. Mr Aquilina in NSW in the Legislative Assembly debate on the Surrogacy Bill 2010 observed:

> that only a few members have opted to contribute to debate on this Bill. That is not surprising because I think members are feeling emotionally exhausted from the substantial amount of legislation that is being brought forward that requires them to look deeply into their consciences and to provide a personal response to issues that will have a huge impact on the individual lives of many people in this State.[43]

It is clear that the justifications given in favour of passing the ACT, NSW and Queensland extraterritorial provisions are sparse. The following four justifications are the clearest enunciations supporting the passage of the restrictive laws.

The first is the view that children should know their ancestry: 'I believe very much that a child has an absolute right to know who they are and where they come from and that's not possible if they're a surrogate child from overseas.'[44] The second is the view that commercial surrogacy is not available 'in our backyard' and therefore nor should it be available in anyone else's: 'This amendment would simply ensure a consistent standard: commercial surrogacy is not supported in New South Wales, therefore citizens in New South Wales should not be able to circumvent the law by engaging in commercial surrogacy arrangements overseas.'[45]

The third view is that surrogacy – especially commercial surrogacy – encourages exploitation. Ms Burney stated:

> In some countries where commercial surrogacy is allowed, such as the United States, some regulation is in place to protect the wellbeing of surrogate mothers. In other countries regulation is mostly absent. In my mind it would be irresponsible and indeed immoral to legislate in New South Wales but to be

42 ACT, *Parliamentary Debates*, Legislative Assembly, 19 May 1994, 1732 (Mr Connolly).

43 NSW, *Parliamentary Debates*, Legislative Assembly, 10 November 2010, 27 583 (Mr Aquilina).

44 Linda Burney, ABC Radio, *AM*, 4 December 2010, available at http://www.abc.net.au/am/content/2010/s3084682.htm, accessed 9 February 2015.

45 NSW, *Parliamentary Debates*, Legislative Assembly, 10 November 2010, 27 598 (Ms Burney).

> silent on the potential exploitation by our own citizens of vulnerable women overseas, especially in the face of mounting evidence that commercial surrogacy is a growth industry in many countries.[46]

Former Sex Discrimination Commissioner Pru Goward shared Burney's view:

> Women are not cows; they are not animals and their job is not to bear children for money because other people want children. If it is good enough to ensure that Australian women cannot be exploited commercially for this purpose, out of respect for women around the world – particularly the vulnerable women of Asia and other countries where commercial surrogacy flourishes – we should be particularly mindful that if we do not support this amendment, effectively we are saying that there is one rule for our women and another rule for women in poor countries. That is not good enough. Whilst this Parliament does not have a leading role in international relations and affairs, it should, as much as it is able, uphold Australian values, which must mean respect for all and the rights of all to live lives free of exploitation. Voting the right way will reflect our commitment to women in those poor countries and reinforce their rights as human beings.[47]

The fourth rationalisation is a simple one that merely observes that surrogacy is bad: 'The Government ... wants to give the strongest message possible to the people of Queensland that it believes that surrogacy and the problems that are caused by it are bad.'[48]

IV. Justifying the Justifications?

In one sense the above justifications miss the point entirely. There is not only a marked absence of discussion as to the applicability of extraterritorial provisions applying to enforce moral sovereignty over commercial surrogacy but there is also no debate as to the appropriateness of criminal law restricting liberty with respect to reproductive choice.[49]

Indeed there is a lack of proof that criminal law works in this area of highly personal choice. Paternoster and Simpson note[50] that criminologists focus on two

---

46 Ibid.

47 NSW, *Parliamentary Debates*, Legislative Assembly, 10 November 2010, 27 599 (Ms Goward).

48 Queensland, *Parliamentary Debates*, Legislative Assembly, 7 September 1988, 686 (Mr McKechnie).

49 Jenni Millbank, 'From Alice and Evelyn to Isabella: Exploring the Narratives and Norms of "New" Surrogacy in Australia' (2012) 21 *Griffith Law Review* 101.

50 Raymond Paternoster and Sally Simpson, 'Sanction Threats and Appeals to Morality: Testing a Rational Choice Model of Corporate Crime' (1996) 30 *Law & Society*

informal costs, the 'shame for doing something which the actor considers morally wrong', and 'social censure or disapproval by significant others' and observe that both have the potential to shape behaviour and encourage or discourage compliance with the law. The difficulty with the application of criminal law to assisted reproduction is that both sites are complex. There is shame associated with infertility and social censure and disapproval in relation to the childless. It is not surprising that criminal law does not operate to dissuade individuals from pursuing all available options of family formation available to them – including possibly illegal commercial surrogacy – as in the eyes of the infertile individual and society the worse crime is often that of being childless. It is therefore difficult to argue that the extraterritorial criminal legislation will meet the objective of preventing commercial surrogacy. As Keenan states:

> The decision to commit a crime is complicated and influenced by many factors, among them the probability of being caught, the expected legal sanction, the probability of actually suffering the legal sanction, and social norms. Norms against committing a crime must be stacked next to the other reasons that a person might commit a crime. It is wrong to assume that persons who have decided to commit a crime are not influenced by positive norms.[51]

Rendering commercial surrogacy illegal will not promote openness and transparency. If criminal law will not stop the practice the result is that it will be driven underground. The result of evasive reproductive practice will clearly not end in the justification stated where children know their genetic heritage.[52] Indeed, as is seen from the referrals to the Director of Public Prosecutions in Queensland, the provisions in the ACT, NSW and Queensland may turn some parents into criminals. As Mr Wells stated in the Queensland parliamentary debates:

> If a Queensland resident went to Victoria or South Australia to legally undergo a [surrogacy] and then returned to Queensland, in principle that person could be thrown into gaol for three years. The legislation is silent about what would happen to the child who was born as a result of that act, an act which was perfectly legal in the place where it was carried out.[53]

Problematic, too, is the language of exploitation used to justify the extraterritorial illegality of the practice. The root of the assertion is that infertile individuals

---

Review 549, 579.

51 Patrick J. Keenan, 'The New Deterrence: Crime and Policy in the Age of Globalization' (2006) 91 *Iowa Law Review* 505, 537.

52 See Paula Gerber and Katie O'Byrne's Chapter 6 in this volume entitled 'Souls in the House of Tomorrow: The Rights of Children Born via Surrogacy'.

53 Queensland, *Parliamentary Debates*, Legislative Assembly, 7 September 1988, 683 (Mr Wells).

take advantage of liberties which are not available in their home jurisdiction and travel from their own developed 'sending' country to another, often less developed, 'receiving' country[54] to engage in exploitative reproduction. Under this rationalisation a resident of the ACT, NSW and Queensland will owe their state or territory obedience no matter where they are, and any effort to take advantage of other legal regimes is an improper evasion of this obligation. This view borrows support from the traditional terminology applied in this area. For example, the Standing Committee of Attorneys-General Joint Working Group referred to travel for reproductive purposes as 'forum shopping'.[55] This language, alongside terms such as 'sex tourism', 'reproductive tourism', 'fertility tourism' and 'procreative tourism'[56] indicates a casual, enjoyable and blasé misuse of power. This terminology thus embodies notions of choice – that the infertile individuals who travel to access commercial surrogacy do so as a matter of choice and from a position of power. It follows therefore that their 'choice' must involve equal gain for themselves and exploitation of others, and that to enforce the 'at-home' restrictive policy the international pursuit of the practice must be illegal.

This assumption of exploitation is problematic for a number of reasons. First, the condemnation of commercial surrogacy seems ad hoc – there are other illegal Australian reproductive practices that remain legal to seek overseas, such as sex selection.[57] Second, application of exploitative terminology to characterise the infertile is not consistently applied. For example, the dialogue of exploitation has shifted in the ACT between 1994 and 2012. On 19 May 1994 the Australian Capital Territory Attorney-General and Minister for Health, Mr Connolly, stated in the parliamentary debate with respect to the passing of the Substitute Parent Agreement Bill 1994 that 'commercial agreements involve making a business and a profit out of the perceived needs of others'.[58] But this was a reference to surrogacy agencies making a business and a profit out of the needs of the infertile rather than the infertile exploiting the weaknesses of others.

Finally, Van Hoof and Pennings suggest that the reasons why international commercial surrogacy is exploitative have little to do with the practice itself and are solely grounded in the poor economic situation of the surrogate.[59] It is, of course, possible to access surrogacy in well-regulated international jurisdictions

---

54 Marianna Brungs, 'Abolishing Child Sex Tourism: Australia's Contribution' (2002) 8(2) *Australian Journal of Human Rights* 101.

55 Standing Committee of Attorneys-General Joint Working Group, *A Proposal for a National Model to Harmonise Regulation of Surrogacy* (January 2009), 14.

56 Zeynep B. Gürtin and Marcia C. Inhorn, 'Introduction: Travelling for Conception and the Global Assisted Reproduction Market' (2011) 23 *Reproductive Biomedicine Online* 535.

57 Whittaker, above n. 6, 614.

58 ACT, *Parliamentary Debates*, Legislative Assembly, 19 May 1994, 1730 (Mr Connolly).

59 Van Hoof and Pennings, above n. 3.

where there is a body of empirical research into the soundness of the practice. For example, California has a well-regulated practice of commercial surrogacy and an equivalent country background yet the practice of surrogacy in that jurisdiction was not mentioned in any of the parliamentary justifications for extraterritorial laws in Australian jurisdictions. The exploitation justification is therefore flawed with respect to commercial surrogacy as there is the possibility of non-exploitative legal regulation of its practice.

V. Conclusion

In the Australian context there is an absence of discussion as to the international consequences of extraterritorial criminal law applying to surrogacy and a lack of inquiry into the criminalisation of the practice. Indeed, in Queensland and NSW, this lack of discussion is highlighted by the fact that the most recent extraterritorial prohibitions are the result of government inquiries into altruistic surrogacy which had expressly excluded commercial surrogacy from their terms of reference.[60]

Extraterritorial legislative prohibition upon surrogacy in the ACT, NSW and Queensland condemns the practice both morally and legally. This has been done without extensive debate as to whether laws which restrict reproductive choice are justifiable given 'international law, comity and practice'. Further, there has been little attempt to be informed by individuals who have engaged in cross-border reproductive travel. This is despite the fact that research by Millbank has determined, through media reporting, that a significant number of Australians engage in cross-border commercial surrogacy. From the period 2007–10, 69 distinct families had been involved in surrogacy. Of these 69 cases, travel to 'evade restrictive local laws or to access donor gametes unavailable in home jurisdictions occurred in 44 cases'.[61] Travel to another Australian state was reported in 9 arrangements while international travel occurred in 35 cases. The omission to speak to people who have engaged in cross-border reproductive travel is significant, especially as a UK study found that participants 'saw the ability to access treatment wherever they choose to as an important right in a liberal democracy'.[62]

Australian legislators have disregarded any consideration of such a right in creating ad hoc exceptions in favour of extraterritoriality for specific offences and in extending the law of the state to offences outside state geographical borders.

---

60 Queensland, *Investigation into Altruistic Surrogacy*, Report (October 2008); NSW, Standing Committee on Law and Justice, *Legislation on Altruistic Surrogacy in NSW*, Report 38 (May 2009).

61 Millbank, above n. 7.

62 Nicky Hudson and Lorraine Culley, 'Assisted Reproductive Travel: UK Patient Trajectories' (2011) 23 *Reproductive Biomedicine Online* 573, 579. Australian research is currently underway see: Sam Everingham, Martyn Stafford-Bell & Karin Hammarberg, 'Australian's use of surrogacy' (2014) 201(5) *Medical Journal of Australia* 1–4.

Senz and Charlesworth state that '[e]xtraterritorial legislation is a controversial category of law'[63] that impinges upon the sovereignty of the country where the criminalised conduct takes place, suggesting that it is an underhand means of promoting foreign policy objectives. Here, the exact foreign policy objectives of reproductive commercial surrogacy laws are ill-defined. While there is an international obligation not to push our unwanted practices into other countries,[64] there is also an obligation to the residents of a home jurisdiction to ensure that laws which will restrict their offshore choices are passed in a principled and considered policy environment. Both aspects have been sorely lacking with respect to the extension of moral sovereignty being applied to restrict access to cross-border commercial surrogacy.

63 Deborah Senz and Hilary Charlesworth, 'Building Blocks: Australia's Response to Foreign Extraterritorial Legislation' (2001) 2 *Melbourne Journal of International Law* 69, 70.

64 Richard F. Storrow, 'Quests for Conception: Fertility Tourists, Globalization and Feminist Legal Theory' (2005–06) 57 *Hastings Law Journal* 295.

Chapter 6

Souls in the House of Tomorrow: The Rights of Children Born via Surrogacy

Paula Gerber* and Katie O'Byrne**

Your children are not your children.
They are the sons and daughters of Life's longing for itself.
They come through you but not from you,
And though they are with you yet they belong not to you …
You may give them your love but not your thoughts,
For they have their own thoughts.
You may house their bodies but not their souls,
For their souls dwell in the house of tomorrow …
For life goes not backward nor tarries with yesterday

Khalil Gibran[1]

I. Introduction

The above passage, written by the Lebanese philosopher Khalil Gibran in 1923, provides a useful starting point for a discussion about children's rights, particularly in the surrogacy context. Reflecting on the psychological, bodily and spiritual autonomy of the child, it encapsulates the responsibility of the child's parent(s), and also of the wider community, to love and safeguard the child while nurturing its individuality. Gibran's revelation that all children are born 'of Life's longing for itself', coming 'through you but not from you', is a reminder that, whatever their parentage or the means of their conception and birth, children are not property, but human beings and rights-holders in law.

This is also the message proffered by Michael Freeman, a modern-day children's rights philosopher. Freeman suggests that children's rights mirror certain responsibilities incumbent on parents and the community, particularly

* Associate Professor, Law Faculty, Monash University and Deputy Director of the Castan Centre for Human Rights Law.

** Barrister, Doughty Street Chambers, London, UK.

1 Khalil Gibran, 'On Children', in *The Prophet* (Heinemann: London, 1926), 20.

when it comes to novel areas of law and medical ethics.[2] Freeman argues that the focus of debate on children's rights should be about establishing structures to protect their integrity.[3] Applying that proposition to children born via surrogacy is the focus of this chapter.

The urge to have children is, of course, the most vital of human desires. Surrogacy sees this desire manifested in a complex web of science, ethics, human rights and law. The resulting child, while typically longed-for and deeply loved, is also the object or product of the transaction. Viewed from a human rights perspective, the interests of the child born via surrogacy may compete with the interests of other participants in the surrogacy arrangement. The child's interests may also be vulnerable to the operation of immigration, family and criminal laws in the country or countries where the birth takes place or where citizenship is sought for the child. Careful consideration of the human rights of children born in that position is warranted in order to evaluate whether the legal infrastructure around surrogacy is effectively protecting and promoting the rights of the child.

This chapter is presented in four parts. Part II identifies the human rights most relevant to children born via surrogacy, as embodied in the UN Convention on the Rights of the Child ('CRC').[4] It analyses the content of these obligations in relation to children born via surrogacy under four headings: non-discrimination, best interests, identity and sale of children. Part III uses Australia as a case study, evaluating whether Australian domestic laws are compliant with the international norms set out in CRC. This analysis involves looking not only at surrogacy legislation, but also at other relevant areas of law such as immigration and citizenship, family law and criminal law. Part IV concludes with recommendations for reform aimed at ensuring that surrogacy practices are consistent with the norms set out in the CRC. It is beyond the scope of this chapter to examine the issue of whether there should be a new international treaty regulating surrogacy, which has been explored by others.[5]

---

2 Michael Freeman, *The Moral Status of Children: Essays on the Rights of the Child* (The Hague: Kluwer Law International, 1997), 185.

3 Ibid., 188.

4 *Convention on the Rights of the Child*, adopted 20 November 1989, UNGA Res 44/25, entered into force 2 September 1990, 1577 UNTS 3 ('CRC'). While other international conventions contain provisions relevant to children's rights, the analysis in this chapter is largely confined to the CRC.

5 See, for example, Carolyn McLeod and Andrew Botterell, 'A Hague Convention on Contract Pregnancy (or "Surrogacy"): Avoiding Ethical Inconsistencies with the Convention on Adoption' (2014) 7(2) *International Journal of Feminist Approaches to Bioethics* 219; and Katarina Trimmings and Paul Beaumont (eds), *International Surrogacy Arrangements: Legal Regulation at the International Level* (Oxford: Hart Publishing, 2013). Note that, since 2010, the Permanent Bureau of The Hague Conference on Private International Law has been undertaking a project entitled 'The private international law issues surrounding the status of children, including issues arising from international surrogacy arrangements'. The project is looking at what a treaty on surrogacy might cover.

II. The Convention on the Rights of the Child

Before embarking on a detailed consideration of the rights of children born via surrogacy, it is important to address the question: what is a child? Surprisingly, this simple question does not have a simple answer. Article 1 of the CRC provides: 'For the purposes of the present Convention, a child means every human being below the age of eighteen years', but does not specify when childhood begins. The Preamble to the CRC adds to the ambiguity by quoting from the Declaration of the Rights of the Child:[6] 'the child … needs … appropriate legal protection, *before as well as after birth*' (emphasis added). During the CRC negotiations, the issue was a controversial one that was ultimately left open for each State Party to determine.[7] Australia, for example, has taken the approach that a foetus has no legal personality until it is born.[8] For the purposes of this chapter, 'child' is taken to refer to the child already born via surrogacy, rather than the unborn foetus in the uterus of the surrogate[9] – though some of the discussion applies equally to the foetus as to the child itself.

The CRC was adopted by the UN General Assembly in 1989, whereupon states began to sign and ratify it at a rapid rate. The CRC now has 195 parties, including all the members of the United Nations except Somalia and the United States, giving it near-universal acceptance.

The CRC does not make specific reference to children born via surrogacy, or indeed, any form of assisted reproductive technology, but several of its provisions have special relevance for the rights of such children. This chapter considers four key provisions as outlined in Figure 6.1 below.

This Part analyses the obligations of States Parties most relevant to children born via surrogacy, namely to guarantee non-discrimination (Article 2); prioritise a child's best interests (Article 3); register all births and respect a child's right to a nationality and to know and be cared for by one's parents (Article 7); and the right to identity and family relations (Article 8). Consideration is also given to whether the practice of compensated surrogacy amounts to the selling of children in violation of Article 35

Further information can be accessed here: http://www.hcch.net/index_en.php?act=text.display%tid=178, accessed 10 February 2015.

6 Adopted 10 December 1959, UNGA Res 1386 (XIV), 14 UN GAOR Supp. (No. 16) at 19, UN Doc A/4354 (1959).

7 See Adam Lopatka, 'Introduction', *Legislative History of the Convention on the Rights of the Child* (Geneva: Office of the High Commissioner for Human Rights, 11 June 2007), xli, explaining that this insertion was essentially a compromise measure.

8 *Attorney-General (Qld) (ex rel Kerr) v T* [1983] 1 Qd R 404, 406–407, affirmed on appeal in *Attorney-General (Qld) (ex rel Kerr) v T* (1983) 46 ALR 275.

9 Cf., for example, Rita Joseph, 'CRC Legislative History and the Child before Birth', *Human Rights and the Unborn Child* (Leiden: Martinus Nijhoff Publishers, 2009).

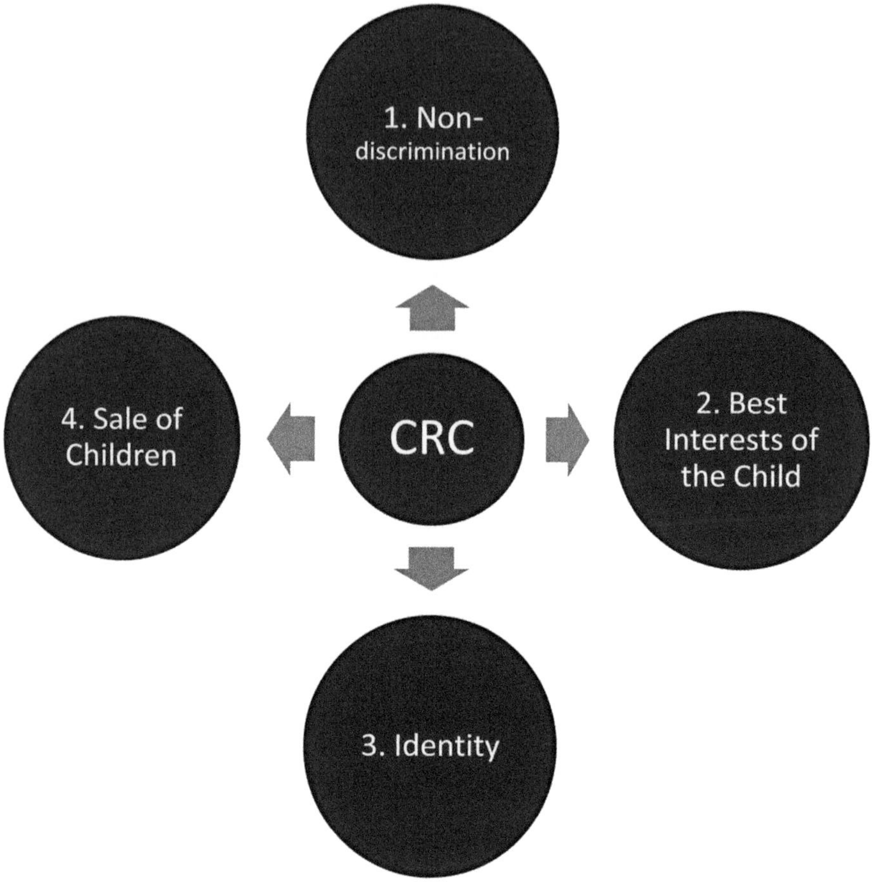

Figure 6.1 Key provisions of the CRC relevant to a consideration of surrogacy

of the CRC and the Optional Protocol on the Sale of Children, Child Prostitution and Child Pornography ('OP').[10]

A. Non-discrimination

Grounded in the bedrock principle of equality, non-discrimination is a foundational standard of international human rights law.[11] All major human rights treaties

10 Adopted 25 May 2000, UNGA Res 54/263, entered into force 18 January 2002, 2171 UNTS 227.

11 United Nations, Secretary-General, 'The Main Types and Causes of Discrimination: Memorandum submitted by the Secretary General', UN Doc E/CN.4/Sub.2/40/Rev.1 (1949).

include non-discrimination or non-distinction provisions,[12] and it is recognised as a norm of customary international law.[13]

Article 2 of the CRC provides:

1. States Parties shall respect and ensure the rights set forth in the present Convention to each child within their jurisdiction without discrimination of any kind, irrespective of the child's or his or her parent's or legal guardian's race, colour, sex, language, religion, political or other opinion, national, ethnic or social origin, property, disability, birth or other status.
2. States Parties shall take all appropriate measures to ensure that the child is protected against all forms of discrimination or punishment on the basis of the status, activities, expressed opinions, or beliefs of the child's parents, legal guardians, or family members.

Thus, the CRC places a child-specific obligation on States Parties to ensure that, in the implementation of the rights in the CRC, there is no distinction, exclusion, restriction or preference on the basis of any specified status that impairs the enjoyment of rights.[14] In other words, the principle of non-discrimination applies to the whole of the CRC.

Article 2 protects the child against discrimination based on specified characteristics of that child, relevantly including 'social origin ... birth or other status'. The categories of 'birth' and 'other status' arguably encompass being born via surrogacy. Article 2 also protects the child against discrimination based on specified characteristics of that child's parent or legal guardian, relevantly including 'sex ... disability', 'status, activities, expressed opinions, or beliefs'.[15]

---

12 See, for example, *Universal Declaration of Human Rights*, adopted 10 December 1948, UNGA Res 217 A (III), Art 2; *International Covenant on Civil and Political Rights*, adopted 16 December 1966, UNGA Res 2200A (XXI), entered into force 23 March 1976 (except Art 41 on 28 March 1979), 999 UNTS 171 ('ICCPR'), Arts 2(1) and 26; and *International Covenant on Economic, Social and Cultural Rights*, adopted 16 December 1966, UNGA Res 2200A (XXI), entered into force 3 January 1976, 993 UNTS 3, Art 2(1). The protected grounds in the CRC show some expansion in the concept, for example, by the extension to disability, which was not a ground explicitly protected in the earlier treaties.

13 See, for example, *South-West Africa Cases (Ethiopia v. South Africa; Liberia v. South Africa)*, Second Phase (1966) ICJ Rep 3, 293 per Judge Tanaka.

14 Here we adopt the formulation of the Human Rights Committee, General Comment 18, UN Doc HRI/geN/1/Rev. 5 (1989), [7], as distilled by Bruce Abramson, 'Article 2: The Right of Non-Discrimination', in André Alen et al. (eds), *A Commentary on the United Nations Convention on the Rights of the Child* (Leiden: Martinus Nijhoff Publishers, 2008), 19 [36].

15 See Samantha Besson, 'The Principle of Non-Discrimination in the Convention on the Rights of the Child', in Michael Freeman (ed.), *Children's Rights: Progress and Perspectives: Essays from the International Journal of Children's Rights* (Leiden: Martinus Nijhoff Publishers, 2011), 102.

A child may be discriminated against because he or she is a child (vis-à-vis adults)[16] or because s/he is a member of a class of children having a particular characteristic (vis-à-vis other classes of children). In the surrogacy context, discrimination is likely to take shape as discrimination between classes of children, though it may be difficult to separate the different types. Discrimination can be direct or indirect, and can be particularly damaging when it occurs on two or more intersecting bases. That said, the CRC does not require identical treatment in every situation. Article 2 can be used to justify 'asymmetrical measures'[17] or special treatment to ensure substantive equality between different classes of children. For example, a surrogate child may require particular measures to ensure that they can benefit equally from the rights to birth registration, nationality and identity.

The scope of Article 2, and of the CRC as a whole, is subject to jurisdictional limits. Under Article 2(1), States Parties promise to respect and ensure the rights in the CRC, without discrimination, to 'each child within their jurisdiction'. 'Jurisdiction' in international law refers to the judicial, legislative and administrative competence of a state.[18] While jurisdiction is presumptively coextensive with national territory, it may extend beyond territorial borders in some circumstances, including to nationals overseas.[19]

In contrast to the ICCPR, the CRC's jurisdiction clause does not contain any territorial limit.[20] 'Jurisdiction' under the CRC is not confined to citizens, so non-national children, at least within territory, can still be regarded as being within jurisdiction and entitled to the benefit of the CRC. This would include children born via overseas surrogacy who enter the territory of a State Party on a visa rather than as a citizen of that country. Further, the CRC applies to children who are lawfully within jurisdiction as well as to children who have been brought within jurisdiction by irregular means.[21]

16 Susan Marks and Andrew Clapham, *International Human Rights Lexicon* (Oxford: Oxford University Press, 2005), 19.

17 Besson, above n. 15, 108.

18 Ian Brownlie, *Principles of Public International* Law (Oxford: Oxford University Press, 7th edn, 2008), 299.

19 Traditionally it has been thought that extra-territorial jurisdiction can be founded on a limited number of exceptional bases (the effects doctrine, the nationality principle, the passive personality principle, the protective principle and the universality principle), but these are usually applied in the criminal law context and do not translate well to the context of protecting children born via surrogacy.

20 The prohibition on discrimination in ICCPR, Art 2(1) must be guaranteed by a state party to persons 'within its territory and subject to its jurisdiction'. Nonetheless, this phrase has been given a disjunctive reading (see, for example, Human Rights Committee, General Comment 31, UN Doc CCPR/C/21/Rev.1/Add.13 (2004), [10], indicating a willingness on the part of interpreters to extend jurisdiction beyond territory.

21 The CRC applies to certain vulnerable groups whose presence within a state's jurisdiction may be irregular, such as children in trouble with the law and refugee children;

As noted above, Article 2 is concerned not only with discrimination based on the characteristics of the child, but also discrimination based on the status or activities of the child's parent. The UN Committee on the Rights of the Child has affirmed, in General Comment 7, that States Parties must 'monitor and combat' the consequences for children of discrimination against their parents, 'for example if children have been born out of wedlock or in other circumstances that deviate from traditional values'.[22] Parents who pursue surrogacy may already encounter social stigma; for example, because of infertility or sexual orientation (sometimes called 'social infertility'), or may be characterisd as 'deviant'[23] or 'selfish' for pursuing the human urge to generate life.

It is well established that discrimination against a person or persons on the basis of their sexual orientation falls within 'other status' and is therefore prohibited.[24] While not explicitly specified in Article 2(1) or (2), medical infertility could, applying the interpretive principle of *ejusdem generis*, be considered sufficiently similar to the other specified grounds to qualify as prohibited grounds within the scope of Article 2. Arguably, at least on the basis of his or her parents' 'activities', a child who suffered damage or differential treatment because the parents entered into a compensated surrogacy arrangement could claim a breach of Article 2(1).

Further, States Parties to the CRC are responsible for preventing discrimination against children born via surrogacy to same-sex parents. Homophobia may be the source of unlawful discrimination by state or non-state actors, whether against the child directly or against the parents in a way that affects the rights of the child.[25] The Committee has reiterated the entitlement of all children to enjoy rights regardless of the identity or structure of their family:

> the family has always been shaped in a diversity of ways and naturally faces different challenges or living conditions ... Could it be considered that only in certain circumstances would the family or family life have decisive social value? ... Would it be possible to favour a perspective where only under certain conditions would children be given the opportunity to enjoy rights, which in fact are inherent to the dignity of their human nature?

---

it would similarly apply to a child born via surrogacy who is within territory but without citizenship, visa or passport.

22 Committee on the Rights of the Child, General Comment 7, UN Doc CRC/C/GC/7/Rev.1 (2006), [12].

23 Freeman, above n. 2, 192–4, though it is not clear that he is using the word pejoratively.

24 *Young v Australia*, Communication No. 941/2000, UN Doc CCPR/C/78/D/941/2000 (2003), [10.4]. See also *Toonen v Australia*, Communication No. 488/1992, UN Doc CCPR/C/50/D/488/1992 (1994), [8.7].

25 On this issue, see Tami Dower, 'Redefining Family: Should Lesbians Have Access to Assisted Reproduction?' (2001) 25 *Melbourne University Law Review* 466.

> … All these questions seem to place the essential value of the principle of non-discrimination in the forefront of the general discussion.[26]

This recognition by the Committee on the Rights of the Child is under threat by the 2014 Resolution of the Human Rights Council entitled 'Protection of the Family'.[27] On its face the language appears innocuous but use of the term 'the family' in the singular is based on a philosophy that there is only one family structure and fails to recognise the diversity of family forms including same-sex parents who have children via surrogacy.[28] This may lead some states to believe that it is legitimate to discriminate against such families, including their children.

All laws relating to surrogacy must be evaluated against the non-discrimination standard in Article 2 of the CRC. How some laws may discriminate against children born via surrogacy is illustrated in the Australian case study in Part III.

B. Best Interests of the Child

Article 3(1) of the CRC provides that '[i]n all actions concerning children, whether undertaken by public or private social welfare institutions, courts of law, administrative authorities or legislative bodies, the best interests of the child shall be a primary consideration'. Under Article 3(2), states are obligated to take legislative and administrative measures to ensure the child's well-being, taking into account the rights and duties of parents and legal guardians. Under Article 3(3), states must also ensure that childcare institutions, services and facilities comply with prescribed standards.

The 'best interests' principle is undoubtedly the cornerstone of the child-rights regime. Yet the CRC does not define 'best interests'. The 'best interests' principle derived from the same or similar principles in national jurisdictions,[29] and featured

---

26 Committee on the Rights of the Child, Day of General Discussion on the Role of the Family, UN Doc CRC/C/34 (1994), 36 [190]-[191].

27 Human Rights Council, 'Protection of the Family', UN Doc A/HRC/26/L.20/Rev.1 (2014).

28 The resolution was introduced by countries hostile to rights for sexual minorities, many of which still criminalise homosexual conduct, including, for example, Angola, Egypt, Ethiopia, Lebanon, Nigeria, Qatar, Sri Lanka, Tunisia, Uganda, and Zimbabwe. Attempts by countries such as Chile, France, Ireland and Uruguay to amend the resolution to explicitly recognise that families come in various forms were defeated by a 'no action' motion by Russia. See Article 19 et al., 'Joint Statement: Discussion of 'protection of the family' at Human Rights Council must reflect diversity and focus on human rights' (1 July 2014), available at http://www.article19.org/resources.php/resource/37609/en/joint-statement:-discussion-of-%E2%80%9Cprotection-of-the-family%E2%80%9D-at-human-rights-council-must-reflect-diversity-and-focus-on-human-rights, accessed 10 February 2015.

29 See, for example, Michael Freeman, 'Article 3: The Best Interests of the Child', in André Alen et al. (eds), *A Commentary on the United Nations Convention on the Rights of the Child* (Leiden: Martinus Nijhoff Publishers, 2007), 26; Philip Alston, 'The Best Interests

prominently both in the 1959 Declaration on the Rights of the Child[30] and in all draft versions of the CRC.[31] The delegates seemed to assume that the meaning of 'best interests' was self-evident, and almost no time was dedicated to discussing it.[32] Principle 2 of the 1959 Declaration made reference to 'special protection … to enable [the child] to develop physically, mentally, morally, spiritually and socially'. These dimensions are similar to the universal concepts to which Gibran alludes to in his poetry quoted at the start of this chapter.

The CRC stipulates only that the best interests of the child shall be '*a* primary consideration' in actions concerning children. Proposals to elevate best interests in Article 3(1) to '*the* paramount consideration' or even '*the* primary consideration' were rejected during the negotiations,[33] although 'the paramount consideration' was agreed as the relevant standard in relation to the adoption of children in Article 21. In all other situations, the CRC does not require the best interests of the child to be the single overriding consideration[34] but rather that States Parties must promote a child-centred approach by 'asking whether the force of any other consideration outweigh[s] it'.[35]

Surrogacy regulation creates particular challenges for identifying the 'best interests' of the child precisely because it involves decision-making in relation to children who have not yet been born, or children who have been born very recently. Article 3(1) of the CRC requires that best interests must be considered 'in *all* actions concerning children' (emphasis added). Therefore, a rigorous child-centred approach to surrogacy regulation would arguably impose an initial best-interests inquiry prior to conception, asking whether it is in the child's best interests to be conceived in the first place. This is a difficult question to answer, as it involves assessing the best interests of a hypothetical child. It also engages deeper philosophical challenges about whether children have a right *not* to be born.[36] After the birth of the child, a best-interests inquiry must be undertaken to determine how issues about the child's legal status and parenting arrangements ought to be decided.

With that in mind, the lack of definition of 'best interests' in the CRC may be beneficial in the context of surrogacy, because it allows for the term to expand and adapt to new developments over time, and to play a role in mediating normative

---

Principle: Towards A Reconciliation of Culture and Human Rights' (1994) 8 *International Journal of Law and the Family* 1, 11.

30 Declaration of the Rights of the Child, adopted 20 November 1959, UNGA Res 1386 (XIV), Principle 2.

31 Office of the United Nations High Commissioner for Human Rights, *Legislative History of the Convention on the Rights of the Child* (United Nations: New York and Geneva, 2007) ('Legislative History'), 335–48.

32 Alston, above n. 29, 11.

33 Legislative History, above n. 31, 339, 344, 346.

34 Alston, above n. 29, 12.

35 *Minister for Immigration and Ethnic Affairs v Teoh* (1995) 183 CLR 273, 292 per Mason CJ and Deane J.

36 Freeman, above n. 2, 195 and ch. 9.

conflict and filling gaps where necessary.[37] For a convention with near-global ratification, a plurality of perspectives on best interests allows for differences in cultural values.[38] This carries the risk, however, that the general nature of the term may give rise to subjective interpretations based on 'the value system of the decision maker'[39] or on 'purely nationalist content'.[40] Interpretations may clash in a single case,[41] creating inconsistency and uncertainty.

There is no doubt that such dilemmas will continue to play out with particular intensity in surrogacy cases, because societies and individuals take a wide spectrum of views on whether, and under what circumstances, surrogacy should be allowed by the state. In any case, decision-makers must attempt to make the assessment by standing in the shoes of the child. The best interests of the child can be better understood, if not defined, by reference to the other rights in the CRC.

C. Identity

Freeman notes that '[t]here can be few more basic rights than a right to one's identity'.[42] Article 7 of the CRC provides:

> 1. The child shall be registered immediately after birth and shall have the right from birth to a name, the right to acquire a nationality and. as far as possible, the right to know and be cared for by his or her parents.
> 2. States Parties shall ensure the implementation of these rights in accordance with their national law and their obligations under the relevant international instruments in this field, in particular where the child would otherwise be stateless.

---

37 Alston, above n. 29, 16; Stephen Parker, 'The Best Interests of the Child – Principles and Problems' (1994) 8 *International Journal of Law and the Family* 26, 27.

38 See, for example, Freeman, above n. 29, 33–40; Philip Alston and Bridget Gilmour-Walsh, *The Best Interests of the Child: Towards a Synthesis of Children's Rights and Cultural Values* (Florence: UNICEF, 1996), 39.

39 See, for example, *Department of Health and Community Services v JWB* (1992) 175 CLR 218, 271 per Brennan J, noting that 'in the absence of legal rules or a hierarchy of values, the best interests approach depends upon the value system of the decision maker'.

40 Legislative History, above n. 31, 341.

41 See, for example, Freeman, above n. 29, 28–9, citing *Painter v Bannister* 140 N.W. 2d 152 (1966) and *Re M and R* [1996] 2 FLR 195.

42 Freeman, above n. 2, 196. See further Jaap E. Doek, 'Article 8: The Right to Preservation of Identity and, and Article 9: The Right Not to Be Separated from His or Her Parents', in André Alen et al. (eds), *A Commentary on the United Nations Convention on the Rights of the Child* (Leiden: Martinus Nijhoff Publishers, 2006), 7–10; Claire Breen, 'Human-Assisted Reproduction and the Child's Right to Identity', in *Age Discrimination and Children's Rights* (Leiden: Martinus Nijhoff Publishers, 2006), 73.

Under Article 8(1) of the CRC, States Parties must respect a child's right 'to preserve his or her identity, including nationality … and family relations as recognised by law without unlawful interference'. Under Article 8(2), States Parties must act to assist and protect a child who is illegally deprived of elements of his or her identity.

The right to identity is best understood by considering three separate aspects of this right, namely: (1) the right to birth registration, (2) the acquisition and preservation of nationality, and (3) the right to parental relations (family relations and the right to know and be cared for by one's parents).

1. Birth registration

Birth registration is the process of the state recording the details of the child's birth. Alongside Article 7 of the CRC, Article 24(2) of the ICCPR provides that '[e]very child shall be registered immediately after birth and shall have a name'. Because registration assists in establishing the legal personality of a child as well as being 'a first step in ensuring the rights to survival, development and access to quality services for all children', the Committee on the Rights of the Child recommended in General Comment 7, on implementing child rights in early childhood, that States Parties take all necessary measures to ensure universal registration of births.[43] The Commentary on Article 7 notes that '[t]he drafters have separated the right to registration, name and acquisition of citizenship', with registration acting as a 'minimum guarantee' of rights.[44] The Committee emphasised that registration processes should not discriminate between children entitled to citizenship and non-citizens or refugee children.[45] Accordingly, registration should generally be regarded as a preliminary process separate to the further determination of legal parentage and nationality in surrogacy arrangements.

For a child born via surrogacy in a country different to that of his/her intended parents, birth registration will depend on the national laws in the country of birth.[46] Problems arise where the birth certificate does not record the intended parents, or where the authorities in the intended parents' home country do not recognise the foreign birth certificate. For example, in 2010, a Spanish court refused to

43 Committee on the Rights of the Child, General Comment 7, UN Doc CRC/C/GC/7/Rev.1 (2005), [25].

44 Ineta Ziemele, 'Article 7: The Right to Birth Registration, Name and Nationality, and the Right to Know and Be Cared for by Parents', in André Alen et al., *A Commentary on the United Nations Convention on the Rights of the Child* (Leiden: Martinus Nijhoff Publishers, 2007), 23 [44].

45 Committee on the Rights of the Child, *Concluding Observations: Cambodia*, UN Doc CRC/C/15/Add.128 (2000), [30]; see also Committee on the Rights of the Child, *Concluding Observations: Estonia*, UN Doc CRC/C/15/Add.196 (2003), [29].

46 See CRC, Art 7(2).

recognise Californian birth certificates of twins born in San Diego via surrogacy which recorded a Spanish gay couple as the children's parents.[47]

Stark suggests that a child may be left in a precarious position where the law stipulates that a child born of surrogacy cannot acquire the nationality of his/her intended parents.[48] Joslin suggests that such uncertainty may be dealt with by reforming domestic laws,[49] but this may be easier said than done.

2. Acquisition and preservation of nationality

Every child has a right to acquire a nationality under Article 7(1) of the CRC and to preserve that nationality under Article 8(1). Given the qualifier 'in accordance with their national law' in Article 7(2), the status of this principle as a positive obligation on states has been called into question.[50]

For children born to intended parents via overseas surrogacy arrangements, the issue of nationality is particularly acute. Under Article 7(2), special efforts must be made in respect of nationality if children will otherwise be left stateless. This was the case in *Re X & Y (Foreign Surrogacy)*[51] where twins born in Ukraine via surrogacy to intended parents from Great Britain were considered under Ukrainian law to be the children of the British couple, while British law considered them the children of the Ukrainian surrogate and her husband. Justice Hedley observed that:

> The effect was that the children were marooned stateless and parentless whilst the applicants could neither remain in the Ukraine nor bring the children home ... It was as well in this case that there was no pressing need for medical treatment.[52]

These conflict of laws problems create complexities in affording children a nationality in accordance with Articles 7 and 8 of the CRC. Storrow asserts that denying citizenship to children of parents who travelled abroad to have children via surrogacy is a 'particularly draconian and disproportionate response to the problems a country fears may arise from the violation of its surrogacy proscriptions abroad.'[53] He suggests that the doctrine of comity provides the best solution, since it requires the countries recognise foreign judgments and administrative acts and

---

47 *La Ley* 152885/2010, Court of First Instance n. 15 of Valencia, Judgment of 15 September 2010.

48 Barbara Stark, 'Transnational Surrogacy and International Human Rights Law' (2012) 18 *ILSA Journal of International and Comparative Law* 1, 16.

49 Courtney G. Joslin, 'Protecting Children: Marriage, Gender, and Assisted Reproductive Technology' (2010) 83 *Southern California Law Review* 1177, 1228.

50 Ziemele, above n. 44, 23 [46].

51 [2008] EWHC 3030 (Fam).

52 Ibid., [10].

53 Richard F. Storrow, "'The Phantom Children of the Republic': International Surrogacy and the New Illegitimacy' (2012) 20(3) *Journal of Gender, Social Policy and Law* 561, 602.

accept them as conclusive evidence (absent fraud or strong public policy grounds).[54] Thus, under the principle of comity courts would recognise parentage and afford citizenship to children born via surrogacy in countries where it is legal to do so, including, for example, giving effect to a Californian birth certificate recording a child's parents as two gay dads. Such an approach would be consistent with the CRC, and a distinct improvement from the approach of some countries to use 'the denial of citizenship and parentage recognition as blunt instruments in a battle against international surrogacy'.[55]

As well as a potential violation of Articles 7 and 8 of the CRC, denying children nationality may also constitute discrimination between children born via surrogacy and children born overseas by some other means. It also arguably constitutes harm to the best interests of the child by reason of discrimination based on the child's parents' infertility. The problem could be addressed by creating a new visa category for such cases. Again, this debate draws on the tension between efforts to prohibit compensated surrogacy and the best interests of the child.

3. Parental relations

The right to 'family relations'[56] and particularly 'to know and be cared for by [one's] parents'[57] raises the question as to the identity of the child's parents. Does it refer to biological or gestational parents, or commissioning or relational parents, or both? The use of the qualifier 'as far as possible',[58] means that this proposition is particularly complicated in surrogacy arrangements[59] where there may be up to five parent-like people: two intended parents, a sperm donor, an egg donor and a surrogate (to that we could add a sixth: a surrogate's male partner (if any), who in most jurisdictions will be considered the father and who may or may not be part of the surrogacy 'team').

It may be that 'parents' should be defined differently depending on the functional attributes of the relevant right. It is suggested that, in line with adoption practice, the right 'to know' one's parents includes, but is not limited to, biological and gestational parents.[60] This is a question of the child's genetic identity, where science is key. Some exchanges between the CRC Committee and States Parties in the framework of the periodic reporting process suggest that the CRC Committee takes the view that the term 'parents' in the context of Article 7, and the aims of the CRC, includes biological parents and that the child has the right to know, as far as

54 Ibid.
55 Ibid.
56 CRC, Art 8(1).
57 CRC, Art 7(1).
58 CRC, Art 7(1).
59 See Stark, above n. 48, 2.
60 Ziemele, above n. 44, 26–7 [51]–[55].

possible, who they are.[61] By contrast, the right 'to be cared for' by one's parents, in the surrogacy context, may refer to the commissioning parents who have undertaken parental responsibility for raising the child. This question is about the care of the child, which is more qualitative than scientific. Superficial responses to the content of Article 7(1) tend to gloss over the finer points of this distinction.[62]

If the child born via surrogacy is to have the right to know his or her biological and gestational parents, they must be made aware of the existence and identity of the persons who contributed to their making. The right to know one's origins is described by Freeman as a 'moral right in the 'ideal' sense' that should not be denied.[63] The moral right is said to derive primarily from the child's interest in understanding their own identity, though other motivations such as health concerns, property interests and even anxiety about accidental consanguineous marriage have also been raised.[64] Persons conceived as a result of assisted reproductive treatment have often attested to psychological damage and loss of agency as a result of the withholding of their genetic origins.[65]

In the surrogacy context, this would therefore mean that any child born via surrogacy has a right to know the identity of the surrogate, egg donor and sperm donor (if any). In order to give effect to this right, records must be kept and made available to the child, when the child reaches an appropriate age, should they desire access to such information. Registers should be kept of the source of donations of eggs and/or sperm in order to protect a child's right to know their origins.[66] The 2009 documentary *Google Baby* exposed a disquieting trend of importing sperm and eggs from Eastern European countries before shipping embryos to India for gestation. A child resulting from such an arrangement would have little to no prospect of identifying his or her genetic origins, and therefore this practice would be inconsistent with Article 7 of the CRC.

The right of the child to be cared for by his or her parents, in the surrogacy context, means that States Parties should recognise that relationship, if to do so is in the best interests of the child. As Isterevych notes, 'in cases of surrogacy the question of parenthood should be interpreted not as a biologically proven fact,

---

61 Ibid.

62 Cf., for example, Tim Cannon, 'Surrogacy: A Black Hole for Children's Rights' (2009) 30(2) *Australian Family Association Journal* 27, 34.

63 Freeman, above n. 2, 204.

64 See generally Katherine O'Donovan, 'A Right to Know One's Parentage?' (1998) 2(1) *International Journal of Law, Policy and the Family* 27.

65 See, for example, John Tobin, *The Convention on the Rights of the Child: The Rights and Best Interests of Children Conceived through Assisted Reproduction* (Victorian Law Reform Commission, 2004), 44, and the sources cited therein.

66 See *Gaskin v United Kingdom* (1989) 12 EHRR (no 16, ser A) 36. For discussion of development of the right under the CRC and European Convention on Human Rights, see Samantha Besson, 'Enforcing the Child's Right to Know Her Origins: Contrasting Approaches under the Convention on the Rights of the Child and the European Convention on Human Rights' (2007) 21(2) *International Journal of Law, Policy and the Family* 137.

but as a social construct based on considerations of the best interest of the child.'[67] However, as the Australian case study in Part III demonstrates, commissioning parents are not uniformly recognised as parents of a child born via surrogacy. Courts can require the child's parents to present extensive evidence about the surrogacy agreement. While this creates a hurdle for the recognition of parentage, it is arguably justifiable as it is directed at ensuring that a bona fide parent-child relationship exists, and that a child can know its biological origins, consistent with Article 7(1) and with the best interests of the child.

D. Sale of Children?

Article 35 of the CRC is a very short provision that simply states that:

> States Parties shall take all appropriate national, bilateral and multilateral measures to prevent the abduction of, the sale of or traffic in children for any purpose or in any form.

This norm has been elaborated upon in the OP, Article 2 of which provides that:

> For the purposes of the present Protocol:
>
> (a) Sale of children means any act or transaction whereby a child is transferred by any person or group of persons to another for remuneration or any other consideration.

The remainder of the substantive provisions of the OP are concerned with the prohibition and punishment of numerous acts aimed at the exploitation of children, including offering, delivering or accepting a child for the purposes of sexual exploitation, transfer of organs or forced labour.[68] Article 8 of the OP provides for the needs of child victims of these crimes.

Whether compensated surrogacy amounts to the selling of children under international law is an issue that has been hotly contested. There are experts who argue that compensated surrogacy constitutes the sale of children.[69] John Tobin, for example, suggests that:

---

67 Tetiana Isterevych, *International Surrogacy Arrangements: The Problem of Recognition of Legal Personhood* (2013) LLM Thesis, Central European University, 53, available at www.etd.ceu.hu/2014/isterevych_tetiana.pdf, accessed 27 February 2015.

68 OP, Art 3.

69 See Sonia Allan's Chapter 7 in this volume; and John Tobin, 'To Prohibit or Permit: What is the (Human) Rights Response to the Practice of International Commercial Surrogacy?' (2014) 63(2) *International and Comparative Law Quarterly* 317.

> The ordinary meaning of terms such as 'transfer', 'remuneration' and 'consideration' indicates that a commercial surrogacy will fall within the definition of the sale of a child. Put simply, such an arrangement contemplates that a child will be carried to term and delivered by one person (the surrogate mother) and given (transferred) to another (the intending parent(s)) in exchange for money (remuneration).[70]

Others argue that compensated surrogacy involves remuneration to the surrogate for her services in carrying and giving birth to the child, rather than payment for the purchase of a child.[71]

This chapter adopts the latter view, with some qualifications. As a matter of both principle and practice, it is submitted that the proposition that compensated surrogacy *in general* constitutes the sale of children suffers from a number of flaws. Where there is an absence of proper regulation, there is a risk that a compensated surrogacy arrangement, especially one involving traditional rather than gestational surrogacy, may amount to the sale of a child under international law. The UN Committee on the Rights of the Child has considered this issue in the context of unlawful adoption of children from their birth parents,[72] noting that without clear regulation compensated surrogacy 'can lead to the sale of children'.[73] This may be the case where, for example, payments were used to induce a surrogate who was also the genetic mother to give up the child at birth without her informed consent.

However, a more general proposition is difficult to sustain. It is significant that, having considered substantial evidence on the practice of compensated

70 Tobin, above n. 69, 335.

71 See, for example, Jason K.M. Hanna, 'Revisiting Child-based Objections to Commercial Surrogacy' (2010) 24(7) *Bioethics* 341.

72 Committee on the Rights of the Child, *Concluding observations on the report submitted by India under article* 12, *paragraph* 1, *of the Optional Protocol to the Convention on the Rights of the Child on the sale of children, child prostitution and child pornography*, UN Doc CRC/C/OPSC/IND/CO/1 (2014), in the context of unlawful adoption, notes concern at 'unregulated informal adoption', that this 'may give rise to the sale of children for adoption purposes' and that commercial surrogacy 'can lead to the sale of children': [23]; Committee on the Rights of the Child, *Concluding observations on the second periodic report of the United States of America submitted under article* 12 *of the Optional Protocol to the Convention on the sale of children, child prostitution and child pornography, adopted by the Committee at its sixty-second session*, UN Doc CRC/C/OPSC/USA/CO/2 (2013) indicates, in the context of economic incentives for adoption, that 'if not clearly regulated' surrogacy can amount to sale of children: [29(b)].

73 Committee on the Rights of the Child, *Concluding observations on the report submitted by India under article* 12, *paragraph* 1, *of the Optional Protocol to the Convention on the Rights of the Child on the sale of children, child prostitution and child pornography*, UN Doc CRC/C/OPSC/IND/CO/1, [23].

surrogacy,[74] the Committee on the Rights of the Child has restricted its findings to the context of unlawful adoption where there is a lack of regulation, and has not made any statement to the effect that compensated surrogacy constitutes the sale of children per se.

Reading the terms of Article 35 and the OP in their context, it appears that that the prohibition on sale of children is primarily aimed at offences enumerated in the OP and other harmful activities that compromise the best interests of the child. The Preamble to the OP locates these practices in the context of 'international traffic in children'.[75] It could not be said that the named offences are in any way analogous to compensated surrogacy arrangements, at least where properly regulated. The context, process and consequences of surrogacy, which is a planned process to bring a child into an intended family, are wholly different in character to those associated with the activities expressly covered in the OP.

It is true that the States Parties to the OP did not explicitly confine the definition of 'sale of children' to activities carried out with an exploitative purpose.[76] However, there remains the more fundamental requirement to interpret treaty terms in their context and in the light of the object and purpose of the treaty.[77] It is clear that the object and purpose of the CRC and OP is to prevent harm to children, to protect children's rights and to promote their best interests. Article 35 should be read accordingly, as proscribing harmful activities.

The interpretation of Article 35 as effectively rendering all compensated surrogacy arrangements unlawful sidelines a more nuanced consideration of children's rights and best interests in this context, both in individual cases and as a matter of policy. Such side-lining is unhelpful in practice for at least two reasons. First, as Millbank notes, 'the social science evidence ... demonstrates that payment alone cannot be used to differentiate 'good' surrogacy arrangements from 'bad' ones'.[78] Longitudinal studies have tended to demonstrate that surrogacy of

---

74 See Office of the High Commissioner for Human Rights, 'Committee on Rights of Child examines reports of India under the Convention and Protocols on Children in armed conflict, sale of children' (3 June 2014), available at http://www.ohchr.org/EN/NewsEvents/Pages/DisplayNews.aspx?NewsID=14663&LangID=E#sthash.MxeQFYbK.dpuf, accessed 10 February 2015.

75 Preamble to the OP, para. 3.

76 Tobin, above n. 69, 336, fn. 72, analysing the drafting history.

77 *Vienna Convention on the Law of Treaties*, adopted 23 May 1969, entered into force 27 January 1980, 1155 UNTS 331 ('Vienna Convention'), Art 31(1).

78 Jenny Millbank, 'Rethinking "Commercial" Surrogacy' (2014) *Journal of Bioethical Inquiry doi* 1, 1. See also Jenny Millbank, 'Resolving the Dilemma of Legal Parentage for Australians Engaged in International Surrogacy' (2013) 27 *Australian Journal of Family Law* 135, 139, fn. 17, quoting Amrita Pande, 'Commercial Surrogacy in India: Manufacturing a Perfect Mother-Worker' (2012) 35 *Signs* 969: 'surrogacy is not a moral dilemma to be solved, it is a structural reality to be understood'; we would add 'and appropriately regulated'.

itself is not contrary to a child's best interests.[79] Millbank concludes that 'there is no research to suggest that the amount of money, if any, received by surrogates has an impact upon the well-being of children or the quality of their relationship with either the surrogate or the intended parents'.[80] Second, for a surrogacy arrangement that has already occurred, the child's best interests must be the priority. Courts are regularly called upon to determine the best interests of children already born as a result of surrogacy arrangements, whether lawful or not. Superimposing a gloss to the effect that all intended parents engaging in compensated surrogacy are effectively participating in child trafficking may interfere with determining where best interests lie in real cases.

A more subtle and realistic view is that a compensated surrogacy arrangement is not premised on a 'transfer' of 'entitlement',[81] but on an allocation of responsibility between the parties to the arrangement as to the care of the child at different points in time, with the aim of bringing the child into its intended family. Regulation helps to ensure that such arrangements are formulated and implemented in accordance with the best interests of the child.

At least in regulated environments, gestational compensated surrogacy arrangements are made up of several layers of agreement in which all parties contribute to the outcome. Intended parents make financial, medical and logistical arrangements, not only with donor(s) and the surrogate, but also with doctors, clinics and other professional intermediaries. All are remunerated for their services. The biological material of one or both of the intended parents often contributes to the genetic makeup of the child. Where an egg or sperm donor contributes genetic material, the agreement with the donor is separate to the agreement with the surrogate. The fact that payment to the surrogate is generally made in instalments spanning the processes of conception, pregnancy, labour and birth tends to confirm that the payment is for services, not for the child itself. When the child is born, the surrogate's role ceases and the intended parents take up the full extent of their obligations and responsibilities to protect and care for the child.

The multi-layered character of compensated surrogacy complicates the meaning and applicability of the concept of 'transfer' in this context. Tobin identifies[82] but does not appear to address this issue, save to state that 'physical' transfer of the child 'facilitated by remuneration' will be sufficient to meet the definition.[83] Even assuming, in the absence of any legal authority, that physical transfer is sufficient, there is no nexus between 'transfer' and 'remuneration' (as

79 The most comprehensive and authoritative research on this point is the Golombok longitudinal study; see most recently Susan Golombok et al., 'Children Born through Reproductive Donation: A Longitudinal Study of Psychological Adjustment' (2013) 54 *Journal of Child Psychology and Psychiatry* 653.

80 Millbank (2014), above n. 78, 5.

81 Tobin, above n. 69, 341.

82 Ibid., 335.

83 Ibid., 340.

required by the word 'for' in the definition) unless the payment is regarded as being in direct exchange for the child itself. This assumption does not fit neatly with the purpose and structure of surrogacy arrangements as identified above.

To undermine the argument that a compensated surrogacy contract is a contract for services and not a sale, Tobin submits that if the surrogate decided she would not transfer the child, realisation of the purpose of the contract (transfer of the child) 'would only be possible through specific performance of a contract of sale'; this, he says, reveals that transfer of the child is the fundamental purpose of the contract.[84] This hypothesis is unsupported by authority and not borne out in practice. In the rare cases where a dispute has arisen because the surrogate refused to relinquish the child, courts have not approached surrogacy agreements as contracts of sale, nor engaged in a discussion of specific performance or contractual purpose, nor awarded remedies on those bases. Rather, courts dealing with such situations have made determinations about allocation of responsibility for care of the child based on the best interests of that child,[85] notwithstanding extraneous considerations.

An authoritative interpretation of the application of Article 35 of the CRC and the OP to compensated surrogacy arrangements would be welcome. Until then, the better view is that such practices, when properly regulated, do not constitute the sale of children, and do not violate the CRC.

III. Case Study: Australia

Australia ratified the CRC on 17 December 1990 and is accordingly bound in international law to perform the treaty in good faith.[86] International law holds that the conduct of a state organ shall be considered an act of that state, whether it is an organ of central government or a territorial unit.[87] Therefore, Australia is liable under international law for breaches of the CRC, whether by federal, state or territory governments. Australia has not enacted specific legislation to implement the CRC; rather, many different pieces of federal and state legislation have provided piecemeal compliance with some of the rights it contains. This

84 Ibid., 341.

85 See, for example, *Johnson v Calvert* 851 P.2D 776 (1993) (Supreme Court of California). *Rusken & Jenner* [2009] FamCA 282 is the only Australian reported case where a foreign surrogate resiled from her agreement to relinquish the child and where the relationship between the birth parents had ended. In considering the position of the parents, Bell J held 'It is not his rights that we are concerned about. It is not her rights we are concerned about. It is the child's.': at [42]. Bell J ordered that the intended father should have sole parental responsibility in the best interests of the child, in the absence of 'one jot of evidence' that the child's welfare would be advanced by returning to South Africa with the surrogate: at [45]. It was relevant that the surrogate 'was paid to become pregnant': at [44].

86 Vienna Convention, Art 26.

87 International Law Commission, Articles on State Responsibility, *Yearbook of the International Law Commission* (2001), vol. II (Part Two), Art 4.

Part uses the CRC as a lens through which to examine four distinct aspects of Australian domestic law relevant to children born through surrogacy, namely, surrogacy legislation, immigration and citizenship, family law and criminal law.

A. Surrogacy Legislation

Surrogacy statutes in Australia's six states[88] and the Australian Capital Territory[89] permit altruistic surrogacy and prohibit compensated surrogacy, while the Northern Territory does not regulate surrogacy. The legislation presumes that the surrogate and her partner are the parents of the child at birth, but allows intended parents in altruistic surrogacy arrangements to apply to a court for a 'parentage order' which transfers the legal status and responsibilities of parenthood to the intended parents, subject to various preconditions.[90] Preconditions variously include the identification of intended parents, age requirements, residency requirements, registration of the birth and consent of the birth parents.

Overseas compensated surrogacy arrangements are excluded from domestic surrogacy legislation. Intended parents in those arrangements must instead apply for 'parenting orders' in the federal Family Court. Numerous studies and commentators have recognised that cross-border surrogacy is common in Australia, and that international arrangements are more common than domestic arrangements.[91] By failing to address cross-border situations, operation of the state surrogacy legislation is confined to a very small proportion of surrogacy arrangements commissioned by Australians. The prevalence of parenting orders, discussed in Section C on family law below, illustrates the relative ineffectiveness and under-utilisation of state and territory surrogacy legislation.

For the small number of arrangements to which it applies, the standard imposed by state surrogacy legislation goes further in some respects than the standard imposed by Article 3(1) of the CRC (best interests as 'a primary consideration'). Queensland has created a 'guiding principle' stipulating that, in the administration

88 *Surrogacy Act* 2010 (NSW); *Surrogacy Act* 2010 (Qld); *Family Relationships Act* 1975 (SA); *Surrogacy Act* 2012 (Tas); *Assisted Reproductive Treatment Act* 2008 (Vic); *Status of Children Act* 1974 (Vic); *Surrogacy Act* 2008 (WA).

89 *Parentage Act* 2004 (ACT).

90 *Surrogacy Act* 2010 (NSW), s 39; *Surrogacy Act* 2010 (Qld), s 39(2); *Family Relationships Act* 1975 (SA), s 10HB(13); *Surrogacy Act* 2012 (Tas), s 26(1); *Status of Children Act* 1974 (Vic), s 19; *Surrogacy Act* 2008 (WA), s 26(1); *Parentage Act* 2004 (ACT), s 29. Parentage orders are recognised under federal legislation: *Family Law Act* 1975 (Cth), s 60HB(1).

91 See the various statistics reported in Anna Whitelaw, 'Hundreds pay for overseas surrogacy', *The Sydney Morning Herald*, 3 June 2012; see further Mary Keyes, 'Australia', in Trimmings and Beaumont, above n. 5, 38; Jenny Millbank, 'The New Surrogacy Parentage Laws in Australia: Cautious Regulation or "25 Brick Walls"?' (2011) 35(1) *Melbourne University Law Review* 165, 191; Australian Families Through Gestational Surrogacy, 'Statistics on Babies Born to Australians' (2011).

and implementation of the surrogacy legislation, 'the wellbeing and best interests of a child born as a result of a surrogacy arrangement, both through childhood and for the rest of his or her life, are paramount'.[92] NSW has a similar 'guiding principle' based on 'the best interests of the child of [a] surrogacy arrangement',[93] while Victoria's 'guiding principle' is expressed in respect of the child's 'welfare and interests'.[94] Victoria is alone in setting out detailed procedures for the pre-approval of individual surrogacy arrangements by the Patient Review Panel. This Panel was established pursuant to the Assisted *Reproductive Treatment Act 2008* (Vic) to determine complex and sensitive applications for medical procedures that attempt to procure pregnancy in a woman by means other than sexual intercourse. Thus, one of the functions of the Panel is to consider applications for surrogacy arrangements. In deciding such applications, the Panel must have regard to whether the proposed procedure 'is consistent with the best interests of a child who would be born as a result of the treatment procedure'.[95]

In all cases where a parentage order is sought, the court must be satisfied that making the order is in the best interests of the child.[96] In New South Wales, Queensland and Tasmania the legislation permits the court to dispense with one or more of the other statutory preconditions if consistent with the child's best interests.[97] The discretionary approach is arguably preferable to mandatory enforcement of all conditions, since the assessment of best interests will always be fact-specific and may require a particular balance to be struck. The Northern Territory, in failing to regulate surrogacy at all, does not comply with the best interests test.

Not all state surrogacy laws require a 'best interests' assessment 'in *all* actions concerning children' (emphasis added), as mandated by Article 3(1) of the CRC. The application of best interests to the whole of the legislation in Queensland, NSW and Victoria is preferable to confining it to the context of parentage orders as in South Australia, Western Australia and the ACT, even if this is the dominant context in which legislative duties are imposed. Victoria's Patient Review Panel promotes the most rigorously child-centred approach by asking, not just after the child's birth but prior to its conception, whether the contemplated procedure is in the best interests of the resulting child in each case. Notwithstanding the vagaries of assessing the best interests of a hypothetical child, this approach seeks to avoid as far as possible using the child as a means to an end by placing determinative

---

92 *Surrogacy Act* 2010 (Qld), s 6(1).

93 *Surrogacy Act* 2010 (NSW), s 3.

94 *Assisted Reproductive Treatment Act* 2008 (Vic), s 5(a).

95 *Assisted Reproductive Treatment Act* 2008 (Vic), s 15(3)(b)(ii).

96 *Surrogacy Act* 2010 (NSW), s 22(1); *Surrogacy Act* 2010 (Qld), s 22(2)(a); *Family Relationships Act* 1975 (SA), s 10HB(6); *Surrogacy Act* 2012 (Tas), s 16(2)(k); *Status of Children Act* 1974 (Vic), s 22(1)(a); *Surrogacy Act* 2008 (WA), ss 13(1), 21(2)(g); *Parentage Act* 2004 (ACT), s 26(1)(a).

97 *Surrogacy Act* 2010 (NSW), s 18(2); *Surrogacy Act* 2010 (Qld), s 23(2); *Surrogacy Act* 2012 (Tas), s 16(3).

emphasis on the child's rights from the outset. This approach is better able to secure compliance with Article 3(1) in all actions concerning children born via surrogacy, including the eligibility of the prospective parents for surrogacy and the approval by the state of the surrogacy agreement. For example, if the 'Baby Gammy' case[98] had taken place as a domestic surrogacy arrangement in Victoria, it is highly unlikely that the intended parents would have been approved by the Patient Review Panel to undertake surrogacy because of the father's two convictions for indecently dealing with children under the age of 13.[99]

In relation to the principles of non-discrimination in the CRC, Millbank notes that Article 2 of the CRC has been incorporated into only some of the surrogacy statutes in Australia.[100] Section 6(2)(b) of the *Surrogacy Act* 2010 (Qld) states the principle that:

> the same status, protection and support should be available to a child born as a result of a surrogacy arrangement regardless of –
> (i) how the child was conceived under the arrangement; or
> (ii) whether there is a genetic relationship between the child and any of the parties to the arrangement; or
> (iii) the relationship status of the persons who become the child's parents as a result of a transfer of parentage.

Section 6(2)(d) further provides that 'the autonomy of consenting adults in their private lives should be respected'. These principles would seem to be consistent with the CRC.

To take a less successful example, s 5(e) of the *Assisted Reproductive Treatment Act* 2008 (Vic) provides that 'persons seeking to undergo treatment procedures must not be discriminated against on the basis of their sexual orientation, marital status, race or religion'. This principle proscribes discrimination only against intended parents, rather than its potential effect on children born via surrogacy.

---

98 Baby Gammy is a twin born to a surrogate in Thailand. The intended parents, David and Wendy Farnell brought Gammy's twin sister back to Australia, but allegedly left Gammy behind because he has Down's Syndrome. See http://www.abc.net.au/news/2014-08-04/wa-couple-denies-they-abandoned-baby-gammy/5644850, accessed 10 February 2015.

99 ABC 7.30, 'Baby Gammy's biological father revealed as convicted paedophile, raises surrogacy law questions', 5 August 2014, available at www.abc.net.au/7.30/content/2014/s4062904.htm, accessed 10 February 2015. See also the Victorian Court of Appeal decision in *Patient Review Panel v ABY & ABZ* [2012] VSCA 264 where the Court overturned a decision of the Victorian Civil and Administrative Tribunal (VCAT) which allowed an appeal from the Patient Review Panel denying access to fertility services for a couple where the male partner had served time in jail for sexual offences involving a teenager in his care. The Court of Appeal held that VCAT had applied the wrong test by not using the best interests of the child to be born from the treatment as the paramount consideration.

100 Millbank, above n. 91, 167.

The other states and territories have not included any explicit non-discrimination provisions in their surrogacy legislation.

Australian jurisdictions could be doing much more to implement Australia's obligations under Article 2 of the CRC in respect of children born via surrogacy. The Queensland approach could be used as a possible model. Consistently foregrounding non-discrimination in surrogacy legislation would create a more robust legislative structure to protect the integrity of children's rights and to promote a child-centred approach.

B. Immigration and Citizenship

A child born via surrogacy overseas would not immediately come 'within [the] jurisdiction' (Article 2) of Australia so that he or she is owed obligations by Australia under the CRC. At birth, such a child is neither present on Australian territory, nor an Australian citizen.

Current practice on international surrogacy arrangements under Australian immigration law is set out in a Fact Sheet published by the Department of Immigration and Border Protection.[101] A person born overseas to an Australian citizen does not obtain Australian citizenship by automatic operation of law.[102] To bring a child to Australia, the intended parents must apply, on the child's behalf, either for Australian citizenship by descent or for a permanent visa.[103] Where a child becomes an Australian citizen by descent, the intended parents must also apply for an Australian passport for the child.[104] Because this is the same treatment received by other children born overseas to Australian parents, it does not constitute discrimination against children born via surrogacy in the protection of the right to nationality.

In international surrogacy cases where neither of the intended parents is a biological parent, the child will not ordinarily be eligible for Australian citizenship by descent. In such cases, the parents must apply for a visa for the child to enter and remain in the country. The appropriate visa is an adoption visa, so at least one intended parent would need to formally adopt the child under the law of the country in which the child was born before applying for the visa.[105]

However, there are significant practical difficulties with this approach. The Fact Sheet published by the Department of Immigration and Citizenship states that '[i]t is rare for a child born of an international surrogacy arrangement to be able to meet the immigration requirements for an expatriate adoption and the subsequent

---

101 Department of Immigration and Border Protection, Fact Sheet 36a – International Surrogacy Arrangements, available at http://www.immi.gov.au/media/fact-sheets/36a_surrogacy.htm.

102 Ibid.

103 Under the *Australian Citizenship Act* 2007 (Cth) and the policy guidelines set out in the Australian Citizenship Instructions.

104 Department of Immigration and Border Protection, above n. 101.

105 Ibid.

grant of an Adoption visa'.[106] This is because to be eligible for an adoption visa, 'the overseas adoption must have been arranged through an Australian state or territory adoption authority and there is no provision to grant a visa to a child outside Australia who has been adopted under private arrangements'.[107]

This reflects the more general point that executive and judicial decisions in relation to the legal and immigration status of a child born via surrogacy may also impact on the child's best interests. At the executive level, at least when it comes to public policy, best interests may be just one factor in designing regulatory frameworks. For example, in 2013, India changed its visa regulations to prevent same-sex couples or single persons from obtaining a medical visa to enter the country for the purpose of commissioning a surrogacy agreement.[108] In response to this change, the Australian Government stated that '[o]ur ability to provide assistance in such circumstances would be extremely limited'.[109] Denying a visa to a child born in India to Australian intended parents would be unlikely to be consistent with the best interests of that child.

In this respect, it is not clear that Australia is wholly complying with its international obligations. Children born via overseas surrogacy arrangements that used donors for both egg and sperm may not be able to enter or acquire Australian nationality, notwithstanding that both intended parents are Australian. Chief Federal Magistrate John Pascoe has noted, citing *Wilkie and Anor & Mirkja,* that:[110]

> '[M]any Australian couples have been left 'stranded' overseas after having a child through a surrogate mother, as they are unable to apply for citizenship for the child under the Australian *Citizenship Act*'.[111]

There is also evidence indicating that the laws are being applied inconsistently: Keyes notes that '[s]ome application for Australian citizenship for children born overseas in surrogacy arrangements on the basis of their biological father's citizenship have been successful, whereas others have not'.[112] This is despite the fact that in most Australian jurisdictions the biological father is presumed *not*

---

106 Ibid.

107 Department of Immigration and Border Protection, Fact Sheet 36 – Adopting a Child from outside Australia, available at https://www.immi.gov.au/media/fact-sheets/36adopting.htm, accessed 10 February 2015.

108 See Chapter 9, 'Surrogacy in India: A Globalised Demand Meets (a lack of) Local Laws', by Normann Witzleb and Anurag Chawla in this volume.

109 See Australian High Commission, India, 'International Commercial Surrogacy', available at http://www.india.embassy.gov.au/ndli/consular2013.html, accessed 10 February 2015.

110 [2010] FamCA 667.

111 Chief Federal Magistrate J. Pascoe, 'The Rise of Surrogate Parenting: Family Law and Human Rights implications in Australia and Internationally', *LawAsia*, 10 October 2011.

112 Keyes, above n. 91, 41–2 and fn 124.

to be the child's parent at birth, as discussed further below. The lacunae in both surrogacy and immigration law as regards the status of children born via overseas surrogacy are not in the best interests of the child, meaning that the child can end up with insecure legal identity or a lack of formal status, or as Millbank aptly describes it, 'both stateless and parentless'.[113]

C. Family Law

Intended parents may also apply for legal recognition of parental responsibility through a parenting order or adoption order under federal family law in the Family Court.[114] Parenting orders are different from parentage orders under surrogacy legislation, since they determine responsibility rather than status. Section 60CA of the *Family Law Act* 1975 (Cth) entrenches the general principle of best interests, which governs the making of parenting orders: 'In deciding whether to make a particular parenting order in relation to a child, a court must regard the best interests of the child as the paramount consideration'.

Section 60CC of the *Family Law Act* sets out detailed provisions on how a child's best interests should be determined in the context of parenting orders. Subsection (2) provides that the primary considerations are the 'benefit to the child of ... a meaningful relationship with both ... parents' and 'the need to protect the child from physical or psychological harm'. Additional considerations include:

a. the views of the child;
b. the nature of the relationships at stake;
c. the likely effects and practical difficulties of change;
d. the capacity of the parents to provide for the child;
e. the maturity, sex, lifestyle and background of the child and either parent; and
f. any family violence.[115]

This list of considerations could be enhanced by including a reference to the rights set out in the CRC as a relevant factor.

However, overall, the articulation of the best interests of the child in Australian family law legislation exceeds the standard in Article 3(1) of the CRC. This is because, rather than ranking among a number of potentially important factors, the child's best interests are considered 'paramount', and therefore determinative. However, Keyes notes a clear tension between 'the dominant policy requiring decisions to be made in the child's best interests ... and the policy of controlling

113 Millbank (2013), above n. 78, 137.

114 *Family Law Act* 1975 (Cth), Pt VII.

115 For an example of application of the 'best interests' test under the *Family Law Act* resulting in a grant of parental responsibility to a same-sex couple, see *Re Mark* (2004) 31 Fam LR 162.

altruistic surrogacy and prohibiting commercial surrogacy'.[116] She concludes: 'The priority of the child's best interests suggests that the prohibition of commercial surrogacy is futile.'[117]

Family law judges, in grappling with these issues, are now guided by the best practices principles for surrogacy cases set down by Ryan J of the Family Court, in 2012, in *Ellison and Anor & Karnchanit*.[118] Ryan J made clear that the court will need to have detailed information about the child's origins in order to determine best interests:

> the children may have been victims of child trafficking for whom unidentified parents searched in vain … [there] are compelling reasons why it is incumbent on agencies (including courts) to be satisfied to a high level that babies brought into the country are who it is claimed they are, about the circumstances of their birth and that the subject children have not been wrongfully taken from their parents.[119]

Based on submissions by the Independent Children's Lawyer, separately representing the child, and the Australian Human Rights Commission intervening, Ryan J then set out a number of best practice principles, requiring, in summary:

- appointment of an Independent Children's Lawyer to represent the child's interests;
- affidavit evidence of the applicant(s) and the birth mother containing details of personal circumstances, the surrogacy agreement and birth;[120]
- independent evidence regarding the identification of the child;
- independent evidence with respect to the surrogate birth mother, including confirmation of counselling and informed consent;
- the preparation of a Family Report addressing relevant relationships; and
- evidence of the legal regime in the overseas jurisdiction.

These practices are undoubtedly beneficial in securing the child's best interests. Busby notes, however, that '[t]he procedural and evidentiary requirements set out in *Ellison* … may prove to be overwhelming, extraordinarily expensive, and

116 Keyes, above n. 91, 43; see also Keyes, 'Cross-Border Surrogacy Agreements' (2012) 26 *Australian Journal of Family Law* 28.

117 Keyes, above n. 91, 45.

118 [2012] FamCA 602.

119 Ibid., [4]–[5].

120 Ryan J granted a certificate under s 128 of the *Evidence Act* 1995 (Cth) so that the parents could give evidence without fear that it might be used against them, for example, to found a prosecution for engaging in commercial surrogacy overseas in the three Australian jurisdictions where such conduct can constitute a criminal offence.

unworkable',[121] which she suggests may affect the willingness of intended parents to apply for parenting orders where their child has already been granted citizenship.

Judicial decisions have tended to prioritise the best interests of the child even where the surrogacy agreement itself has been illegal. There is now a line of cases where parenting orders were deemed to be in the best interests of the child in cases of illegal compensated surrogacy,[122] though there is no guarantee that this approach will be taken in future cases. In most, but not all cases, judges either did not mention the illegality of the agreement or held it to be immaterial to the assessment of best interests.[123] Ryan J noted in *Ellison*:

> the AHRC is demonstrably correct in its submission that 'the court is faced with having children in front of it and needs to make orders that are in the best interests of those children, and at that stage it's probably too late to ask whether – or to inquire into the legality of the arrangements that had been made. The court really needs to take children as it finds them.'[124]

Millbank points out another problem of inconsistent application in practice: s 60(1)(d) of the *Family Law Act* provides that a provider of genetic material is not a legal parent, but:

> in some cases the genetic father applied on the basis that he was a legal parent, or sought orders declaring him as such, with mixed results. Some judges have rejected this claim … while others have taken a liberal or 'enlarging' view of parenthood … in order to find that a male genetic parent in surrogacy arrangements is a legal parent without the need for a transfer process.[125]

This again leads to unprincipled decision-making and uncertainty, creating what Millbank refers to as 'limping' legal parentage and failing to grapple with the child's reality.[126]

It is important to emphasise that being raised by same-sex parents, as is the case for some children born via surrogacy, cannot be said as a matter of fact or law to run counter to a child's best interests. Empirical evidence concludes that

---

121 Karen Busby, 'Of Surrogate Mother Born: Parentage Determinations in Canada and Elsewhere' (2013) 25(2) *Canadian Journal of Women and the Law* 284, 311.

122 See for example *Re Mark* (2003) 31 Fam LR 162; *Ellison and Anor & Karnchanit* [2012] FamCA 602.

123 But see the order in *Dudley and Anor & Chedi* [2011] FamCA 502; *Findlay & Punyawong* [2011] FamCA 503, which is further discussed below.

124 [2012] FamCA 602, [87].

125 Millbank (2013), above n. 78, 145.

126 Ibid., 155.

childhood development is not negatively affected by having same-sex parents.[127] Further, there is no right in treaty law or in the jurisprudence of international bodies to have a male parent and a female parent. Sundberg J rejected such an argument proffered by the Catholic Church in the case of *McBain* in the Federal Court of Australia.[128] As John Tobin points out, 'there is nothing in the drafting history of the [CRC] to suggest that the term 'parents' was necessarily to be defined or indeed confined to a man and woman, or to a child's biological parents'.[129] Studies now suggest that the best interests of the child are served by a sense of family and security brought about through responsible and loving relationships that foster a child's development, and are not dependent on the status or orientation of those relationships.[130]

As well as recognising heterosexual couples as parents, all states and territories now recognise female co-mothers as birth parents of children born as a result of assisted reproductive treatment.[131] Male couples who arrange altruistic surrogacy using one partner's sperm may be legally recognised as parents in the Australian Capital Territory, New South Wales, Tasmania, Queensland and Victoria, but not in South Australia, Western Australia or the Northern Territory.[132] Under current laws, it may be difficult for some same-sex parents to be recognised as legal parents, particularly the non-biological male partner in a same-sex relationship, who will usually have to resort to step-parent adoption in order to be recognised as the legal parent of a child born via surrogacy. This may interfere with the parent's

127 See, for example, Jenni Millbank, *Meet the Parents: A Review of the Research on Lesbian and Gay Families* (Sydne : Gay and Lesbian Rights Lobby (NSW) Inc, 2002), 4; Nanette Gartrell and Henny Bos, 'US National Longitudinal Lesbian Family Study: Psychological adjustment of 17 year old adolescents' (2010) 126(1) *Pediatrics* 28; Loes van Gelderen et al., 'Quality of Life of Adolescents Raised from Birth by Lesbian Mothers' (2012) 33(1) *Journal of Developmental and Behavioral Pediatrics* 1; Susan Golombok, 'Adoption by Lesbian Couples: Is it in the Best Interests of the Child?' (2002) 324 *British Medical Journal* 1407; and Simon R. Crouch et al., 'Parent-reported Measures of Child Health and Well-being in Same-Sex Parented Families: A Cross-sectional Survey' (2014) 14 *BMC Public Health* 635.

128 *McBain v State of Victoria* (2000) 99 FCR 116.

129 Tobin, above n. 65, 8.

130 Millbank, above n. 127, 4. CRC, Art 18 recognises that the primary responsibility for the child's upbringing and development is held commonly between the parents but is also shared with institutions, facilities and services. See further Kristen Walker, '1950s Family Values vs Human Rights: In Vitro Fertilisation, Donor Insemination and Sexuality in Victoria' (2000) 11 *Public Law Review* 292, 301.

131 *Parentage Act* 2004 (ACT), s 11(4); *Status of Children Act* 1996 (NSW), s 14(1A); *Status of Children Act* 1979 (NT), s 5DA; *Status of Children Act* 1978 (Qld), ss 19B-19E; *Family Relationships Act* 1975 (SA), s 10C(3); *Status of Children Act* 1974 (Tas), s 10C; *Status of Children Act* 1974 (Vic), ss 13, 14; *Artificial Conception Act* 1985 (WA), s 6A.

132 See *Family Relationships Act* 1975 (SA), s 10HA(2)(b)(iii) and *Surrogacy Act* 2008 (WA), s 19(2).

ability to perform their role, for example in the event of death or separation from the recognised parent.

The way that the law deals with recognising parents of children born via surrogacy may be changing. In August 2014, the Family Law Council released its much anticipated *Report on Parentage and the Family Law Act*.[133] Surrogacy and parentage is dealt with very comprehensively in Chapter 3, with the Council acknowledging that there are divergent and passionately held views across the community, but ultimately there is a:

> need for reform to address the lived reality for children born as a result of commercial surrogacy arrangements, and to ensure they are not disadvantaged by the way in which their family was formed or the status of the adults who are raising them. Council concluded that the paramount concern for the family courts must remain the best interests of the child, and that decisions regarding the prohibition or regulation of commercial surrogacy are a matter for government.[134]

The Council made five recommendations regarding law reform in relation to surrogacy, including:

> *Recommendation 12*
> The proposed new federal *Status of Children Act* contain provisions specifically dealing with applications for transfer of parentage in surrogacy cases where state and territory Acts do not apply. This should be based on a transfer of parentage process and not a presumption of parentage.
>
> *Recommendation 13*
> The provisions in the new federal *Status of Children Act* dealing with the transfer of parentage in surrogacy cases where state and territory Acts do not apply should contain a set of minimum requirements based on the proposals considered by Ryan J in *Ellison and Anor & Karnchanit* [2012] FamCA 602 with the aim to ensure compliance with Australia's international human rights obligations, including the following:
>
> - That any order is subject to the best interests of the child;
> - Provision is made for when the parties change their minds;
> - Evidence of the surrogate mother's full and prior informed consent;
> - Evidence of the surrogacy agreement, including any sums paid;

---

133 Family Law Council, *Report on Parentage and the Family Law Act* (2014), available at http://www.ag.gov.au/ FamiliesAndMarriage/ FamilyLawCouncil/ Documents/ family law-council-report-on-parentage-and-the-family law-act-december2013.pdf, accessed 10 February 2015.

134 Family Law Council, above n. 133, 99.

- Consideration should be given to whether the intending parents have acted in good faith in relation to the surrogate mother;
- Evidence of the intending parent/s actions in relation to ensuring the child will have access to information concerning the child's genetic, gestational and cultural origins;
- Provision is made that where a surrogacy arrangement involves multiple births, orders must be made in relation to all children born;
- The legality of the surrogacy arrangement should be a relevant consideration for the court when determining parentage (footnotes omitted).

These factors appear appropriate and consistent with seeking to protect the best interests of the child as well as the interests of all parties involved, by, for example, requiring a demonstration of good faith of the intended parents towards the surrogate.

At the time of writing, there is no indication of whether the Australian Government intends to enact legislation to give effect to these recommendations. It is hoped that it will, since such measures would go a long way to filling the existing legislative gaps in recognising parentage of children born overseas via compensated surrogacy.

D. Criminal Law

The question of criminalisation of compensated surrogacy arrangements is comprehensively covered by Anita Stuhmcke in Chapter 5 of this collection. Only two brief points need be made here.

First, laws that make prosecution of parents possible or likely are not in the best interests of the child. While there is debate about the legitimacy of the policy considerations surrounding the banning in Australia and extraterritorial criminalisation of compensated surrogacy it is submitted that whether or not the surrogate was paid for the use of her uterus is per se irrelevant to the best interests of the child. Enforcement of compensated surrogacy, prohibitions by prosecution and punishment of parents who have engaged in it is clearly not in the best interests of the child born via surrogacy.

Keyes notes: 'The priority that Family Court judges are required to give to the best interests of the child, in applications for parenting orders, has had the consequence of subverting the prohibition of commercial surrogacy.'[135] The contradiction and competition between the prohibition and the protection of best interests is illustrated by the cases of *Dudley & Chedi* and *Findlay & Punyawong* decided in 2011.[136] Watts J made the parenting orders requested by the intended parents, noting that the paramount consideration was the child's best interests, but also noted that two of the intended parents who resided in Queensland appeared to have breached Queensland law and directed that a copy of his reasons be conveyed to the Queensland Director

135 Keyes, above n. 91, 48.

136 *Dudley and Anor & Chedi* [2011] FamCA 502; *Findlay & Punyawong* [2011] FamCA 503.

of Public Prosecutions. No prosecution was forthcoming in that case, and indeed there has never been a prosecution for engaging in extraterritorial compensated surrogacy. This is notwithstanding research that indicates that, in 2011 alone, there were 270 babies born to Australians via overseas surrogacy.[137]

Second, it is arguable that Article 2(1) of the CRC may be breached if a child suffers damage or differential treatment because his or her parents were subject to prosecution for entering into a compensated surrogacy arrangement. This might occur, for example, if parents refrain from seeking certain entitlements, including legal recognition of parentage, for fear of prosecution. Both Millbank[138] and Keyes[139] draw a possible link between the strict approach taken by Watts J and an apparent decline in the number of parents presenting to the courts seeking parental recognition, since 2011.

IV. Conclusion

In our view, compensated surrogacy does not, per se, breach the CRC, but Australian jurisdictions have fallen short of fully implementing its provisions in respect of children born via surrogacy. As Galloway notes in Chapter 3 in this volume, surrogacy is not 'intrinsically contrary to the dignity of the child, provided safeguards are in place to ensure that the child's best interests are paramount'.[140]

There is, however, an urgent need for appropriate regulation of compensated surrogacy practices, based on international human rights standards. We must move away from the highly emotive language and dialogue that dominates discussion regarding surrogacy, and instead develop evidence-based policies and laws that are informed by and comply with international human rights norms, particularly the CRC.

Research suggests that generally children born via surrogacy do well, despite potential, or actual, complications surrounding their legal status and formal recognition of the parent/child relationship.[141] But there is significant scope for improvement in domestic laws and policies to ensure an end to practices that are inconsistent with the rights of the child as set out in the CRC.

In particular, all laws purporting to regulate surrogacy should not discriminate against a child on the basis of the method of his/her conception or birth, or the conduct of his/her parents in engaging in compensated surrogacy. Denying

---

137 Sam G. Everingham et al., 'Australians' Use of Surrogacy' (2014) 201(5) *Medical Journal of Australia* 1.

138 Millbank, above n. 91, 206.

139 Keyes, above n. 91, 47.

140 Chapter 3, Kate Galloway, 'Theoretical Approaches to Human Dignity, Human Rights and Surrogacy', 26.

141 See, for example, Vasanti Jadva et al., 'Surrogacy Families 10 Years on: Relationship with the Surrogate, Decisions over Disclosure and Children's Understanding of their Surrogacy Origins' (2012) 10 *Human Reproduction* 1; Susan Golombok et al., 'Families Created through Surrogacy: Mother–Child Relationships and Children's Psychological Adjustment at Age 7' (2011) 47(6) *Developmental Psychology* 1579.

children citizenship or refusing to recognise their parentage is unlikely to ever be in a child's best interests. As Busby notes, concerns about possible exploitation of women acting as surrogates should be addressed via ethical frameworks that ensure voluntary and informed consent, autonomy throughout the pregnancy and protection of financial interests from a point prior to conception, not only by creating barriers to the realisation of the rights of children born via surrogacy.[142] Refusing to allow children to travel to, or enter, their parents' home country because they were born through surrogacy should not be tolerated. The case of the Balaz twins, stranded in India for two years because neither the German nor Indian Governments would grant them citizenship, is a vivid illustration of what happens when courts and governments elevate public policy over the best interests of the child.[143]

The analysis in this chapter has shown that the standards in the CRC are sufficient to protect children's rights and promote a child-centred analysis when applied properly. Regulation is vital to ensure that rights are protected and children are not commodified. This chapter, and this book more broadly, suggest that the human rights approach holds the answer to many concerns about surrogacy. If human rights including children's rights are prioritised, the scientific process and legal regulation of surrogacy can be regarded as merely facilitative.

In surrogacy, we see that '[m]odern science and medical skill surrounding the creation of life are now well ahead of legal, social and legislative policy.'[144] The answer is 'not to ban commercial surrogacy entirely but to subject it to appropriate safeguards.'[145] Domestic legislation must move forward in order to ensure that the protections around the integrity of children's rights are sufficiently robust. By adhering to the CRC, the laws surrounding surrogacy can remain principled while offering full protection to the children of tomorrow.

142 Busby, above n. 121, 313.

143 Usha R. Smerdon, 'Birth registration and citizenship rights of surrogate babies born in India' (2012) 20(3) *Contemporary South Asia* 341.

144 *Lowe & Barry and anor* [2011] FamCA 625, [5] per Benjamin J.

145 Sarah Mortazavi, 'It Takes a Village to Make a Child: Creating Guidelines for International Surrogacy' (2012) 100 *Georgetown Law Journal* 2249, 2284.

Chapter 7
The Surrogate in Commercial Surrogacy: Legal and Ethical Considerations

Sonia Allan*

I. Introduction

Surrogacy is the term most often used to describe arrangements in which a woman who is, or is to become, pregnant agrees permanently to surrender the child(ren) born of that pregnancy to another person or couple (the commissioning persons(s)).[1] Surrogacy may be 'altruistic' (where the surrogate receives no payment or restricted reimbursement of 'reasonable expenses' associated with her pregnancy) or 'commercial' (where the surrogate is paid a fee beyond expenses and costs).[2] Over the past half century, as assisted reproductive technologies developed,[3] and commercial surrogacy occurred in some jurisdictions, ethical and legal issues surrounding the practice were hotly debated.[4] Early debate focused

---

* Senior Lecturer in Law, Macquarie University. I would like to thank Professors Diane Beeson, Therese McDermott, and Denise Meyerson, Susan Carter, as well as the editors of this book, and the anonymous referees for reviewing the chapter and providing useful comments.

1 The terms 'surrogacy' and 'surrogate' are used throughout this chapter. However, the terminology chosen is in itself controversial. For example, Debra Satz, of Stanford University, makes the point that 'the so-called surrogate mother is not a surrogate, she is the biological and/or gestational mother' and that the more accurate description of what is being discussed is 'contract pregnancy': see Debra Satz, 'Markets in Women's Reproductive Labor' (1992) 21(2) *Philosophy and Public Affairs* 107, fn. 2. In addition, many people use the term 'commissioning parent(s)'. This chapter uses the term 'commissioning person(s)' as it is not a foregone conclusion that the people who engage a surrogate will in fact, or in law, be the 'parent(s)' of the child born.

2 In commercial surrogacy a third-party broker or agent who brings the commissioning parent(s) and surrogate together may also be paid a fee: see Amy M. Larkey, 'Redefining Motherhood: Determining Legal Maternity in Gestational Surrogacy Contracts' (2003) 51 *Drake Law Review* 608.

3 Assisted reproductive technologies enabled broadened contexts for surrogacy moving beyond 'traditional' surrogacy in which a surrogate was impregnated with the sperm of a commissioning male or donor, to practices in which the use of ova from a commissioning woman or 'donor', or an embryo, was also possible.

4 For examples concerning early debate see John Robertson, 'Surrogate Mothers: Not so Novel after All' (1983) 13 *Hastings Center Report*; Department of Health and

primarily upon whether commercial surrogacy commodifies women and children, and whether a surrogate should be required to relinquish the child should she change her mind. The majority of countries that chose to regulate on the matter, moved to prohibit commercial surrogacy, made surrogacy contracts void and unenforceable, and in some instances accepted altruistic arrangements subject to certain criteria being met.

In recent years, the debate has again been enlivened in the context of commissioning person(s) travelling overseas to enter commercial surrogacy arrangements in countries that either allow commercial surrogacy by law, or have no regulation.[5] The focus of renewed discussion has been particularly on issues concerning how to determine legal parentage and citizenship of the resulting child in such circumstances. Some commentators have also called for more permissive laws than currently exist regarding commercial surrogacy.[6] However, the issues raised by commercial surrogacy continue to be far more complex than resolving how to determine legal parentage and citizenship for children, and 'fertility tourism' by some people is not in itself reason to change laws. Ethical and legal issues continue to exist regarding whether commercial surrogacy commodifies women and children; and the social and financial pressures that may lead women to enter such agreements. In addition, the global surrogacy trade has made racial, cultural and social disparities more salient; exposed risks and realities regarding human trafficking; and made questions of autonomy and consent more pronounced. It is only by considering all such complexities that international and domestic

Social Services (UK), *Report of the Committee of Inquiry in Fertilisation and Embryology* (1984) (The 'Warnock Report'); Derek Morgan, 'Making Motherhood Male: Surrogacy and the Moral Economy of Women' (1985) 12 *Journal of Law and Society* 219; D. Brahms, 'The Hasty British Ban on Commercial Surrogacy' (1987) 17 *Hastings Center Report* 16; Larry Gostin (ed.), *Surrogate Motherhood: Politics and Privacy* (Bloomington, IN: Indiana University Press,1990).

5 This has been attributed to such things as legal restrictions or prohibitions in the country in which the commissioning person(s) are usually domiciled; or high costs in the commissioning person(s) country of origin. It has also been a result of increased ability to travel; the wealth of commissioning person(s); cheaper costs of commercial surrogacy arrangements in some destination countries; and the rise in alternative family types in some nations.

6 For examples, see Anemona Hartocollis, 'And baby makes 3: In New York a push for compensated surrogacy', *New York Times*, 19 February 2014, accessed on 10 June 2014, available at http://www.nytimes.com/2014/02/20/fashion/In-New-York-Some-Couples-Push-for-Legalization-of-Compensated-Surrogacy.html; Julia Medew, 'Surrogacy's painful path to parenthood', *The Age*, 23 March 2013, accessed 10 June 2014, available at http://www.theage.com.au/national/surrogacys-painful-path-to-parenthood-20130322-2glhn.html. (Note a simple search of popular media will find a number of analogous stories, with picture of commissioning couple and child(ren). The surrogate is most often absent from such pictures, and is mentioned only briefly within the story.)

regulation of commercial surrogacy can be decided. This chapter therefore adds to current discourse.

In doing so, I was asked to focus particularly upon the surrogate mother. However, it is not possible to speak meaningfully of the surrogate without reference to the child. The chapter therefore also raises some issues regarding the children born of such arrangements albeit not exploring them in depth.[7] Other parties involved in surrogacy agreements are mentioned, as the discussion requires. Section II highlights the ethical and legal issues that continue in modern-day commercial surrogacy practice. Section III examines general approaches and trends in the current regulation of surrogacy agreements worldwide, and considers calls for an international convention on surrogacy. It is contended that, on balance, given the strong ethical quandaries that exist, and the reality that commercial surrogacy presents unacceptable risks for some women and children, prohibitions against commercial surrogacy are acceptable, in those countries that choose to have them. Beyond this, the difficulty in reaching global consensus is recognised. As such, recommendations are made in relation to minimum standards that might be included universally in domestic laws. The multilateral convention that has been proposed by some as a possible way to regulate current trans-national practices is also discussed. Suggestions are proffered with the view that laws that aim to prevent discrimination, exploitation and risk of serious harm, should be encouraged, and that such laws have advanced the position of women and children in other areas tremendously.[8]

II. Ethical and Legal Issues Pertaining to Surrogacy

A. Is the Surrogate Involved in the Sale or Commodification of Children?

There has been international recognition that the sale of children is ethically and morally repugnant as it counters principles of human dignity, respect for persons, and the common good. Legally, the sale of children is prohibited in many countries.[9] The

7 Issues concerning legal parentage or citizenship of children are beyond the scope of the chapter. The provision of information and possibility of ongoing contact with donors and surrogates is also something fundamental to this issue but is not discussed in depth herein.

8 For example, laws that protect people from unconscionable conduct when entering contracts and make void and unenforceable contracts that are against public policy are acceptable. Similarly, laws that ensure people's well-being are in other health and safety contexts very seldom criticised.

9 UNICEF, *Handbook on the Optional Protocol on the Sale of Children, Child Prostitution and Child Pornography* (The United Nations Children's Fund, February 2009) notes that 'many States Parties have legislation prohibiting trafficking in persons, but lack legislation specifically prohibiting the sale of children', 9.

question for this section therefore, is whether the surrogate in commercial surrogacy arrangements is involved in the sale or commodification of children (whether or not she herself is also the subject of exploitation, coercion, or otherwise).

The question is particularly relevant as for decades there have existed ethical, policy and legal statements across the globe that commercial surrogacy commodifies the resulting child, and that this, in itself, is reason enough to deny the practice. For example, in 1984, the United Kingdom Warnock Committee[10] said that 'a [commercial] surrogacy agreement is degrading to the child who is to be the outcome of it, since, for all practical purposes the child will have been bought for money'.[11] In 1988, the New York State Task Force on Life and the Law in its public policy inquiry into surrogacy stated that 'the exchange of money for possession or control of children ... threatens to erode the way that society thinks about and values children, and by extension all human life'.[12] In Germany surrogacy continues to be treated both judicially and by statute as a form of illegal adoption that 'violates the child's and mother's human dignity and reduces both to objects of commercial contracts'.[13] In Australia, legislation exists in all states and the Australian Capital Territory, prohibiting commercial surrogacy,[14] based upon 'a deep discomfort with the commodification of children, women and reproductive services' (amongst other things).[15]

In recent years, prohibitions concerning commercial surrogacy[16] have also been listed by the Australian Government as being 'an explicit prohibition of the sale of children' pursuant to Australia's obligations under the Optional Protocol to the United Nations Convention on the Rights of the Child on the sale of children,

---

10 The UK Government convened the Warnock Committee shortly after the first IVF baby was born in 1978. Its purpose was to consider recent and potential developments in medicine and science related to human fertilisation and embryology; to consider what policies and safeguards should be applied, including consideration of the social, ethical and legal implications of these developments; and to make recommendations.

11 The Warnock Committee, above n. 4, [8.11].

12 New York State Task Force on Life and the Law, *Surrogate Parenting: Analysis and Recommendations for Public Policy* (New York: New York, 1988), 233.

13 Susanne L. Gossl, 'Germany', in Katarina Trimmings and Paul Beaumont (eds), *International Surrogacy Arrangements* (Oxford and Portland, OR: Hart Publishing, 2013), 131–2.

14 See *Parentage Act* 2004 (Tas); *Surrogacy Act* 2010 (NSW); *Surrogacy Act* 2010 (Qld); *Statutes Amendment Act (Surrogacy) Act* 2009; *Surrogacy Act* 2012 (Tas); *Assisted Reproductive Treatment Act* 2008 (Vic); *Surrogacy Act* 2008 (WA).

15 Mary Keyes, 'Cross-border Surrogacy Agreements' (2012) 26 *Australian Journal of Family Law* 42.

16 *Surrogacy Act* 2010 (NSW), s 8.

child prostitution and child pornography (OPCC).[17] Such a view flows from the Convention on the Rights of the Child, which requires that States Parties take 'all appropriate national, bilateral and multilateral measures to prevent the ... sale of or traffic in children for any purpose or in any form'.[18] Article 2 of the OPCC further defines the sale of children as 'any act or transaction whereby a child is transferred by any person or group of persons to another for remuneration or any other consideration'.[19] Commercial surrogacy thus has been seen to fall within the definition of sale of a child as it is *an act* or *transaction* whereby a child *is transferred by any person* or group of persons (the surrogate, the clinics, the brokers) *to another* (the commissioning person(s)) *for remuneration or any other consideration.*[20]

However, this view is not accepted by all. A number of arguments have been put forward that either discount or move away from issues of the sale or commodification of children by framing the surrogate's relationship to the child in particular ways. For example, it has been argued that there is no sale or commodification involved in 'gestational' arrangements because of the lack of genetic relationship between surrogate and child.[21] Larkey states that as the surrogate carries the genetic child

17 Attorney-General's Department (Commonwealth), Australia's response to the List of Issues – *Optional Protocol to the Convention on the Rights of the Child on the Sale of Children, Child Prostitution and Child Pornography*, 4–5 June 2012, accessed 10 June 2014, available at http://www.ag.gov.au/RightsAndProtections/HumanRights/TreatyBodyReporting/Pages/default.aspx.

18 *Convention on the Rights of the Child*, opened for signature 20 November 1989, 1577 UNTS 3 (entered into force 2 September 1990), art 35.

19 *Optional Protocol to the Convention on the Rights of the Child on the Sale of Children, Child Prostitution and Child Pornography*, opened for signature 25 May 2000, 2171 UNTS 227 (entered into force 18 January 2002), art 2(a).

20 Note there have been issues raised in Australia regarding family law judges making legal parentage orders in transnational surrogacy cases, contrary to Australia's reported stance that laws against commercial surrogacy meet our obligations under the OPCC (and contrary to some state laws that prohibit entering into such agreements extraterritorially). In such situations the judges have deemed legal parentage as being 'in the best interests of the child' in the circumstances. Such orders do not resolve the question of sale or commodification, they simply reflect the difficult situation courts are faced with once a child is brought back into the country. Further discussion of this point is beyond the scope of this chapter.

21 It is now possible for a woman to become pregnant as a result of nine different combinations of possible use of eggs and sperm: (a) the egg and sperm of a commissioning heterosexual couple; (b) the egg of a commissioning woman and donor sperm; (c) the egg of a donor and the sperm of a commissioning male (be he part of a couple or a single person); (d) both donor egg and sperm (unrelated to the commissioning person(s)); (e) the egg of a donor and sperm from the surrogate's partner; (f) her own egg and the sperm of a commissioning male; (g) her own egg and the sperm of a donor; or (h) her own egg and the sperm of her partner. (a)–(e) entail some form of 'gestational' surrogacy, in which

of the commissioning person(s) and 'has no biological connection to the child', the surrogate is not the child's 'mother' and therefore is 'not in a position to sell what is not hers'.[22] Rather, payment is proposed to be for services rendered by the surrogate in providing the commissioning person(s) 'their' child.

However, there exists a logical flaw in trying to distinguish gestational surrogacy from instances of traditional surrogacy, in which a genetic connection does subsist between the child and the mother. Larkey's view is premised on the assumption that the child may be viewed as something that is 'owned' based upon who contributed the genetic material, the status of the surrogate as 'gestational', and the existence of an agreement (or in some jurisdictions a 'contract'). The logical conclusion of such arguments is that in cases of traditional surrogacy (the comparator), the child would be the surrogate's and therefore she would be in a position to sell what is hers – namely, the child. Surely the act in both instances is the same, and this is an odd distinction to draw.[23]

Second, in cases of 'gestational surrogacy' to deny that any connection exists between the surrogate and child, or to define relationships (and or acceptability of practice) simply by focusing upon who contributed the gametes or embryo, is an over-simplification. Regardless of genetic connection, the gestational mother provides many biological resources during the pregnancy. As the pregnant woman breathes and feeds and her heart beats the child may grow, and is significantly affected (positively or negatively) by the biological environment in which it exists. During pregnancy, there is also a physical connection provided by the placenta, an organ built of cells from both the woman carrying the pregnancy and the foetus, which serves as a conduit for the exchange of nutrients, gases and wastes. Cells may additionally migrate through the placenta, and may have a broad range of impacts on mother and child, from tissue repair and cancer prevention to sparking immune disorders.[24] There are also significant physical and psychological changes that take place within a pregnant woman's body that cause her to bond with, and connect to the baby as it grows in utero (and vice versa). It is therefore invalid to claim that 'gestational' commercial surrogacy resolves commodification issues[25] simply by denying a connection between the child and the surrogate mother.

---

the woman is not genetically related to the child; (f)–(h) entail what is often referred to as 'traditional' surrogacy, as the woman is genetically related to the child.

22 Larkey, above n. 2, 614.

23 There is also an absurdity if donor gametes or embryos derived from other than the commissioning person(s) are used, as this would lead to questions regarding *whose* child the surrogate is carrying, and after birth, handing over.

24 Robert Martone, 'Scientists discover children's cells living in mother's brains: The connection between mother and child is even deeper than thought', *Scientific American* (4 December 2012), accessed 10 June 2014 at http://www.scientificamerican.com/article/scientists-discover-childrens-cells-living-in-mothers-brain/.

25 Or other issues raised by commercial surrogacy.

Similarly, arguments that try to justify payment by suggesting we move beyond discussion of genetics and consider how the surrogate views herself, are unsatisfactory. For example, Millbank states:

> a baby created via surrogacy is not the baby of the birth mother, not because of the operation of contracts, or genetic link to intended parent(s) combined with lack of genetic link to the surrogate; rather the baby is not hers because she says so and believes this to be so, before, during and after the pregnancy in which she gestates that child into life.[26]

The claim follows that it is only 'fair' for the surrogate to be compensated (beyond reasonable expenses) for the burden she endures by conceiving (or having an embryo implanted in her), carrying the pregnancy and bearing a child that she does not view as her own.[27] The view is similar to that espoused in the United States two decades ago by Ragone, who emphasised 'intentionality' and 'choice' of the surrogate, and separated out the biological function of conception, pregnancy and birth with the social function of parenting.[28]

However, views that the surrogate does not consider herself as a 'mother', is simply 'renting out' her womb,[29] providing her 'services',[30] or being paid a moderate sum for the burden she bears,[31] do not satisfactorily resolve concerns about the sale or commodification of the child. Emphasis upon 'choice', 'intent',

26 Jenni Millbank, 'Resolving the Dilemma of Legal Parentage for Australians Engaged in International Surrogacy' (2013) 27 *Australian Journal of Family Law* 138–9. Note here Millbank refers to the work of A. Campbell, *Sister Wives, Surrogates and Sex Workers: Outlaws by Choice* (Farnham: Ashgate, 2013).

27 Such distinctions have been discussed and debated for decades, and are often reiterated in current day debates by those who suggest that commercial surrogacy should be made legal in their own jurisdiction. For example, see Jenni Millbank, 'Paying for birth: The case for (cautious) commercial surrogacy', *The Guardian*, 22 September 2013, accessed 10 June 2014 at http://www.theguardian.com/commentisfree/2013/sep/02/australia-commercial-surrogacy. Note, Millbank does not go so far as to discount that the woman who gives birth to the child should be treated as the legal parent at birth, and is careful not to completely treat gestation and birth as irrelevant.

28 H. Ragone, *Surrogate Motherhood: Conception in the Heart* (Boulder, CO: Westview Press, 1994), 127. Note the difference in current family formations to the arrangements studied by Ragone is that there may not be an intended social *mother*.

29 Joseph Pelzman, '"Womb for Rent": International Service Trade Employing Assisted Reproduction Technologies (ARTs)' (2013) 21(3) *Review of International Economics* 387–400.

30 Ibid.

31 Millbank, 'Paying for Birth: The case for (cautious) commercial surrogacy', above n. 27.

or a surrogate's perception of self, have been seen by some as problematic,[32] and as simply a way to circumvent laws that prohibit the sale of children.[33] The difficulty is that, no matter what language is used to describe the transaction (including whether we call the commercial aspect of it 'payment', 'compensation' or a 'gift'), no matter what the viewed relationship of the woman called a 'surrogate' to the child, the literal interpretation of the law is the rendering of pregnancy and birth, and the delivery of a child to others *for remuneration or other consideration*, by definition, equates to sale or commodification.[34]

It is also flawed to emphasise the surrogate's view of self without considering the views of resulting offspring. For example, Smerdon quotes one nearly 18-year-old boy born as a result of commercial surrogacy who wrote:

> How do you think we feel about being created specifically to be given away? … I don't care why my parents or my mother did this. It looks to me like I was bought and sold … When you exchange something for [m]oney it is called a commodity. Babies are not commodities. Babies are human beings. How do you think this makes us feel to know that there was money exchanged for us? Because somewhere between the narcissistic, selfish or desperate need for a child and the desire to make a buck, everyone else's needs and wants are put before the kids['] needs. We the children become lost … .[35]

Clearly, this statement reflects the offspring's view that his birth mother was involved in his sale. Alternatively, the view of a 14-year-old girl is noted ' … it doesn't really matter how I was born and that my mother didn't actually carry me.

---

32 Susan Berke Fogel et al., 'Invoking "choice" when discussing surrogacy as a feminist concern is a mistake', *RH Reality Check*, 23 April 2014, accessed 10 June 2014, available at http://rhrealitycheck.org/article/2014/04/23/invoking-choice-discussing-surrogacy-feminist-concern-mistake/.

33 Scott B. Rae, *The Ethics of Commercial Surrogate Motherhood: Brave New Families?* (Westport, CT: Praeger Publishing, 1994), 17.

34 Perhaps it is also here important to note that while there is some evidence that surrogates may psychologically distance themselves from the child they carry (see for example, Olga Van de Akker, 'Psychological Aspects of Surrogate Motherhood' (2007) 13(1) *Human Reproduction Update* 53), research available on the long-term experience, views and outcomes for surrogates is limited. As such foreclosing the view of commercial surrogacy based upon even a present view of whether or not the surrogate views herself as 'mother' during or immediately after birth is problematic. In addition note that issues of commodification also apply to using a woman for the purposes of bearing a child for others in exchange for money (be it for her services, or otherwise).

35 Usha Rengachary Smerdon, 'Crossing Bodies, Crossing Borders: International Surrogacy Agreements between the United States and India' (2009) 39 *Cumberland Law Review* 60.

But it does matter that I am here. I am born.'[36] Noting that research available on the long-term experience, views and outcomes for children is even more limited than that on surrogates (in fact, it is non-existent), the differing voices of the offspring are nevertheless poignant. While such voices may differ, that any child born of such arrangements might feel that they have been 'bought' and 'sold' is nothing short of alarming – and must be acknowledged when determining how to view commercial surrogacy and whether it is acceptable.

Finally, it is also relevant to consider commercial surrogacy in light of situations that have been said to most clearly illustrate the sale and or commodification of children. That is, while in many cases the commissioning person(s) may wish to procure a child that they will love and care for (and do appear to do so very well), the ability to procure a child by payment in commercial surrogacy arrangements, has given rise to clear examples of exploitation and abuse.[37] There have also been recent cases in which children have been abandoned, when they have not meet the expectations of the commissioning persons. In one such case, the Australian commissioning persons left a child with Down's Syndrome behind, while taking his healthy sister, reportedly asking for their money to be refunded. In another case, an Australian couple, decided to keep only one twin based upon its gender,

---

36 Ibid. NB. In these two statements the first child was born as a result of 'traditional 'surrogacy, and the latter a 'gestational' agreement. See discussion above as to why the distinction may be flawed when discussing whether the exchange of money related to the relinquishment of the child equates to sale or commodification.

37 Detailed discussion of concerns about commercial surrogacy and child trafficking and abuse is beyond the scope of this chapter. However, the author notes two recent examples in which commercial surrogacy has raised concern in relation to children. In June 2013, the Israeli National Council for the Child brought to the attention of authorities, an Israeli man, recognised by the authorities as a paedophile (and who had served time in prison for molesting children in his care), who had been given legal custody of a 4-year-old girl following an arrangement with a commercial surrogate in India. The child could not be removed from the man as he is considered her legal parent. Authorities were 'closely monitoring her well-being while she remains in his care'. See http://www.irtsa.com.ua/en/news/732.html (accessed 10 June 2014). Consider also the case of Mark Newton and Peter Truong, a US/Australian couple who ultimately procured a child via paid adoption in Russia, to exploit sexually. The couple, and a number of other men, abused the boy from 6 weeks to 6 years of age. Newton and Truong had engaged in numerous (failed) commercial surrogacy attempts before finding a woman who was already pregnant and willing to sell them her baby once it was born. Surrogacy nevertheless was a real and tried avenue by the men to procure the child: Department of Justice, United States Attorney Joseph H. Hogsett, Southern District of Indiana 'Hogsett announces charges against four men in international child exploitation conspiracy', 28 June 2013, accessed 10 June 2014, available at http://www.justice.gov/usao/ins/press_releases/Pressrelease13/Newton.20130628.pdf'; *United States of America v Mark Jonathan Newton* (United States District Court, 1: 12-cr-00121-SEB-TAB, 25 June 2013).

and to leave the other one behind. [38] Such instances form part of the 'evidence base' that commercial surrogacy involves the sale and/or commodification of children. Perhaps it is needless to say, that this is so whether or not the surrogate is a wholly autonomous and willing party to the transaction, or whether she is herself exploited in terms of the arrangement. In the latter instance, she could not be held morally culpable, but the nature of the transaction remains the same.

Of course, focusing upon whether the surrogate is involved in the sale or commodification of the child she bears is but one issue raised by commercial surrogacy transactions. What of the surrogate who, in the modern-day world of commercial surrogacy, is often subject to social or cultural imbalances, financial pressures and inequities, and in worse case scenarios human trafficking? She too is at risk. It is to these things that the discussion now turns.

B. Human Trafficking

There is no doubt that in the global commercial surrogacy market poor and vulnerable women have been trafficked for use as surrogates for the profit of agents or brokers. For example, in 2012, Rotabi and Bromfield, provided a stark comparison between inter-country adoption and commercial surrogacy in Guatemala,[39] highlighting that 'in the global environment of assistive technology and the demand for babies ... Guatemalan women are at risk of human sales of their offspring in global surrogacy schemes ... '. Drawing analogies to past practices in inter-country adoption rings, Rotabi and Bromfield noted schemes in which women (often teenage girls) were commonly called 'breeders', and were paid small amounts of money in exchange for their child by merchants.[40] The European Parliament's Joint Motion for a Resolution on Guatemala, in July 2005, recognised such concerns. It stated that according to the Office of the Counsel for Human Rights, 'the abuses occurring in Guatemala include forced or surrogate pregnancies, removal of children from their real mothers, substitution of documents, alteration of public records, and the existence of clandestine 'nurseries' ... '.[41] The emerging practices of commercial surrogacy in such places

---

38 See for example Lindsay Murdoch 'Australian Couple Leaves Down Syndrome Baby with Thai Surrogate' *The Sydney Morning Herald* 1 August 2014, accessed 12 March 2015, available at http://www.smh.com.au/national/australian-couple-leaves-down-syndrome-baby-with-thai-surrogate-20140731-zz3xp.html; see also News Corp Australia, 'Indian Surrogacy Saga: Australian Couple Abandons Baby in India, *News.com.au* 9 October, 2014, accessed 12 March 2015, available at http://www.news.com.au/world/indian-surrogacy-saga-australian-couple-abandons-baby-in-india/story-fndir2ev-1227084223406.

39 Karen Smith Rotabi and Nicole Footen Bromfield, 'The Decline in Intercountry Adoptions and New Practices of Global Surrogacy Global Exploitation and Human Rights Concerns' (2012) 27(2) *Affilia* 141.

40 Ibid., 134.

41 Official Journal of the European Union, 'Trafficking in Children in Guatemala: European Parliament Resolution on Guatemala' (P6_TA(2005)0304), accessed 10 June 2014,

clearly raise significant concerns about 'human rights abuses, including human trafficking and violence against women'.[42]

The example of Guatemala is not unique. Cases of human trafficking of women to work as surrogates have been reported for decades in other places. For example, in 1995, young Polish women were recruited to travel to Holland, Belgium and Germany to work (illegally in some cases) as surrogates.[43] In 2009, women from Myanmar were sold to Chinese men to work as surrogates. The women 'had been lured to China in the hope of finding jobs' but were instead paid $250 to act as surrogates.[44] In 2011, several Taiwanese, Chinese and Burmese people were arrested for allegedly running an illegal surrogacy ring in Thailand. In this instance, some of the 14 Vietnamese women being housed as surrogates, 7 of whom were pregnant, had been tricked or forced into the arrangements and, according to the Public Health Minister, some had been raped.[45] In the same year, three individuals in the United States were convicted of criminal charges relating to paying 'surrogate' mothers to be sent to the Ukraine for implantation with embryos, without any surrogacy arrangements in place. If the pregnancy continued into the second trimester, the unborn children were 'sold' to prospective parents under false representations that they were the result of legitimate surrogacy arrangements in which the original commissioning person(s) had 'backed out'.[46] In 2013, the Bangladesh Country Report on combating human trafficking also

---

available at http://www.europarl.europa.eu/sides/getDoc.do?type=MOTION&reference=P6-RC-2005–0415&language=RO.

42 Rae, above n. 33, 129.

43 Iris Leibowitz-Dori, 'Womb for Rent: The Future of International Trade in Surrogacy' *Minnesota Journal of Global Trade* 6 (1997): 329; Abi Daruvalla, 'Poles hired as surrogate mums in illegal trade', *The Independent* (4 June 1995), accessed 10 June 2014, available at http://www.independent.co.uk/news/world/poles-hired-as-surrogate-mums-in-illegal-trade-1584960.html.

44 Lucy Hornby, 'China deports Myanmar women sold as surrogates', *Reuters* (25 March 2009), accessed 10 June 2014, available at http://uk.reuters.com/article/2009/03/25/us-china-myanmar-idUKTRE52O1I720090325.

45 'Thailand police investigate baby sales ring', *BBC News* (22 February 2011), accessed 10 June 2014, available at http://www.bbc.co.uk/news/world-asia-pacific-12575566; Center for Genetics and Society, 'Thai police free women from surrogate baby ring', *AFP* (24 February 2011), accessed 10 June 2014, http://www.geneticsandsociety.org/article.php?id=5606.

46 Hague Conference on Private International Law, *A Preliminary Report on the Issues Arising from International Surrogacy Arrangements* (Preliminary Document No 10 of March 2012). See also Federal Bureau of Investigation, 'Baby-selling ring busted' (9 August 2011), accessed 10 June 2014, available at http://www.fbi.gov/sandiego/press-releases/2011/baby-selling-ring-busted.

mentioned surrogacy as a form of human trafficking in Bangladesh.[47] Such risks and practices are real, and continue into the modern day.

The above cases are extreme in that they include criminality and abuse, and provide a stark illustration of the risks commercial surrogacy may pose, in both the developing and developed world – including the danger that 'agents' or third parties may use and traffic women for profit. However, the risks associated with commercial surrogacy do not end there. Even in more 'routine' cases, there exists concern about the extent to which women engaged as surrogates are influenced by social and economic pressures, are able to give free and informed consent, and are exploited through racial and cultural inequities.

C. Social and Financial Pressures

As commercial surrogacy occurs in a variety of socially and economically different locations, social and financial pressures that may be faced by women who act as surrogates can take many and different forms; blanket statements are not possible. (Although it could confidently be said that very affluent women do not act as commercial surrogates).

In the developed world, few nations permit commercial transactions, and thus perhaps the most looked upon nation is the United States, in which some states have permitted such practices for some time. There, early studies suggested that women acting as commercial surrogates are 'predominantly white, working class, of Protestant or Catholic background' with 30% of them being 'full-time homemakers, married, and with an average of three children'.[48] In 2005, Beckman and Ciccarelli reviewed twenty seven empirical studies conducted between January 1983 to December 2003 in the United States, and concluded that 'surrogate mother's' family incomes are most often modest (as opposed to low) and they are from working class backgrounds'.[49] In 2007, Driabak et al. noted that the rhetoric in the United States that portrays the surrogate as a reasonably well-educated, financially stable woman motivated by altruism stands in contrast to reality.[50] Driabak found that sociological studies of surrogates conducted between 1997 and 2007 suggest that 'financial motivation may be a primary factor in the decision to participate in surrogacy … [and], because of their financial status, commercial surrogates are susceptible to financial inducement and vulnerable to exploitation'.[51]

47 Minister of Home Affairs, *The Bangladesh Country Report 2013 Combating Human Trafficking* (2013), accessed 6 March 2015, available at http://antitraffickingcell.gov.bd/index.php/en/country-report.

48 Helena Ragone, above n. 28.

49 Janice C. Ciccarelli and Linda J. Beckman, 'Navigating Rough Waters: An Overview of Psychological Aspects of Surrogacy (2005) 61 *Journal of Social Issues* 21.

50 Ibid., 304.

51 Katherine Drabiak et al., 'Ethics, Law, and Commercial Surrogacy: A Call for Uniformity' (2007) 35 *Journal of Law, Medicine and Ethics* 301.

More recently reports from the United States indicate, that depending on the state, between 19% and 50% of women who act as commercial surrogates are military wives, with higher rates in larger states that have sizeable military establishments such as Texas and California. Lower earnings for military families (estimated to be at around $30,000 per year), having to look after children, and the absence of the husband who is serving overseas, may all influence engagement with commercial surrogacy, which may provide an extra $25,000-$30,000 to the family.[52]

In the United States (as with practices elsewhere), given the high costs of surrogacy and the fact that they do not usually have children yet, it is unsurprising to find that the commissioning persons are older, generally more educated and had higher incomes than surrogate mothers and their partners.

In regions and countries where poverty is more pronounced, the disparities are even greater. For example, in a study conducted in 2012, by the Center for Social Research (CSR) in India, in which over 100 surrogates, as well as their families, commissioning person(s), clinics, agents, and other stakeholders, were interviewed, the overwhelming majority of surrogates indicated that they had decided to become a surrogate due to 'poverty'.[53] The study found a system rife with problems and inequalities.[54] Concerns were raised about pressure from others (for example, brokers and/or husbands) for women to become surrogates as they may earn many times their husband's yearly income for one surrogacy (noting, that this does not mean that women are paid well). In addition, the CSR study also highlighted a lack of transparency regarding the fees paid to surrogates and disparity between what the commissioning person(s) believe the surrogate is paid and what she is actually paid.[55] The CSR report concluded that 'in reality the contract between the parties to surrogacy would not exist if the parties were equal'.[56]

It has thus long since been an issue that commissioning persons from relatively affluent economic backgrounds may intentionally, or unintentionally,

---

52 Targeted marketing also takes place including statements that commercial surrogacy ' ... is the ultimate call of duty—military wives carrying a dream.' See for example websites such as 'Find a surrogate mother – Military Wives and Surrogacy', accessed 16 February 2015, available at http://www.findsurrogatemother.com/surrogacy/guide-for-surrogate-mothers/military-wives-and-surrogacy.

53 86.7 per cent in Anand, 88.6 per cent in Surat, and 100 per cent in Jamnagar. See Centre for Social Research, *Surrogate Motherhood: Ethical or Commercial* (March 2012), 37–8, available at http://www.womenleadership.in/Csr/SurrogacyReport.pdf, accessed 16 February 2015

54 Ibid.

55 Note that payments to surrogates in India are arbitrarily decided by the infertility physician of the clinic or hospital, and generally range from 2 to 3.99 Lakhs (approximately US$3,800–$5,700). Ibid., 47.

56 Ibid.

take advantage of indigent women by offering a sum of money that such women desperately need and will not be able to refuse.[57]

Such social and class issues are not limited, however, to financial disparities; they impact upon the way in which surrogacy agreements ('contracts') are negotiated, and are reflected in the racial and cultural disparities rife in such transactions. Such concerns have been raised in relation to all regions in which commercial surrogacy is occurring, including, but not limited to, Ukraine, Russia, India, Guatemala, and some American states.[58]

D. Commercial Surrogacy Agreements: Reduced Bargaining Power and Lack of Informed Consent

Concerns have also been raised about women being able to properly protect their interests, or give free and voluntary informed consent to act as a surrogate mother, when dealing with those that organise commercial surrogacy.[59] As a large and organised market, there is drive (and techniques) to ensure that the majority of profits are directed to agencies, clinics, lawyers, and intermediaries, while ensuring there are enough women to meet demand. In such circumstances, potential surrogates who are in need of finance (and commissioning persons experiencing the anguish of infertility or childlessness) may have diminished bargaining power when dealing with people who work in, and profit greatly from, the commercial surrogacy industry.

For example, within the commercial surrogacy industry, there is much emphasis upon surrogates acting to 'help' others and being 'giving' women, motivated ultimately by altruism[60] rather than financial need or gain. This in turn, may be used to reduce the fee paid to the surrogate to ensure that the total cost to the commissioning persons is not prohibitive, while women who act as surrogates are encouraged to report that money is not their primary motivation.[61]

---

57 See, for example of early discussion on this point *In re Baby M*, 537 A.2d 1227, 1250 (NJ 1988).

58 Note as discussed above that the author recognises differences amongst and between states. The financial starting point of some women in developing countries, for example, would be different to that of a surrogate in the United States. In the United States, the visible disparities may be less pronounced, and amounts paid are far greater – but as noted above, very affluent women do not generally act as surrogates in any such nations.

59 Drabiak, above n. 51, 304.

60 Ruth Macklin, 'What's Wrong with Commodification?', in Cynthia B. Cohen (ed.), *New Ways of Making Babies: The Case of Egg Donation* (Bloomington, IN: Indiana University Press, 1996), 106.

61 See, for example, V. Jadva et al., 'Surrogacy: The Experiences of Surrogate Mothers' (2003) 18(10) *Human Reproduction* 2199, in which only one surrogate mother of 34 interviewed reported payment as a motivating factor; H. Ragone, *Surrogate Motherhood*: above n. 28, 57; J.C. Ciccarelli and L.J. Beckman, 'Navigating Rough Waters: An Overview of Psychological Aspects of Surrogacy' (2005) 61 *Journal of Social Issues* 30, in which surrogates stated they would not have become a surrogate simply for the money, as it is

Potential surrogates may, in some cases, also lack independent representation and therefore be more vulnerable to manipulation (by a broker/agent, the assisted reproductive clinic, or the commissioning person(s)) regarding not only price, but also the terms of the contract, including that the surrogate bears most of the risks.[62] For example, in the above-mentioned CSR study conducted in India, it was found that surrogates were often illiterate and relied on clinics to inform them of the terms of the contract, without independent advice. When asked, surrogates could not explain or recall many of the terms of the contract they had entered into. Contracts were often not signed until mid-way through the fourth month of a pregnancy meaning the surrogates would bear all risks and losses if the pregnancy miscarried or was aborted due to foetal abnormalities. Clinics often were not party to the contract, allegedly to avoid accountability.

When commercial surrogacy does not require women to have experienced previous pregnancy and birth other issues regarding free and informed consent may arise. A potential surrogate may enter an agreement due to the offer of, what is to her is a large sum of money, without understanding the physical or psychological effects of acting as a surrogate.[63] Walker suggests that women who have not previously borne children could never really give informed consent to participate in a surrogacy agreement as they will not be able to predict the bond they may feel with the child.[64]

However nor does a requirement for previous births resolve the issues. All women are exposed to risks that include a higher maternal morbidity and mortality rate for women who use other women's eggs.[65] Each pregnancy is different, and having had a previous child does not mean one can predict risks of future pregnancies. There is also often the potential of placing the surrogate mother in a situation where the baby's life may be given priority over hers should complications arise.

A recent European Parliament study into surrogacy practices also noted that the autonomy of the surrogate mother can be compromised throughout the process by her being required by the commissioning person(s) and/or physicians to undergo sampling tests, amniocentesis or vaginal ultra-sound, to change her

---

'never enough' and another woman echoing, 'I'm not doing this for the money' (as cited in Drabiak, above n. 51).

62 Jennifer Rimm, 'Booming Baby Business: Regulating Commercial Surrogacy in India' (2009) 30 *University of Pennsylvania Journal of International Law* 1449.

63 Ibid., 1443–44.

64 Molly Walker, 'Precommitment in Free-market Procreation: Surrogacy, Commissioned Adoption, and Limits on Human Decision Making Capacity' (2005) 31 *Journal of Legislation* 330.

65 M.L.P. van der Hoorn et al., 'Clinical and Immunologic Aspects of Egg Donation Pregnancies: A Systematic Review' (2010) 16(6) *Human Reproduction Update* 704; F. Olivennes, 'Double Trouble: Yes, Twin Pregnancies is an Adverse Outcome' (2000) 15(8) *Human Reproduction Update* 1663.

diet or lifestyle, and or to terminate the pregnancy in case of a defective foetus or multiples.[66] Women who have entered surrogacy agreements due to a need to support their already existing children, or because of significant financial need, may be particularly vulnerable to such pressures. For example, they may be concerned about their ability to meet their current family's needs if told they will not be paid, or that they will be left with another child. In such circumstances it may be extremely difficult to exercise autonomy and choice. In the above mentioned case in which an Australian couple abandoned a child with Down's Syndrome, the 'surrogate' mother was told to abort. When she refused due to religious beliefs, she was left with the child, who she loved and cared for, in dire circumstances. Many women may not have been able to do even this.

E. Autonomy and Free Choice

However, some argue that perpetuating the idea that women who wish to act as surrogate mothers are unable to 'contract' (or make agreements) freely is paternalistic.[67] Andrews and Elster state that it is 'paternalistic to assume that individuals choosing to be donors or surrogates are incapable of making rational, informed choices'.[68] They cite Richard Arneson who contends that 'the thought that commercial surrogacy should be banned because the poor working women who mostly choose surrogacy are too incompetent to be entrusted to make their own decisions in this sphere has an ugly, elitist sound'.[69] Andrews and Elster argue that 'such paternalism and elitism may do more to devalue, degrade, and exploit women than would payment for their reproductive products and services'.[70] Arneson argues that provided no harm is done to others, prospective parents and potential surrogates should be free to act (and contract) as they wish.[71] The emphasis should be upon the autonomy and free choice of those parties,[72] and upon arguments that surrogates and commissioning persons are satisfied and enriched by the process.[73]

Similarly, it has also been questioned whether the fact that a surrogate's decision being influenced by financial need is enough to discount the practice of

---

66 European Parliament, Director General for Internal Policies, Policy Department Citizen's Rights and Constitutional Affairs, *A Comparative Study on the Regime of Surrogacy in EU Member States* (2013).

67 Lori B. Andrews and Nanette Elster, 'Regulating Reproductive Technologies' (2000) 21(1) *Journal of Legal Medicine* 41.

68 Ibid., 41.

69 R.J. Arneson, 'Commodification and Commercial Surrogacy' (1992) 21 *Philosophy and Public Affairs* 132, as cited in Andrews and Elster, above n. 67, 41.

70 Andrews and Elster, above n. 67, 41.

71 R.J. Arneson above n. 69, 158.

72 Ibid.

73 Pamela Laufer-Ukeles, 'Mothering for Money: Regulating Commercial Intimacy, Surrogacy, Adoption' (2013) 8(4) *Indiana Law Journal* 1223.

commercial surrogacy as unacceptable. Pande, for example, quotes the realities of one 25-year-old housewife's 'compulsion' to become a surrogate:

> Who would choose to do this? I have had a lifetime's worth of injections pumped into me. Some big ones in my hips hurt so much. In the beginning, I had almost 20–25 pills almost every day. I feel bloated all the time. But I know I have to do this for my children's future … This is not work, this is *majboori* [a compulsion]. Where we are now, it can't possibly get any worse … In our village we don't have a hut to live in or crops in our farm. The work is not ethical, it's just something we have to do to survive. When we heard of this surrogacy business, we didn't have clothes to wear after the rain … and our house had fallen down. What were we to do?[74]

Such compulsion is not viewed as leading the woman to be unable to make independent decisions. Some argue therefore that she is simply doing what she must, and what she accepts. Pande has thus referred to the labour as equivalent to a woman choosing to do sex-work, in need of the same protections and regulation.

However, arguments such as those made by Andrews, Elster and Arneson (and others) concerning a woman's 'freedom' appear to ignore that in many circumstances such freedom *is* constrained by poverty, unequal bargaining power, and social and cultural circumstances and pressures – all of which may manifest themselves in unacceptable ways in both developed and developing countries. The 'ugly elitism' to which Andrews and Elster refer arguably does not exist in calling for laws that support women and children, but rather exists in the financial and racial disparities, and or cultural exploitation, found in many such arrangements.

Rimm observes that the global surrogacy market 'adds another dimension to the already grim picture that surrounds modern global commercial surrogacy, by introducing the prospect of unacceptable racial distinctions between the commissioning and the commissioned parties'.[75] She argues that international surrogacy is 'especially problematic when performed at 'bargain prices' for wealthy foreigners because it promotes the racist and imperialist view that it is acceptable to exploit and dehumanize women of different origins'.[76] Perhaps speaking loudly to this are recent changes to Thailand's laws, which now prohibit commercial surrogacy, and restrict altruistic arrangements to being made by Thai nationals.[77] A member of Thailand's National Legislative Assembly has been quoted as saying,

74 A. Pande, 'Not an Angel, Not a Whore: Surrogates as Dirty Workers in India' (2009) 16 *Indian Journal of Gender Studies* 160.

75 Rimm, above n. 62, 1446.

76 Ibid.

77 Or if a foreigner, married to a Thai national and resident in Thailand for more than three years. NB. In mid-March 2015, the law was awaiting royal assent.

'This law aims to stop Thai women's wombs from becoming the world's womb'.[78] This speaks not only to the cultural, racial, social and economic disparities that were so clearly pronounced, but also to broader perspectives concerning how, within society, women should (and should not) be viewed.

It is apt here to conclude this section by also returning to issues that may arise for children in such circumstances. In many of the above described circumstances, there continues to be concerns about commodification; access for trafficking or abuse; as well as a child's right to access to information, and connect with siblings, donors and birth mothers. There may also be potential impacts upon the children a 'surrogate' mother already has, as they witness their mother carry a pregnancy and then hand the child to others to parent, in exchange for money.[79] These added complexities all exist in the global market, regardless of freedom, autonomy or choice.

III. Approaches to the Regulation of Surrogacy

Bearing in mind the above issues, this chapter now turns to consideration of how commercial surrogacy is regulated around the globe, with particular focus on how such regulation pertains to the surrogate. As it is not possible in this chapter to discuss specifics of so many jurisdictions, trends in regulation are outlined.[80]

The discussion then turns to whether those jurisdictions that prohibit commercial surrogacy should change their laws to permit it – it being argued that this is not necessary or desirable. In addition, minimum standards for all countries in relation to surrogacy are suggested. To address the global issues examined in this chapter, the proposal for an international convention is also considered. The conclusion reached is that it is not desirable for countries that currently prohibit commercial surrogacy to acquiesce to current practices found in some nations, or to take a laissez-faire approach to regulation. International and domestic prohibitions on commercial surrogacy should be encouraged and/or maintained. They should also

78 ABC News, 'Thailand Bans Surrogacy in a Bid to End 'Rent a Womb' Tourism', 20 February 2015, accessed on 6 March 2015, available at http://www.abc.net.au/news/2015-02-20/thailand-bans-surrogacy-for-foreigners/6163810.

79 In one example cited by a researcher presenting her work at the Institute of Social Studies forum on Inter-country Adoption and Global Surrogacy, held in The Hague in August 2014, a small boy said to his mother 'We don't need the money, can we just keep my brother?' See http://www.iss.nl/research/conferences_and_seminars/periodic_conferences_debates_and_seminars/international_forum_on_intercountry_adoption_global_surrogacy/.

80 The outline of laws was initially drawn from the Permanent Bureau of The Hague (which has for some time been considering issues pertaining to international surrogacy) and uses the four categories of regulation they refer to. See Permanent Bureau, *A Preliminary Report on the Issues Arising from International Surrogacy Arrangements* (March 2012). It has been updated by the author's own commissioned research for the Center for Genetics and Society, Berkeley California under a MacArthur Foundation Grant, in which she identified surrogacy laws and policies in every nation around the world as at March 2015.

be enforced. However, as global agreement on the issue may be elusive, minimum standards for regulation of all surrogacy arrangements, including in those countries that permit the practice, is also recommended.

A. A Snapshot of Worldwide Regulation

Four broad approaches have been used to categorise laws and policies of various nations regarding surrogacy.[81] They are as follows:

1. *to prohibit all surrogacy arrangements*. This approach is taken in a significant number of nations via laws and policies.[82] The ethos underpinning such bans range from statements that surrogacy 'is a violation of the child's and surrogate mother's human dignity' to fear that if surrogacy is permitted legally, social and ethical chaos will ensue.[83] If surrogacy were to occur in any of these jurisdictions, the birth mother would be considered the legal mother of any resulting child, and the surrogacy arrangement would be void and unenforceable. Criminal sanctions may apply to the parties involved in the arrangement or, more commonly, for any intermediaries and/or medical institutions facilitating the arrangement.
2. *to leave surrogacy largely unregulated.*[84] Under this approach, there is no express prohibition in law concerning surrogacy, but a contractual obligation for a surrogate to surrender a child to commissioning person(s) would be void and unenforceable under general law. In addition, in some such jurisdictions commercial surrogacy is banned either through express legal provision or general laws pertaining to, for example, child trafficking.[85]

---

81 Ibid.

82 Such nations include Afghanistan, Albania, Algeria, Austria, Bahrain, Bangladesh, China (mainland), Croatia, Egypt, El Salvador, Ethiopia, Finland, France, Germany, Iceland, Indonesia, Italy, Jordan, Kuwait, Malaysia, Maldives, Malta, Mauritius, Mexico (Queretaro), Malodva, Marocco, Norway, Oman, Portugal, Qatar, Saudi Arabia, Serbia, Singapore, Slovenia, Spain, Sweden, Switzerland, Syrian Arab Republic, Taiwan, Tajikistan, Tunisia, Turkey, Turkmenistan, the United Arab Emirates, some jurisdictions within the United States of America (for example, Arizona, District of Columbia), Vietnam and Yemen. Note that the law in China simply bans trade in fertilised eggs and embryos and forbids hospitals from performing surrogacy procedures. It is reported that such regulations are not adhered to by some. See for example, Xinhua, 'China's female lawmakers call for surrogacy ban', *ChinaDaily.com* (3 August 2012), accessed 10 June 2014, available at http://www.chinadaily.com.cn/china/2012-03/08/content_14782835.htm.

83 Permanent Bureau, above n. 80, 9.

84 This approach is taken by countries including (but not limited to) Argentina, Belgium, Brazil, the Czech Republic, Ireland (which is considering introducing laws to prohibit commercial surrogacy), Japan, Mexico (Mexico City) and some jurisdictions in the United States of America (for example, Michigan and New York) and Venezuela.

85 For example, Turkmenistan and Azerbaijan.

3. *to expressly permit and regulate 'altruistic' surrogacy*. A number of countries permit only altruistic surrogacy arrangements and provide criminal sanctions regarding commercial surrogacy.[86] A number of these countries, however, allow reimbursement of 'reasonable expenses'. The Permanent Bureau notes that under this approach there is also a 'strong trend' to permit only surrogacy arrangements where at least one commissioning person is genetically related to the child, and in some jurisdictions only 'gestational' surrogacy is permitted. In several jurisdictions, women must meet certain criteria before being able to act as a surrogate. These may include such things as age requirements, satisfactory completion of medical and psychological screening, having already had a living child and/or having completed her family, civil status and having received independent legal advice.
4. *A permissive approach to surrogacy, including commercial surrogacy*. Countries in this category include Armenia, Georgia, India, Israel,[87] Kyrgyzstan, Russia,[88] Uganda, Ukraine and 18 jurisdictions in the United States of America.[89] In these jurisdictions:

- commercial surrogacy is permitted and practised;
- following a surrogacy arrangement, there are usually procedures in the State which enable legal parentage to be granted to one or both of the intending parent(s);
- there may not be a domicile or habitual residence requirement for intending parents; and
- differences are found regarding who is permitted to enter into such agreements, and requirements such people must meet.[90]

86 Such countries include Australia (all states and territories except the Northern Territory, where surrogacy is not practiced), Belarus, Belgium, Brazil, Bulgaria, Canada, Denmark, Greece, Hungary, Latvia, some states in Mexico, the Netherlands, New Zealand, South Africa, South Korea, Thailand, the United Kingdom and Peru.

87 Israel authorises monthly 'compensation payments' to the surrogate for pain and suffering which are seen by many as thus placing it in the category of permissive states.

88 Note there have been recent calls in Russia to prohibit surrogacy.

89 There is affirmative case law or legislation allowing commercial surrogacy in California, Maryland, Massachusetts, Ohio, Pennsylvania, South Carolina (case law); and Alabama, Arkansas, Connecticut, Illinois, Iowa, Nevada, North Dakota, Oregon, Tennessee, Texas, Utah, West Virginia (statutes). Within the mentioned jurisdictions some are considering introducing legislation to further regulate commercial surrogacy – for example, India is considering laws that will facilitate commercial surrogacy arrangements.

90 For example, in Russia the prospective parents must be a heterosexual couple or single woman, who meet certain medical criteria regarding inability to conceive, carry or deliver a child. Stipulations regarding who may act as a surrogate also exist (regarding age; requirement of previous health child; medical certification of good health; among other things).

Policy perspectives in countries that permit commercial surrogacy vary – for example in India there has been an economic policy of encouraging 'medical tourism', while in the United States constitutional or legal protections (as above-mentioned) may influence the legal culture. What has occurred therefore is that while the vast majority of jurisdictions around the world express grave concerns about, and opposition to, commercial surrogacy and, as a result, have adopted a stance that prohibits such practices, this has not led to a global situation in which women or children are safe from actual or potential exploitation or harm.

The Permanent Bureau of The Hague notes that:

> the prohibitive or restrictive legal approach of many States to surrogacy (in particular, commercial surrogacy), combined with the liberal approach of a minority, means that prospective intending parents are often using surrogacy services abroad because they are prohibited or restricted at home. Other motivating factors may be lower costs or fewer perceived risks abroad … A further layer of complexity, however, is the fact that the growth of international surrogacy in some States also results from 'the ready availability of poor surrogates'.[91]

In other words, absent uniform legislation worldwide, combined with the ability of some people to travel to countries in which commercial surrogacy may occur, there has been increase in 'fertility tourism' and the potential for exploitation of women who are economically, socially or legally disadvantaged – many of whom live in developing nations.[92] The Permanent Bureau notes in this regard '[t]he unease expressed by some concerning the practice of engaging surrogates in States with emerging economies to bear children for more wealthy intending parents … has dimensions similar to those discussed in the preparatory reports on inter-country adoption'.[93]

B. Suggestions for the Future Regulation of Surrogacy

How should we address concerns that surrogacy may pose risks to women and children, in light of the issues discussed in Section II? This final section considers briefly regulatory suggestions regarding commercial surrogacy (both domestically and internationally).

91 Permanent Bureau, above n. 80, 7.
92 Leibowitz-Dori, above n. 43, 329.
93 Permanent Bureau, above n. 80, 7.

i. Domestic regulation

What legal position should jurisdictions take toward commercial surrogacy practices? As stated above, some people have argued that the solution is to permit commercial surrogacy, rather than continue to prohibit it, in their own jurisdictions.[94]

In Australia, Millbank suggests 'cautious' commercial surrogacy or a flat rate compensatory fee, as the way to resolve such issues.[95] She proposes a set fee for profit – which is not too low, but not too high – to prevent exploitation. Allegedly, the minimum (small) payment will serve to avoid 'unfair inducements', while being fair compensation for surrogates for the risk and burden they take. However, this would not address the ethical issues that have been discussed in this chapter. Who would act as a surrogate in such circumstances? The risk is that it might be the most vulnerable or financially needy, the low-income single mother, immigrant, unemployed woman, or mother unable to work and care for the children at the same time – induced by the minimum payment that moves above reimbursement of reasonable expenses. Perhaps what will follow will be arguments that accepting low payments for commercial surrogacy reflects that surrogates are not really doing it for the money after all – noting again that such rhetoric is often used to keep the price of surrogacy low.

One may also question arguments that focus upon the 'plight' of commissioning persons and claims that people who desire children may face 'serious harms' due to being 'excluded from their preferred or only available, family formation avenue'.[96] Even if some such people seek to engage in practices elsewhere that are prohibited in their home state, this in itself is no reason to move to accepting commercial surrogacy in their country of origin. Building families, in all shapes and sizes, is wonderful; however, it should not be at the expense of, or risk to, others – including the surrogate mother and/or the children. Laws should not be changed on the basis that some people will break them. There are also broader social values adopted in many nations regarding how such actions are viewed, that would not support such a move.

Further, while people travelling abroad to engage in commercial surrogacy arrangements has led to questions of how to resolve the legal parentage and citizenship of the resulting children, this is only one consideration. Analysis of the broader ethical and legal issues raised by such practices should not be lost when considering regulatory options.

Permitting commercial surrogacy in jurisdictions that currently ban it may further risk broadening a practice (or 'market') that reflects the financial, social

94 For example, see Loane Skene, 'Why legalising commercial surrogacy is a good idea', *The Conversation* (10 December 2012), accessed 10 June 2014, available at http://theconversation.com/why-legalising-commercial-surrogacy-is-a-good-idea-11251.

95 Millbank, 'Paying for birth: The case for (cautious) commercial surrogacy', above n. 27.

96 Millbank, 'The New Surrogacy Parentage Laws in Australia: Cautious Regulation or "25 Brick Walls"?' (2011) 35(1) *Melbourne University Law Review* 189.

and cultural disparities between commissioning person(s) and surrogates. It may serve the agents, lawyers, and clinics that stand to profit greatly, but would not serve women or children. It certainly would not address issues surrounding the nature of the transaction for example, regarding the sale or commodification of women and children, the human rights issues raised by such practices, nor risks and realities related to their trafficking.

It is here important to note that commissioning person(s) may also vulnerable. They may be 'sold' the idea that commercial surrogacy is simply a business transaction that can be performed with ease. There is clear, and extensive marketing to them, including conferences held in Europe, London and Australia to sell the idea of commercial surrogacy being their 'path to parenthood'. They may be told they will achieve emotional fulfilment and a family of their own using commercial surrogates who are really giving, altruistic women, who want to help (for a fee/compensation). Interestingly, in an environment in which only altruistic surrogacy is available, the ready availability of such giving, altruistic women, is rather limited, and perhaps is evidence in itself that it is the commercial nature of transactions elsewhere that increases participation.

Nevertheless, there is scope for domestic laws to be improved. For example, there is a need to create consistency in countries that permit reimbursement of reasonable expenses to ensure that such 'reasonable expenses' are not a guise for commercial (that is, 'for profit') arrangements. Clear statements and uniform agreement upon what expenses may be reimbursed are also needed. It is also necessary to ensure that laws apply equally to all, regardless for example of sexuality. Clearly, in cases where people have moved beyond the law, and/or engaged in commercial surrogacy abroad, considerations concerning their actions, as well as the child's status and legal parentage, must also be addressed. The legislature needs to speak to these things, noting, at a minimum, it will still most likely be that each case must be assessed by a court of law, regarding whether:

a. it is in the best interests of a child to be parented by people who may have broken the law (if this has been the case);
b. such commissioning person(s) had any (or no) regard for the circumstances of the woman who gave birth and the egg donor if there was one;
c. there may have been fraud, coercion, or even trafficking; and
d. whether there is concern about information available to the child, and the possibility of future release of information and or relationships between the child, gamete donors and surrogate.[97]

That said, there are, of course, problems with any approach in which the law prohibits a practice, and yet courts 'outline the principles that are necessary to ensure legal recognition of, and by implication, legitimacy for the practice'. Tobin

97 Mary Keyes and Richard Chisholm, 'Commercial Surrogacy – Some Troubling Family Law Issues' (2013) 27 *Australian Journal of Family Law Issues* 117.

refers to this as 'signal failure', and indicates that continued recognition of legal parentage in such circumstances is unsatisfactory and unsustainable.[98]

It may be argued therefore, that in jurisdictions in which laws prohibit engagement in commercial surrogacy arrangements, including extra-territorially, that legal parentage should never be granted to commissioning persons(s) if they have acted contrary to the law. This is however what has led to the current debate about commercial surrogacy, and is the perennial question that society and legislators face. The surrogate's legal status as mother may be recognised, but she may not be in the position to parent the child, may not wish to do so, or, in some circumstances, may not be able to be found. Who will parent the child in such circumstances, thus needs to be resolved.[99] Perhaps as increasingly we see nations pass restrictive laws, the incidence of such problems will reduce, but one cannot naively hope that this will be the case. The market is driven by significant profits, and pushes into nations that have no regulation and often lack the infrastructure to protect women and children. Countries have thus moved to consider how they will resolve legal parentage issues while also continuing to (or even introducing laws that will) prohibit commercial surrogacy.

There should also be a focus on how to address the actions of lawyers, brokers and other agencies who make a business (and handsome profit) out of giving 'advice' to people about commercial surrogacy arrangements abroad. Such people may encourage or facilitate people to engage in commercial surrogacy transactions that are against the laws of their state. They may further be responsible (in some circumstances) for placing the commercial transaction above the health, safety and well-being of women and children. The large sums of money such people can make also encourages them to advocate for an expansion of practice. Thus pro bono systems might be considered to ensure that lawyers, brokers, and other agencies are not driving the industry due to their own financial interests.

For those countries that continue to prohibit commercial surrogacy within their borders, there is the option to introduce prohibitions that apply extraterritorially. That is, residents of those jurisdictions would be committing a crime if they travelled elsewhere to engage in practices that are prohibited in their own territory. This is the position taken in three Australian states (New South Wales, the Australian Capital Territory and Queensland),[100] Malaysia, and Turkey.[101] Arguably, such extraterritorial prohibition may lead to a reduction in forum shopping and limit

98 John Tobin, 'To Prohibit or Permit: What is the (Human) Rights Response to the Practice of International Commercial Surrogacy?' (2014) 63(2) *International and Comparative Law Quarterly* 340, 349.

99 This may, for example, be via adoption of the child. Further exploration of this issue is necessary, but is beyond the scope of the chapter's focus upon the surrogate.

100 *Surrogacy Act* 2010 (NSW), s 11; *Parentage Act* 2004 (ACT), s 45; *Surrogacy Act* 2010 (Qld), s 54.

101 R. Storrow, 'Assisted Reproduction on Treacherous Terrain: The Legal Hazards of Cross-border Reproductive Travel' (2011) 23 *Reproductive Biomedicine Online* 538.

the number of people willing to engage in such practices abroad. However, the counter-argument is that extraterritorial laws are extremely difficult to enforce,[102] and there are clearly dilemmas regarding the status of children when such laws are breached.[103] Some people also continue to travel to engage in commercial surrogacy, despite such laws. Perhaps, another alternative or simultaneous option is to encourage countries that choose to allow commercial surrogacy,[104] to restrict access to people permanently domiciled in that jurisdiction. That is, such countries should not offer their own citizens for commercial surrogacy arrangements with people from countries where the practice is banned. (Note, there are such residency requirements in some countries in relation to the altruistic arrangements they permit).

In addition, all states that currently do not have any form of regulation should pass laws on surrogacy. Some may choose to prohibit all forms of surrogacy, while others may pass laws that permit the form(s) of surrogacy they are willing to accept. Whether altruistic or commercial surrogacy is permitted, all suchstates should pass laws that set at least minimum standards to protect women and children. Such regulation should include:

a. *A requirement for independent legal advice*, which would help to protect the surrogate from exploitative contracts and aid the informed consent process (provided the advice given is thorough and comprehensible). It is noted, however, that issues of access to such advice (for example, whether there would be public funding) would also need to be addressed.
b. *Ensuring some measure of uniformity* in regard to the payment of 'reasonable expenses' in countries that permit 'altruistic surrogacy' – including specifying which expenses and costs related to the pregnancy and birth are to be reimbursed, and setting minimum/maximum thresholds. It is imperative in such circumstances to ensure that reimbursement of expenses does not act as a guise for commercial arrangements.
c. *Consideration of who 'brokers' the arrangements:* in regard to the problems posed by brokers, lawyers, and others who stand to greatly profit from surrogacy arrangements, countries that permit commercial or altruistic surrogacy could introduce a statutory restriction on the organisations that can legally receive payment for arranging surrogacy contracts, or preferably prohibit payments for brokering such arrangements all together.[105] Perhaps allowing charities, or possibly governmental organisations to act as intermediaries 'would dramatically reduce the risk to surrogates that [paid] intermediaries introduce'.[106] Rimm states that 'this solution would

102 Ibid.

103 Refer to comment above n. 20.

104 On the assumption that total prohibition globally might not become a reality.

105 Rimm, above n. 62.

106 Rimm, above n. 62, 1458.

protect potential surrogates both from the possibility of their exploitation by for-profit private agencies and from the black market industry that would develop if brokering surrogacy contracts was completely outlawed'.[107] Here I would suggest caution however toward agencies that set up as not-for-profit as a way around prohibitions, while having the potential to make significant profits by directing people to private companies or businesses.

d. *Screening and eligibility requirements:* determining who may enter into a surrogacy agreement is also an issue. Laws that govern whether any, or all, parties to a surrogacy arrangement should have to meet particular criteria before being able to enter into a surrogacy arrangement may therefore also be introduced. It is beyond the scope of this chapter to discuss such criteria in depth, however, some jurisdictions already include such things as limiting altruistic surrogacy to gestational arrangements;[108] requirements concerning how old the surrogate must be (for example, over 25); satisfactory completion of medical and psychological screening; requirements that the surrogate has already had a living child; and/or requirements that she has completed her family.[109] In addition, extensive screening requirements of the commissioning person(s) might also apply (for example, in terms of criminal record, and child protection orders, as well as a family assessment report).[110] Consideration of (and possible counselling) about such issues as the provision of medical treatment to the woman, foetal reduction, and life insurance of the surrogate mother may also be required prior to entering into a surrogacy agreement.
e. *Provisions that address the legality and enforceability of contracts:* whether surrogacy contracts will be deemed legal and enforceable, legal and unenforceable, or neither legal nor enforceable, is also of utmost importance as it will often define not only whether once an agreement is made, the parties must follow through, but most importantly may contribute to how a jurisdiction will proceed in terms of determining legal parentage. Most jurisdictions to this end make void and unenforceable any agreement (except

---

107 Ibid.

108 But note the objection above to classifying 'gestational' surrogacy as something that does not involve biology or connection to the surrogate.

109 Note above discussion that recognises that requiring that a woman has already had children may raise other issues such as how her current children will experience her acting as a surrogate mother and handing the child over after birth, as well as vulnerabilities of a woman who has entered into such an arrangement due to an attempt to meet her current family's needs.

110 The author notes that laws that purport to protect surrogates by restricting access to commercial surrogacy to heterosexual married couples do nothing to protect surrogates or children. Such laws have recently been enacted in India; they unacceptably discriminate against people in same-sex relationships and fail to address the real issues raised by commercial surrogacy for women and children.

in relation to reimbursement of reasonable expenses incurred by the surrogate mother), and recognise the surrogate mother as the legal mother of the child until such time as legal parentage is lawfully transferred.

f. Provision for information recording and sharing regarding donors and surrogates which may be accessed by the offspring, should they choose to do so.

In practice, however, whether developing countries have the capacity and will to establish, and effectively enforce, such a regulatory framework has been questioned.[111] Therefore, this too will need to be addressed in order to resolve the above-discussed ethical and legal issues.

ii. International regulation

The Permanent Bureau of the Hague Conference on Private International Law has expressed doubt about whether any individual state can provide a complete solution to the problems arising out of international surrogacy.[112] There are some views that unilateral solutions have not proven sufficient as, for example, laws prohibiting commercial surrogacy in some jurisdictions – including extraterritorially – have not prevented some people from travelling abroad to engage in commercial arrangements. At a global level, therefore, some have called for a multilateral, legally binding instrument that would establish 'a global, coherent and ethical practice of international surrogacy'.[113] One suggestion has been that a convention could provide a minimum framework for cooperation between governments regarding some of the issues raised by transnational surrogacy, particularly in relation to parentage of children born via such agreements and other minimum standards of practice. Whether this is feasible or desirable is, as yet, undecided, and is a matter for state parties to decide. There are a number of issues that will need to be further explored.

---

111 Tobin, above n. 98, 347.

112 Hague Conference on Private International Law, *A Preliminary Report on the Issues Arising from International Surrogacy Arrangements* (Preliminary Document No. 10 of March 2012), [44].

113 Katrina Trimmings and Paul Beaumont, 'International Surrogacy Arrangements: An Urgent Need for Legal Regulation at the International Level' (2012) 7(3) *Journal of International Private Law* 627, 633 citing T. Krim, 'Beyond Baby M: International Perspectives on Gestational Surrogacy and the Demise of the Unitary Biological Mother' (1996) 5 *Annals of Health Law* 193; Lebowitz-Dori, above n. 43; S. Fiandaca, 'In Vitro Fertilization and Embryos: The Need for International Guidelines' (1998) 8 *Albany Law Journal of Science and Technology* 337; W. Davis and J. Dalessio, 'Reproductive Surrogacy at the Millennium: Proposed Model Legislation Regulating "Non-Traditional" Gestational Surrogacy Contracts' (2000) 31 *McGeorge Law Review* 673; R.L. Lee, 'New Trends in Global Outsourcing of Commercial Surrogacy: A Call for Regulation' (2009) 20 *Hastings Women's Law Journal* 275; and *X & Y (Foreign Surrogacy)* [2008] EWHC 3030 (Fam), 29.

For instance, if such a convention were to be developed, it is important that all states are engaged in the process but, as noted, one of the complexities with commercial surrogacy is that there are significantly disparate views and practices across the globe. A convention serves no purpose if states are not willing to ratify it.[114] In addition, the suggested type of multilateral agreement is also complex. Such instruments are human rights instruments, transnational in nature, which require judicial and administrative cooperation, and states to take joint responsibility for each adoption made under the convention.[115] This is not easy to achieve. Further, a convention on its own may not be enough. Implementation in some states is automatic, while in others requires further legal enactment.[116] Ultimately we return to the fact that domestic laws and action will be required.

In addition, as approximately 62 of the 71 nations with current laws or policies on surrogacy *prohibit* commercial surrogacy (with many prohibiting all forms of surrogacy), it is doubtful that they would accede to an instrument that may facilitate such practices. Thus, it is important to consider how a convention would be framed, and its scope, noting that resolution of such questions will ultimately lie with states parties.

One proposal that has been put forward is that of Trimmings and Beaumont.[117] They suggest a convention on surrogacy should establish 'a framework for international co-operation with emphasis on the need for substantive safeguards and on procedures for courts, administrative authorities and private intermediaries'.[118] Trimmings and Beaumont emphasise oversight to ensure the safety of women and children, however they also advocate that 'a generous approach should be taken with respect to the recognition of cross-border surrogacy arrangements and their effects within the framework of cooperation established by the Convention'.[119] They thus suggest that detailed regulation should be left to bilateral agreements between

---

114 Hannah Baker, 'A Possible Future Instrument on International Surrogacy Arrangements: Are There Lessons to be Learnt from the 1993 Hague Inter-country Adoption Convention?' in Katarina Trimmings and Paul Beaumont (eds), *International Surrogacy Arrangements* (Oxford and Portland, OR: Hart Publishing, 2013), 417–18. Note, initial consideration was given by The Hague Permanent Bureau on Private International Law as to whether HIAC was applicable to commercial surrogacy; however, it was determined that it was not, due to the significant differences between adoption and surrogacy. It is also noted that the success of HIAC was made possible because the starting point was general international consensus that adoption is an acceptable practice in certain circumstances. Clearly this differs regarding commercial surrogacy, in that there is no such consensus.

115 Baker, above n. 114, 420–21.

116 For example, in Australia, federal legislation needs to be created by parliament for a convention to be binding, and depending on the area of law states and territories may also be required to introduce relevant legislation, whereas, in the United States, a treaty becomes part of domestic law upon ratification.

117 Trimmings and Beaumont, above n. 113.

118 Baker, above n. 114, 635.

119 Ibid.

Member States, giving states 'maximum flexibility to agree on details of international surrogacy arrangements, including issues such as suitability of 'intended parents', suitability of a surrogate mother, and payments in surrogacy arrangements'. The convention therefore, would set minimum standards but would not prevent State Parties from setting higher standards for international surrogacy arrangements.[120]

The suggested convention by Trimmings and Beaumont's is in some ways like the Hague Convention on Protection of Children and Cooperation in Respect of Inter-country Adoption (HIAC),[121] which does not mandate that all states engage in inter-country adoption, but provides for minimum standards if they do. Trimmings and Beaumont's proposal does not however, explicitly oppose the *commercial* nature of global surrogacy transactions. Their view is that this approach reflects the 'lesser of two evils' in that regulating commercial surrogacy is better than no regulation at all.

However, as per the above discussion, there is a majority global view that the risks to women (and children), real and potential, in any situation in which there are financial exchanges in relation to pregnancy and birth, create a situation in which commercial surrogacy is unacceptable. A convention on surrogacy might therefore serve a better purpose if it reflects a united stance against such practices. That prohibiting commercial surrogacy is the preferred approach of many states that have already chosen to regulate on the issue, and also the majority of states that are moving to do so (whether or not they then move to allowing some form of altruistic surrogacy) may be recognised and upheld.[122] Whether issues of legal

120 Ibid.

121 The HIAC operates through a system of national Central Authorities, reinforces the *Convention on the Rights of the Child* (art. 21) and seeks to ensure that inter-country adoptions are made in the best interests of the child and with respect for his or her fundamental rights. It also seeks to prevent the abduction, the sale of, or traffic in children. As at 21 March 2013 there were 90 contracting States to the convention. Haiti, Nepal and The Russian Federation are signatories, but have not ratified. HIAC prohibits anyone from deriving 'improper financial or other gain from an activity related to inter-country adoption'. Note however, while HIAC appears to have reduced inter-country adoptions, and appears to have some significant effects in curbing the sale and exploitation of women and children in such contexts, the practice of commercial surrogacy has risen. HIAC does not govern surrogacy and, more recently, has been found to be inappropriate to use in such cases due to differences between international commercial surrogacy and adoption. Such differences include that adoption 'focuses on finding a family for a child in need, whereas surrogacy involves the creation of a child to meet the needs of adults': Hague Conference on Private International Law, *Private International Law Issues Surrounding the Status of Children, Including Issues Arising from International Surrogacy Arrangements*, Preliminary. Document No. 11 of March 2011), 3.

122 In addition, a prohibition on commercial surrogacy would be consistent with the European Parliament resolution on the trade in human egg cells (P6_TA(2005)0074), adopted 10 March 2005, which affirmed that payment for ova should be prohibited, recognising that the harvesting of egg cells constitutes a high medical risk for the life

parentage of children taken across borders from states that permit commercial surrogacy into those that don't, could be resolved within this framework, needs to be further explored. In the meantime, a number of states are moving to find ways of resolving legal parentage issues, without broadening the scope of, or accepting commercial surrogacy practices within their borders, and some have questioned whether a convention in such circumstances is needed at all.

Finally, the question of whether prohibiting commercial surrogacy would in fact stop the practice, or merely drive it underground is noted.[123] However, while some argue that a ban would create a black market, others argue that laws that regulate surrogacy end up promoting it, and that even if surrogacy was 'outlawed' thereby driving it underground, 'the number of surrogate arrangements would be miniscule compared to the explosive growth that would result from permissive regulation'.[124] Of course, there are black markets in many other prohibited enterprises, but laws are not changed to facilitate them because some people choose to engage in them anyway. A convention, if deemed necessary in such circumstances, would represent a strong and united stance taken by the international community that it wishes to see exploitative and risky practices, that often entail human rights violations, cease.

IV. Conclusion

Advances in assisted reproductive technology, increases in its use, and positive social progress in recognising and accepting different family formations and ways of achieving parenthood have all contributed to an increase in surrogacy arrangements. Surrogacy, however, has also raised many ethical and legal issues and has been the subject of 'heated debate' related to actual, or potential, exploitation of women and children. Arguments exist that women should be free to exploit their reproductive capabilities and to act (or contract) as they wish. This chapter does not argue against that women should be free to contract, bargain, work, and make informed choices about their bodies, nor that opportunities for women to rise out of poverty, provide for their families, and build better lives should exist. However, the world of commercial surrogacy is not a place where this should or does occur. The reality shows us that it is a world of inequality and unequal bargaining power, lack of freedom and less than informed decision-making. In worse case scenarios, it is a world that is exploitative and potentially

---

and health of women; the planned egg cell trade would exploit the economic situation of women who lived in impoverished regions; and despite the possibility of serious effects on women's life and health, the high price paid for egg cells incites and encourages donation, given the relative poverty of the donors. As commercial surrogacy poses virtually the same risks, it is appropriate that it be similarly banned.

123 Keyes and Chisholm, above n. 97, 132.

124 Smerdon, above n. 35, 81–3.

dangerous. Commercial surrogacy is not simply 'labour' or 'work'.[125] While the arguments on both sides regarding how to address such issues are complex, most jurisdictions have decided that commercial surrogacy creates unacceptable risks for women and children, commodifies them, and is not acceptable in light of broader implications concerning how women and children should be viewed. They have therefore prohibited its practice.

Domestic laws should not be changed to permit commercial surrogacy in those jurisdictions that currently prohibit the practice solely based upon dilemmas created by people who have engaged in global surrogacy arrangements (sometimes against the law of their own jurisdiction). Such cases should be dealt with by the courts, on a case-by-case basis; or the legislature should speak as to what should occur. More broadly, the issue remains as to what must be done given the international nature of commercial surrogacy and the problems it raises. This chapter has examined some such issues and made suggestions for regulatory actions that may serve to address discrimination, exploitation, inequities, trafficking, and or commodification of women, while still permitting certain forms of surrogacy, namely, altruistic arrangements. Commercial practices should continue to be prohibited in those jurisdictions that choose to do so. The majority of jurisdictions that have chosen to regulate take this stance. It is recognised, however, that international consensus may be difficult to achieve, as there are a small number of jurisdictions that permit commercial surrogacy. Those jurisdictions should restrict such practices to within their own borders, and implement regulatory standards to protect women and children.

In closing, I note that if the concern is that women should have a way to prosper, support their families, have added income, and or to move out of poverty, other opportunities for them to do so, beyond commercial surrogacy, should be the focus. Similarly, while we should accept and encourage different family formations, commercial surrogacy should not be 'sold' as the preferred option to people seeking to form a family. While many people only seek to love and care for a child, the issues discussed in this chapter, arise and exist beyond individual families, surrogates and circumstances. Decisions about addressing such issues must take precedence over any singular desire to have a family. Market forces should not drive our laws. The profit made by lawyers, brokers and clinics, that drives such an industry needs to be addressed. It is preferable to find ways to support people genuinely seeking to become parents, without their having to resort to commercial surrogacy.

---

125 Tobin states that in many ways viewing what a commercial surrogate is doing as simply 'labour' or 'work' is in itself demeaning to women and children: Tobin, above n. 98: 340.

Chapter 8
Recognition of Parentage in Surrogacy Arrangements in Australia

Alexandra Harland* and Cressida Limon**

I. Introduction

Recognition of legal parentage, and the implications of recognition for the rights of the child, has presented particular challenges for Australian families and Australian courts. As the phenomenon of overseas commercial surrogacy continues to flourish, Australian legal frameworks are increasingly ill-equipped formally to recognise the reality of new family structures. This chapter puts these challenges in context, examines some particular case examples from the Australian Family Courts,[1] and outlines some recommendations for reform.

Australians who cannot have children without the assistance of reproductive technology look increasingly to international surrogacy as a way of creating a family. For some Australian couples and individuals, adoption and IVF are not options that are available to them. Fertility clinics in Thailand and India promote themselves as attractive options.[2] For Australians, part of the attraction of commercial surrogacy in these countries is the affordability of airfares and surrogacy fees (as compared to the United States) and the lack of regulation.[3]

---

* Judge, Federal Circuit Court of Australia. Some of the research for this chapter was undertaken as part of an LLM by Research at the Faculty of Law, University of Technology Sydney. The views expressed in this chapter are the author's own and do not represent the views of the Court. The author would like to thank Professors Jenni Millbank and Anita Stuhmcke for their helpful comments and encouragement.

** Dr Cressida Limon is a Lecturer in the School of Law, University of Western Sydney.

1 The 'Family Courts' refers to both the Family Court of Australia and the Federal Circuit Court of Australia. To date most relevant published decisions have been from the Family Court of Australia.

2 See, for example, http://www.whatclinic.com/fertility/india; http://www.fertilityindia.com/; http://thailandfertility.com/home/; http://www.whatclinic.com/fertility/thailand.

3 Anita Browning, 'As the Stork Flies from India to Australia: Intercountry Commercial Surrogacy Arrangements' (2011) 107 *Precedent* 22.

Australians have continued to travel overseas for surrogacy regardless of whether or not it is illegal in Australia.[4]

However, the lack of regulation is a double-edged sword, and particularly so when it comes to the rights of all the parties involved. It means that couples can access surrogacy services with relative ease, but there can be problems after the child is born. One such hazard is the potential for children to be stateless and/or parentless because of conflicting laws in the country where the surrogacy has taken place and the home country of the intending parents. Australian legal frameworks for the regulation of surrogacy and the legal recognition of parentage are currently uncertain and inconsistent, which compounds the problems of a lack of regulation overseas.

The significance of the questions raised by international surrogacy arrangements is illustrated by the fact that the Hague Conference on Private International Law (HCCH) is currently investigating the issue of international surrogacy. Similarly, the Family Law Council of Australia recently completed a broad inquiry into parentage and the *Family Law Act* which also highlighted a number of concerns in relation to international surrogacy.[5] One of the issues of great concern identified by the HCCH is the status of children, and particularly the establishment or recognition of the child's legal status, which has important consequences for the child including nationality, immigration status and parental responsibility.[6] There have now been several international cases that have highlighted complex problems and consequences for children without a home state. The *Baby Manji Case* is often cited as an example.[7] In that case, lack of regulation and recognition resulted in the child being stranded for two years in India while legal proceedings

4 See for example Anna Whitelaw, 'Hundreds pay for overseas surrogacy', *Sydney Morning Herald* (3 June 2012), available at http://www.smh.com.au/federal-politics/political-news/hundreds-pay-for-overseas-surrogacy-20120602–lzplu.html, accessed 15 June 2014, citing research commissioned by Surrogacy Australia. As to the legality of surrogacy arrangements overseas, see Anita Stuhmcke's Chapter 5, 'Extraterritoriality and Surrogacy: The Problem of State and Territory Moral Sovereignty', in this volume.

5 Family Law Council, *Report on Parentage and the* Family Law Act (December 2013), especially Chapter 3. This Report was released in August 2014 after most of this chapter had been written and so a comprehensive consideration of the Council's recommendations has not been possible. To date, the Federal Government has not responded to the Family Law Council's recommendations.

6 Hague Conference on Private International Law, 'Private International Law Issues Surrounding the Status of Children, Including Issues Arising from International Surrogacy Arrangements' (Preliminary Document No. 11 of March 2011 for the attention of the Council of April 2012 on General Affairs and Policy of the Conference), [3]; Hague Conference on Private International Law, 'The Desirability and Feasibility of Further Work on the Parentage/Surrogacy Project' (Preliminary Document No. 3 B of April 2014 for the attention of the Council of April 2014 on General Affairs and Policy of the Conference).

7 See the detailed discussion of this case provided in Normann Witzleb and Anurag Chawla's Chapter 9 in this volume.

ensued. Unfortunately, the *Baby Manji Case* is not the only example of a child born through surrogacy being stranded and stateless.[8]

Even in less extreme cases, the difficulty with partial solutions is that children may be left with what has been called 'limping' legal parentage, where one parent may not be legally recognised as the child's parent.[9] This can have various impacts on parents and children as they may be confronted with situations where they are not recognised by institutions such as hospitals as being able to authorise treatment for their child, or to enrol their child in school. It may cause an individual to feel less of a parent than one who is legally recognised as a parent. One parent being recognised legally and the other not can cause tension in the relationship. This chapter shows how such issues are contentious in Australia.

The relevance of international human rights law to overseas commercial surrogacy arrangements is a relatively recent area of concern for policy makers in Australia.[10] In part, this is because of the increased visibility of Australians who have travelled overseas for surrogacy arrangements and because of the growing number of cases that have come to the family courts. Overseas commercial surrogacy arrangements raise a range of legal and ethical issues.[11] The focus of this chapter is the legal recognition of parentage under the *Family Law Act* 1975 (Cth) ('*Family Law Act*') and why the current laws need to be reformed. It is within this context that we note that regardless of the regulatory regime in place (for example, the current prohibition of commercial surrogacy in domestic Australian law – and many other jurisdictions) this 'does not provide sufficient justification for ignoring

8 See, for example, *Pawandeep Singh v Entry Clearance Officer* [2005] QB 08; *Re: X & Y (Foreign Surrogacy)* [2008] EWHC 3030; Anil Malhotra and Ranjit Malhotra, 'All Aboard for the Fertility Express' (2012) 38(1), *Commonwealth Law Bulletin* 31.

9 Jenni Millbank, 'Resolving the Dilemma of Legal Parentage for Australians Engaged in International Surrogacy' (2013) 27 *Australian Journal of Family Law* 135; Hague Conference on Private International Law, 'A Preliminary Report on the Issues Arising from International Surrogacy Arrangements' (Preliminary Document No. 11 of March 2011 for the attention of the Council of April 2012 on General Affairs and Policy of the Conference), [33].

10 Yasmine Ergas, 'Thinking "Through" Human Rights: The Need for a Human Rights Perspective with Respect to the Regulation of Cross-Border Reproductive Surrogacy', in Katarina Trimmings and Paul Beaumont (eds), *International Surrogacy Arrangements: Legal Regulation at the International Level* (Oxford and Portland, OR: Hart Publishing, 2013), 427; and John Tobin, 'To Prohibit or Permit: What Is the (Human) Rights Response to the Practice of International Commercial Surrogacy?' (2014) 63(2) *International and Comparative Law Quarterly* 317.

11 See Eric Blyth, Marilyn Cranshaw and Olga van den Akker, 'What are the best interests of the child in international surrogacy?' *Bionews* (2014), 742, available at http://www.bionews.org.uk/page_397263.asp; Pamela Laufer-Ukeles, '"Mothering for Money" Regulating Commercial Intimacy' (2013) 88(1) *Indiana Law Journal* 1.

the basic needs of children born of [Australian citizens]'.[12] Richard Storrow, for instance, has highlighted a potential 'new illegitimacy' for children born as a result of international surrogacy arrangements.[13] For this reason, a complete prohibition on commercial surrogacy does not address the human rights of the children born from such arrangements.[14] In addition, a child's right to genetic information and to know the identity of their gestational mothers is a separate question to the question of legal parentage.[15]

Part II of this chapter explains, as a first step, why legal recognition of parentage is important for the rights of the parties involved – not just to the adult acting in that role but also to the child who is parented. As discussed in Part III, some intended parents of children born as a result of surrogacy arrangements outside Australia opt for informal recognition of parentage, or for no recognition at all. These options carry significant attendant risks and costs. To obtain any legal status in relation to their children, the best that can be achieved for Australian intended parents who have entered into commercial surrogacy arrangements (or who have entered into altruistic arrangements but are unable to comply with the state and territory requirements) is to apply to the family courts for parental responsibility orders. Part IV of this chapter uses several case studies to highlight some of the challenges in doing so. Even where they can be obtained, parental responsibility orders do not provide the same level of protection to a child as having legal parents. Part V draws on comparative approaches in the United Kingdom that have considered the competing public policy issues in relation to commercial surrogacy arrangements and the best interests of the child when determining issues of legal parentage. In the UK, and more recently in Australia, there is a tension between the legal frameworks that make commercial surrogacy unlawful and the need for courts to consider the best interests of the child. In the UK this tension is somewhat alleviated by the exercise of judicial discretion to grant parental orders. There is no similar provision in Australian law. The chapter concludes with a brief exploration of some options and recommendations for reform at the federal level to address some of these problems, including changing the law regarding parentage to ensure that children are not disadvantaged.

---

12 Pamela Laufer-Ukeles, 'The Lost Children: When the Right to Children Conflicts with the Rights of Children' [2015] *Journal of Law and Ethics of Human Rights* (forthcoming), 29.

13 Richard F. Storrow, '"The Phantom Children of the Republic": International Surrogacy and the New Illegitimacy' (2012) 20(3) *Journal of Gender, Social Policy & the Law* 561.

14 We do not agree with the argument that commercial surrogacy involves the 'sale of a child' and is therefore contrary to the Optional Protocol to the Convention on the Rights of the Child on the Sale of Children, Child Prostitution and Child Pornography as asserted by Tobin, above n. 10 and Sonia Allan in her Chapter 7 in this volume.

15 On this point see Deborah H. Wald, 'The Parentage Puzzle: The Interplay between Genetics, Procreative Intent, and Parental Conduct in Determining Legal Parentage' (2007) 15 *American University Journal of Gender, Social Policy & Law* 379.

II. Why is Legal Parentage Important?

The Hague Convention on Private International Law has recently emphasised that the question of legal parentage 'is not a mere legal nicety for children. It is the gateway, today, through which many of the obligations owed by adults to children flow, and it is therefore a legal status from which children derive many important rights, including rights established in international law.'[16] Legal parentage involves a range of obligations and responsibilities ('parental responsibility') that parents have in relation to children.[17] The significance of legal parentage is that it makes a difference to the ability of children to obtain various rights and protections, including:

- citizenship;
- access to Medicare and medical benefits;
- access to medical treatment;
- applications for passports and anything requiring a birth certificate;
- inheritance rights;
- rights to workers compensation entitlements upon the death of a parent;
- access to child support; and
- identity.

Many of these rights are reflected in the United Nations Convention on the Rights of the Child ('CRC').[18] Article 7 states:

> 1. The child shall be registered immediately after birth and shall have the right from birth to a name, the right to acquire a nationality and, as far as possible, the right to know and be cared for by his or her parents.
> 2. States Parties shall ensure the implementation of these rights in accordance with their national law and their obligations under the relevant international instruments in this field, in particular where the child would otherwise be stateless.

Since 2012, the *Family Law Act* has included a specific object to give effect to the CRC to ensure that the best interests of children are met in decisions that affect

16 Hague Conference on Private International Law, 'The Desirability and Feasibility of Further Work on the Parentage/Surrogacy Project' (Preliminary Document No. 3 B of April 2014 for the attention of the Council of April 2014 on General Affairs and Policy of the Conference), [18].

17 For a summary see Victorian Law Reform Commission, *Assisted Reproductive Technology and Adoption: Final Report* (2007), chapter 11.

18 *Convention on the Rights of the Child*, opened for signature 20 November 1989, 1577 UNTS 3 (entered into force 2 September 1990).

them.[19] Crucially, the CRC does not define 'what is a parent', nor does it include any specific articles in relation to assisted reproduction.[20] It is important to note that there is nothing in the CRC that would support the argument that 'parents' means biological parents.[21] The non-discrimination principles enshrined in the CRC (for example, Article 2) further recognise that children should enjoy rights 'without discrimination of any kind irrespective of the child's or his or her parent's or legal guardian's race, colour, sex, language, religion, political or other opinion, national, ethnic or social origin, property, disability, birth or other status'.

As the discussion below demonstrates, the right to a birth certificate and a nationality are also fundamental issues. The *Baby Manji Case* referred to above, and a number of Australian cases discussed below, illustrate that some children born via surrogacy arrangements are being denied these rights and have been rendered stateless because of clashes between the laws of the country where the surrogacy took place and the intended parents' country of residence. These children are not entitled to the nationality of either the intended parents or the surrogate mother.[22] It is in a child's best interests for the reality of the child's family life to be legally recognised, and to recognise that children's human rights are inextricably entwined with the human rights of their parents.[23]

Given the significance of legal parentage the way the law defines 'what is a parent' is obviously crucial. Australian law is complicated in this matter. Although parentage (and birth certificates) are largely a matter for the states and territories,

19 *Family Law Act*, s 60B (4).

20 See John Tobin, 'The Convention on the Rights of the Child: The Rights and Best Interests of Children Conceived through Assisted Reproduction' (Victorian Law Reform Commission, 2004).

21 Ibid., 8. The literature on 'what is a parent' is extensive. See Roxanne Mykitiuk, 'Beyond Conception: Legal Determinations of Filiation in the Context of Assisted Reproductive Technologies' (2001) 39(4) *Osgoode Hall Law Journal* 771; Alison Diduck, '"If Only We Can Find the Appropriate Terms to Use the Issue Will Be Solved": Law, Identity and Parenthood' (2007) 19 *Child & Family Law Quarterly* 458.

22 Intended parents have had difficulties in achieving statehood for their children born as a result of surrogacy arrangements in India and the Ukraine. See, for example, *IJ (A Child)* [2011] EWHC 921 (Fam). The plight of a French couple seeking citizenship for their children born to a surrogate in the Ukraine received significant media attention. See, for example, Nisha Satkunarajah, 'Legal case brings France's surrogacy laws into focus', *Bionews*, 604, accessed 18 June 2014, available at http://www.bionews.org.uk/page_92561.asp. For further discussion of the *Baby Manji Case* and others see Yasmine Ergas, 'Babies without Borders: Human Rights, Human Dignity and the Regulation of International Commercial Surrogacy' (2013) 27 *Emory International Law Review* 117.

23 The Human Rights and Equal Opportunity Commission looked at this issue in the context of non-recognition of same-sex couples, Human Rights and Equal Opportunity Commission, *Same-Sex Same Entitlements: National Inquiry into Discrimination against People in Same-Sex Relationships: Financial and Work-Related Entitlements and Benefits* (May 2007), 91.

there is also a complex set of provisions in the *Family Law Act*. The *Family Law Act* provisions have become relevant as intending parents have turned to the family courts seeking orders in relation to children born overseas as a result of surrogacy arrangements. In order to appreciate the difficult legal issues involved, it is helpful to understand the current framework. There is no single, general definition of a parent in the *Family Law Act*. Instead there are provisions that 'deem' certain people to be parents in certain circumstances for the purposes of the Act. For instance, s 60H deals with children born from 'artificial conception procedures' and s 60HB deals with children born from surrogacy arrangements in certain situations. These provisions are irrebuttable. On the other hand there are a number of rebuttable presumptions of parentage – such as s 69R – which is a presumption based on being named as a parent on a prescribed register of births. In the case of overseas surrogacy arrangements it is possible that a number of provisions might apply and judicial officers have had to work through a range of competing options. The current uncertainty and inconsistency in the application of different provisions is a cause for concern in itself.

III. What are the Options for Parents Seeking Recognition?

There is a hierarchy of options available to parents coming home from overseas with a baby born as a result of a commercial surrogacy arrangement. The first option is to seek no formal recognition at all. If the parents have been able to obtain citizenship for the child they may decide not to seek formal recognition from the courts. It is impossible to know how many parents have chosen this option. As the discussions of Australian cases below demonstrate, going to court may only result in an order for parental responsibility and not legal parentage. In addition, there is a risk of being referred for prosecution.[24] Furthermore, the legal costs may be significant.[25] However, not seeking formal recognition from the courts is risky, because, in the future, the lack of formal recognition may disadvantage the child, for example, child support obligations are generally only imposed on legal parents.

The second option is for parents to rely on informal recognition such as a foreign birth certificate which records at least one intended parent on the child's birth certificate. This is also risky because foreign birth certificates are not recognised as conferring parental status for the purpose of Australian laws.[26] These

24 See *Dudley & Chedi* [2011] FamCA 502 and Anita Stuhmcke's Chapter 5 in this volume.

25 In *Ellison and Anor & Karnchanit* [2012] FamCA 602, Ryan J appointed an Independent Children's Lawyer and ordered a family report. These involve significantly greater costs than a summary hearing dealing with the applications on the papers (that is without cross-examination of witnesses).

26 See *Ellison and Anor & Karnchanit* [2012] FamCA 602 [70] and the discussion below in Part IV.

parents may experience the same difficulties as the parents in the first option. Conversely parents may find that some institutions will accept a foreign birth certificate as evidence of parentage. Parents using options one or two may not encounter any parentage problems for many years. However, if they subsequently find themselves in a situation where they need to approach the court for a parental responsibility order they may face evidentiary difficulties. For example, it may not be possible to find and serve the surrogate mother should the court require it.

The third option is to seek parental responsibility orders from the family courts. A parental responsibility order is a type of parenting order.[27] Anyone who has an interest in the care, welfare and development of a child may apply for parenting orders.[28] Parental responsibility orders do not provide the same level of protection to a child as having legal parents. Parental responsibility gives a person decision-making responsibility for the welfare of the child until the child turns 18.[29] A parental responsibility order at least allows an adult to deal with health, educational and travel issues but it does not address the more fundamental issues discussed in Part VI.

A fourth possibility is to seek a declaration of parentage from the family courts.[30] However, the availability of this option is currently uncertain and has limited application. Obtaining a declaration of parentage is not available to intended mothers as there is no parentage presumption in the *Family Law Act* which applies to intended mothers who have entered into a surrogacy arrangement. The same is true of intended fathers who do not have a biological connection to the child. It is not possible to seek a parentage order from any state or territory courts as the state and territory surrogacy legislation only provides for parentage orders arising out of altruistic surrogacy arrangements.[31] These orders effectively transfer legal parentage from the surrogate mother (and her partner) to the intending parents. In *Ellison and Anor & Karnchanit*[32] Ryan J declared the male applicant to be a parent pursuant to s 69VA of the *Family Law Act*. Section 69VA states that the court may make a declaration of parentage after receiving evidence. In that case the evidence relied on by the court was a DNA test showing the male applicant was the biological father of the children. The surrogate mother was single. If she had been married or in a de facto relationship her partner would have been presumed to be the father.[33] However, in a more recent case, *Mason & Mason and Anor*[34] Ryan J

27 *Family Law Act*, s 64B.

28 *Family Law Act*, s 65C.

29 See *Family Law Act*, ss 61B, 61C.

30 *Family Law Act*, s 69VA.

31 For a comprehensive discussion of state and territory surrogacy legislation, see Tammy Johnson's Chapter 4, 'Through the Looking-Glass: A Proposal for National Reform of Australia's Surrogacy Legislation', in this volume.

32 [2012] FamCA 602.

33 *Family Law Act*, s 60H(1).

34 [2013] FamCA 424.

came to the conclusion that the *Family Law Act* did not permit a declaration of parentage to be made in cases involving surrogacy arrangements that fall outside state and territory laws. The implications of this recent decision are discussed in the next part.

IV. Applications to the Family Courts: The Quest for Recognition

One of the great challenges for people engaging in overseas surrogacy is the differing levels of regulation and, in some countries, lack of regulation. This makes it possible for people to engage in surrogacy arrangements, but the same lack of regulation also results in a denial of legal status to their children. To obtain any legal status in relation to their children, the only option for Australian intended parents who have entered into commercial surrogacy arrangements (or who have entered into altruistic arrangements but are unable to comply with the state and territory requirements), is to apply to the Family Courts for parental responsibility orders. Some couples may be compelled to seek orders because of problems with the immigration status of their children. However, a large majority of parents do not seek formal recognition of their legal status. It has been estimated that over 300 children are now born each year as a result of overseas surrogacy arrangements.[35] However, to date, there have only been 20 reported cases of applications to the family courts.[36] This means that the vast majority of these children do not have a legally recognised parent in Australia.

Analysis of the following cases shows that making an application to the family courts is risky and uncertain. These cases have been selected because each illustrates a number of the more general difficulties involved; namely, the legal gaps leading to inconsistent decision-making, the uncertainties in the definition of what is a parent, and the challenges of balancing the rights of the various parties including, most critically, the rights of the child.

A. Dennis & Pradchaphet and Dudley & Chedi*: Same facts, legal gaps*

The cases of *Dennis & Pradchaphet*[37] and *Dudley & Chedi*[38] involved the same couple. They had three children born on the same day to two different mothers in Thailand. They brought separate applications with respect to the children of the surrogate mothers. In both cases the intended parents sought consent orders providing for the intended parents to have parental responsibility and for the child/

35 Millbank, above n. 9; Amy Corderoy, 'More parents defy law with overseas surrogacy', *The Age* (14 September 2013), citing estimates from the Department of Immigration and Border Protection and community organization Surrogacy Australia.

36 Two of these cases involved 'altruistic' surrogacy arrangements.

37 [2011] FamCA 123.

38 [2011] FamCA 502.

ren to live with them. As these applications were for parenting orders, s 60CA of the *Family Law Act* applied. Section 60CA states that the best interests of the child is the paramount consideration. These two cases are of interest because of the different approaches judicial officers took when faced with the same facts.

Dennis & Pradchaphet was heard by Stevenson J. The application before her was in relation to one of the children. She noted that the birth of each of the three children was registered in Thailand with the details of the male applicant and the relevant surrogate mother on the birth certificate. The male applicant commenced proceedings in Thailand seeking orders that the surrogate mother relinquish her parental rights. This was unsuccessful because under Thai law the mother is not able to relinquish her parental rights until the child reaches the 'age of reason at 7 or 8 years old'.[39] The applicants filed an affidavit by the surrogate mother which was translated by a Thai translator which dealt with the consent documents and an advice she had received about Australian and Thai legislation. Her Thai lawyer also gave evidence to the effect that under Thai law the birth mother is the only parent with any parental rights when the parents are unmarried. In this case the birth mother was not the biological mother as anonymous donor eggs were used. He also deposed that there is no Thai law addressing surrogacy.

Stevenson J made orders for the applicants to have equal shared parental responsibility and for the child to live with them. She found that the male applicant was the father in circumstances where there was a positive DNA test and he was named on the birth certificate. The father had provided his genetic material which was used for IVF and, as noted above, he was named on the birth certificate. Stevenson J explicitly stated that her finding was not to have wider implications for other cases.[40] She was satisfied on the evidence before her that the applicants would provide the child with a high standard of care and that it was in the child's best interests to make the orders sought by the applicants. The applicants also gave evidence that they would ensure the child grew up with an awareness of his Thai culture.

Dudley & Chedi was heard by Watts J. This application concerned the twins born on the same day as their brother. Watts J referred to Stevenson J's judgment. Watts J also noted that the applicants were resident in Queensland and that it was illegal for Queensland residents to engage in surrogacy arrangements.[41] At the time of the surrogacy arrangement the *Surrogate Parenthood Act* 1988 (Qld) was in force. That Act banned all forms of surrogacy and made it illegal for Queensland residents to enter into surrogacy arrangements regardless of whether those arrangements took place in Queensland, interstate or overseas.[42] Watts J

---

39 *Dennis & Pradchaphet* [2011] FamCA 123 [7].

40 Ibid. [19].

41 Ibid. [7].

42 Even if the *Surrogacy Act* 2010 (Qld) (which replaced the *Surrogate Parenthood Act* 1988 (Qld) and recognises altruistic surrogacy arrangements in certain circumstances) applied to them, they would not have been able to rely on the parentage transfer

commented that the material before him was 'starkly deficient'[43] and lacked any details as to the nature of the surrogacy arrangement and any financial provisions. There was no evidence as to any safeguards which may have been in place to protect the surrogate mother. He declined to make a finding that the male applicant was the father for several reasons, discussed further below. While Watts J found it was in the children's best interests to make the orders, as the children needed to be cared for by someone and the evidence was that the applicants could do so very well including addressing the children's need for cultural identity, he referred the matter to the Queensland Director of Prosecutions as the surrogacy arrangement was illegal. Presumably the evidence presented to the Court in both cases was similar, as the same law firm prepared the applications. It is significant that two judges took such different courses of action on the same facts. In both cases it was noted that the applicants had unsuccessfully applied for citizenship by descent for all three children but had obtained visas for the children after a DNA test confirmed that the male applicant was the biological father of the children.[44] The issue of citizenship is considered briefly in the next part.

B. H v Minister for Immigration and Citizenship*: The Need for Citizenship and Who is a Parent?*

Securing Australian citizenship for a child born as a result of an overseas surrogacy arrangement is a significant incentive for seeking parental responsibility orders in relation to that child, as this can assist with the citizenship application.[45] However, the definition of 'parent' in one piece of federal legislation does not automatically apply to other pieces of federal legislation since the purposes of the legislation are often different. The *Australian Citizenship Act* 2007 (Cth) ('*Citizenship Act*') provides that Australian citizenship by descent is derived by a 'child' from a 'parent' who is an Australian citizen.[46]

In this respect, it is useful to examine the decision of the Full Court of the Federal Court in *H v Minister for Immigration and Citizenship*[47] because it considers the meaning of who is a 'parent' in the context of s 16 of the *Citizenship Act*. The *Citizenship Act* does not define the word 'parent'. Section 16 deals with applications for eligibility for citizenship. In this case the Full Court of the Federal Court examined whether the reference to 'parent' in s 16 of the *Citizenship Act*

---

mechanisms therein, because other requirements of the Act, including assessment reports and counselling, had not been fulfilled.

43 *Dennis & Pradchaphet* [2011] FamCA 123 [17].

44 *Dennis & Pradchaphet* [2011] FamCA 123 [6–7], *Dudley & Chedi* [2011] FamCA 502 [11].

45 As was the case in *Dennis & Pradchaphet* [2011] FamCA 123 and *Dudley & Chedi* [2011] FamCA 502.

46 *Citizenship Act*, s 16.

47 [2010] FCAFC 119.

means only a biological parent. The Court rejected the argument that the *Family Law Act* and the *Citizenship Act* covered the same subject matter such that provision in the *Family Law Act* giving parental status to persons who were not biological parents meant that the reference to 'parent' in the *Citizenship Act* could be used in the same way. The Court held that the *Citizenship Act* expressly picked up some *Family Law Act* provisions for its own purposes but this did not diminish the fact that the two Acts cover different subject matters.

The Court did not accept that the specific parentage presumptions in the *Family Law Act* could be applied to other Commonwealth legislation such as s 16(2) of the *Citizenship Act*.[48] The Court stated that the issues relating to artificial conception and surrogacy are relatively new and complex and they require 'clear and specific' provisions.[49] The Court concluded that there was nothing in the objects or the structure of the *Citizenship Act* that led to the conclusion that the reference to 'parent' in s 16(2) referred only to a biological parent. The better view is that parent has an ordinary meaning which may depend on various factors including biological, social and legal relationships.[50] The significance of this case is that it means that a person may be a parent for the purposes of determining the citizenship of a child, but that same person may not be a parent for the purposes of the *Family Law Act* or, for that matter, any other Commonwealth or state legislation.

C. Ellison and Anor & Karnchanit*: A Deeper Analysis and the Human Rights Commission Intervenes*

Up until the decision of *Ellison and Anor & Karnchanit*,[51] no judicial officer in the family courts had undertaken a detailed analysis of the legal issues concerning surrogacy. It is important to appreciate that these judicial officers are usually presented with little information about the surrogacy arrangements. It would seem that applications are filed on the basis that they will be dealt with 'on the papers' without much enquiry, as there is in a contested case. In *Ellison*, although the orders were not contested, Ryan J appointed an Independent Children's Lawyer and invited the Australian Human Rights Commission (AHRC) to intervene. The AHRC accepted that invitation. The Commonwealth Attorney-General's Department was also invited to intervene, but declined.

The applicants had entered into a surrogacy arrangement in Thailand. They went to a Thai fertility clinic where they used an egg from an unknown egg donor. Mr Ellison, one of the applicants, provided the sperm. Embryos were then implanted in the surrogate mother, Ms Karnchanit and, as a result, twins were born. Mr Ellison and the surrogate mother were named as the children's parents

48 Ibid., [82].

49 Ibid., [92].

50 Ibid., [127]–[129]. See also the discussion in Family Law Council, *Report on Parentage and The Family Law Act* (December 2013), 109-110.

51 [2012] Fam CA 602.

on their Thai birth certificates. Ms Solano was Mr Ellison's wife and the other applicant. She had no genetic connection to the children. The applicants initially sought orders for equal shared parental responsibility and that the twins live with them. The applicants and the children lived in Queensland where, as previously noted, it is prohibited for Queensland residents to engage in commercial surrogacy anywhere in the world.[52]

Ryan J was critical of the evidence, or the lack thereof, put forward by the applicants. She commented that this was to 'mask the fact that the children were born as a consequence of an illegal (in Australia) commercial surrogacy arrangement'.[53] At that time commercial surrogacy arrangements were not illegal in Thailand.[54] The effect of the extra-territorial ban on commercial surrogacy was that the applicants were liable for prosecution, which potentially could result in imprisonment.[55] Ryan J resolved this issue by granting the applicants certificates under s 128 of the *Evidence Act* 1995 (Cth), the effect of which is to grant the person privilege with respect to self-incrimination.

The applicants were granted leave to seek a parentage declaration in favour of Mr Ellison. Initially this was to assist in an application for the children to be granted Australian citizenship, although before the case was finished the children were granted citizenship by descent. The AHRC argued that legal parentage was still valuable for the children because of the limits on parental responsibility. Having a legal parent would give them a child/parent status that lasts beyond the age of 18 and reflects their reality.

Ryan J noted that even if Mr Ellison established, on the balance of probabilities, that he was the children's biological father, 'it does not automatically follow that federal and state laws recognise him as their parent', due to the operation of parentage presumptions.[56] Ryan J discussed the interpretation of s 60H(1). This section defines parentage where children are born as a result of artificial conception procedures. It does not contain any geographical limit in its wording. Ryan J expressed the view that s 60H expands the categories of parents and is not exhaustive.[57] In this case if the surrogate mother was in a de facto relationship at the time of conception and her partner consented to the procedure then he would be deemed to be a parent of the children. The evidence about the mother's relationship status was initially unclear, but Ryan J was satisfied in the end that

---

52 *Surrogacy Act* 2010 (Qld), s54. The same is true for NSW residents: *Surrogacy Act* 2010 (NSW), s 11 and ACT residents: *Parentage Act* 2004 (ACT), s 45.

53 *Ellison and Anor and Karchanit* [2012] Fam CA 602 [3].

54 The law in Thailand was changed in early 2015 following the Baby Gammy scandal; see, 'Thailand Bans Commercial Surrogacy', *The Guardian Australia* (20 February 2015), available at http://www.theguardian.com/world/2015/feb/20/thailand-bans-commercial-surrogacy, accessed 10 March 2015.

55 *Surrogacy Act* 2010 (Qld), s54, *Surrogate Parenthood Act* 1988 (Qld), s 3(2).

56 *Ellison and Anor and Karchanit* [2012] Fam CA 602 [17].

57 Ibid., [61].

she was not in a de facto relationship at the time of conception, so s 60H(1) did not apply. Mr Ellison was also not assisted by s 69R with respect to parentage presumptions arising as a result of his name being on the birth certificate because there are no prescribed overseas jurisdictions for the purpose of s 69R.

Section 60HB, which deals with children born under surrogacy arrangements, is much more restrictive. It only operates where a court has made an order under a prescribed law of an Australian state or territory. The prescribed laws are the state and territory surrogacy laws which address altruistic surrogacy. This does not assist anyone involved in commercial surrogacy arrangements. Section 60HB had no application in the cases discussed above as the very reason the applicants came to the family courts was because they could not seek relief under state and territory legislation.

The only parentage provision Mr Ellison could rely on was s 69VA, which enables a court to make a declaration of parentage after having received evidence about the parentage of the child. Once that declaration is made, it is conclusive evidence of parentage for the purpose of all Commonwealth laws.

In *Dudley & Chedi*[58] Watts J declined to make a finding that Mr Dudley was a parent even though he acknowledged it would benefit the children.[59] The AHRC submitted that although it was open to Watts J to take that course of action, it was not in the children's best interests and was inconsistent with the CRC. The AHRC argued that whilst Watts J relied on public policy issues, the Court has to deal with the children who are before the court and what is in their best interests, rather than looking at the legality of the arrangements which brought them into the world.

Ryan J held that in exercising her discretion she could not give greater weight to public policy decisions than to the children's best interests. She noted that a declaration of parentage 'has a wider reach' than parenting orders.[60] A declaration of parentage would also recognise the realities of the children's lives.[61] Nevertheless, the parentage declaration made by Ryan J only applied to Mr Ellison because the DNA test confirmed that he was the children's biological father.

The Independent Children's Lawyer and the AHRC made submissions about developing practice guidelines for international surrogacy cases. They recommended that the following issues be addressed:

- The appointment of an Independent Children's Lawyer. In this case the Independent Children's Lawyer played an important role in gathering evidence.
- Affidavit evidence setting out details of the applicants and birth mother, the circumstances leading up to the surrogacy agreements, and the arrangements after the birth of the child.

58 *Dudley & Chedi* [2011] FamCA 502 [32].
59 Ibid., [32].
60 *Ellison and Anor and Karchanit* [2012] Fam CA 602 [91].
61 Ibid., [87], [92] and [101].

- Independent evidence about the child's identity. This should include parentage testing which complies with the *Family Law Regulations* 1984 (Cth) ('*Family Law Regulations*').
- Independent evidence with respect to the birth mother including confirmation that she received legal advice and counselling before entering into the surrogacy arrangement and evidence taken after the birth about what relationship, if any, she wants with the child.
- A family report detailing the nature of the child's relationship with the applicants and the capacity of the applicants to care for the child long term and promote the child's culture and address any issues of identity.
- Evidence of the legal regime in the overseas jurisdiction where the procedure took place with respect to surrogacy arrangements.
- Evidence of the legal regime in the overseas jurisdiction where the procedure took place with respect to the rights of the birth mother and her partner if applicable.

This decision provided a solution in respect of parental status for Mr Ellison but not for Ms Solano; and thus cannot be said to be a complete solution. It is reminiscent of the era when it was not possible to recognise both same-sex parents as legal parents, with the consequence that children of same-sex parents had a legally invisible parent.[62] In addition, there are other inconsistencies that follow from this decision as a result of the application of the parentage provisions. For instance, as already noted, a declaration of parentage in favour of Mr Ellison could only be made because the surrogate mother did not have a partner. Millbank has argued that this 'creates demand driven pressures for overseas surrogates to be unmarried or divorced'.[63] However, the availability of this partial solution is now uncertain.

In June 2013, Ryan J reconsidered the Family Court's power to make a declaration of parentage in overseas commercial surrogacy arrangements. *Mason & Mason and Anor*[64] was a case where a gay couple had entered a gestational surrogacy arrangement in India with an Indian surrogate mother using anonymous donor eggs. Twins were born in 2011, and were granted Australian citizenship by descent based on a DNA parentage test. The couple applied for parenting orders and Mr A Mason also sought a declaration of parentage in relation to the twins. Ryan J revisited her earlier decision in *Ellison*'s case and held that it was not open to her to make a declaration of parentage even though such an order would be in the children's best interests.[65] Her Honour's reasons were based on principles of

62 See Human Rights and Equal Opportunity Commission, above n. 23. Amendments were subsequently made in the *Family Law Act* in 2008 to recognise same-sex partners as parents: *Family Law Amendment (*de facto *Financial Matters and other Measures) Act* 2008.

63 Millbank, above n. 9, 151.

64 [2013] FamCA 424.

65 Ibid., [6].

statutory interpretation and the scope of ss 60H and 60HB. Briefly, Her Honour considered that the provisions of the *Family Law Act* (s 60H and s 60HB) 'evince an intention by Parliament that the parentage of children born as a result of artificial conception procedures or under surrogacy arrangements will be determined by reference to those provisions and not the general parentage provisions':[66]

> The effect of this is that unless an order is made in favour of the applicant pursuant to the Surrogacy Act [2010 (NSW)], the provisions of the [Family Law] Act do not permit this Court to make a declaration of parentage in his favour. Thus, on reflection, I am inclined to respectfully agree with Watts J in *Dudley and Anor & Chedi* [2011] FamCA 502, where at [29] his Honour determined that ultimately state law will govern the determination of parentage [for children born under surrogacy arrangements] and that state law will be recognised by federal law.[67]

On this point it is also instructive to consider a decision by Crisford J in the Family Court of Western Australia. *Blake & Anor*[68] was an application for adoption. In this case a gay couple had twins through a surrogacy arrangement in India. The intending father, who was not genetically related to the children, applied to adopt the children as a step-parent of the children, pursuant to the state adoption legislation.[69] The issue was whether Mr Blake's partner, Mr Marston, was a 'birth parent' of the children. Mr Marston was the genetic parent of the twins. In the absence of any definition excluding Mr Marston from being considered a parent, Crisford J found that he was a 'birth parent':

> To suggest that Mr Marston is anything other than a parent or a father within its ordinary meaning is to turn a blind eye to the reality of 'family' in present day society. It is also turning a blind eye to the reality of the situation presently before the Court. The objective facts surrounding the birth and the manner in which various agencies have treated those circumstances coupled with the fact of the genetic father acting in that role since the birth of the twins points to the use of an expanded definition of parent.[70]

This decision was based on the relevant state adoption legislation and is therefore not directly relevant to the issue of declarations of parentage made under the *Family Law Act*.[71] Nevertheless, it does demonstrate the lack of consistency of approach to the legal recognition of parentage at both state and federal levels.

---

66 Ibid., [33].

67 *Mason & Mason and Anor* [2013] FamCA 424 [34].

68 [2013] FCWA 1.

69 *Adoption Act* 1994 (WA).

70 *Blake & Anor* [2013] FCWA 1 [51].

71 Although Crisford J referred to the decision in *Ellison*'s case Her Honour also noted that there was no equivalent of s 69VA in the *Family Court Act* 1997 (WA): ibid., [42].

The uncertainty of approach in surrogacy parentage cases before the family courts may deter some couples from commencing court proceedings if they do not have an immediate need for a parental responsibility order. This can arise in situations where a couple is able to obtain citizenship by descent (and an Australian passport) for the children. They may have a foreign birth certificate naming the intended parents on the children's birth certificate. Such a certificate has no legal effect in Australia,[72] but it may be enough to enrol their children in school and so on. In many instances, the male intended parent (or one parent in the case of a gay couple) may be named on a foreign birth certificate but the other intended parent has no legal status at all. This might not cause problems immediately, but may cause problems in future years, for example, if the relationship breaks down or one parent dies. While recognition for one parent may solve most issues in a practical sense, the philosophical and psychological implications for both child and parent of a lack of legal recognition may have a negative impact on the family. The next Part considers how the recognition of legal parentage in overseas surrogacy cases has been approached in the UK.

V. Comparative Approaches in the UK: Public Policy and the Welfare of the Child

The United Kingdom was the first country to introduce surrogacy legislation as a result of the *Baby Cotton Case*.[73] Initially the *Surrogacy Agreements Act* 1985 ('*Surrogacy Agreements Act*') banned and criminalised commerical surrogacy. The *Surrogacy Agreements Act* was later amended to allow approval of payments in some circumstances but to render surrogacy agreements unenforceable as a matter of law.[74]

A significant difference between the environment in Australia and the UK, is the presence of surrogacy organisations such as Childlessness Overcome Through Surrogacy (COTS) in the UK. COTS was founded in 1988 as a non-profit organisation which provides information and support to people interested in surrogacy. It also introduces potential surrogates and intended parents to one another.[75] Although most Australian states and territories now allow altruistic surrogacy, advertising for a surrogate is banned in some states[76] and some of the

---

72 *Family Law Act* 1975 (Cth), s 69R. There are no prescribed jurisdictions for the purposes of this section.

73 Anita Stuhmcke, 'Looking Backwards, Looking Forwards: Judicial and Legislative Trends in the Regulation of Surrogate Motherhood in the UK and Australia' (2004) 18(1) *Australian Journal of Family Law* 1, 8–9.

74 Ibid., 9.

75 See http://www.surrogacy.org.uk/About_COTS.htm, accessed 14 June 2014.

76 *Parentage Act* 2004 (ACT), s 43; *Surrogacy Act* 2010 (NSW), s 10; *Surrogacy Act* 2010 (Qld), s 55; *Family Relationships Act* 1975 (SA), s 10H; *Surrogacy Act* 2012 (Tas),

legislation is unclear as to whether the ban applies only to commercial surrogacy or to altruistic surrogacy as well. As a consequence almost all altrustic surrogacy arrangements are among family and friends. Notwithstanding the existence of agencies such as COTS, finding a surrogate in the UK can be difficult so English couples do look overseas.[77]

English cases such as *Re: X & Y (Foreign Surrogacy)*[78] and *Re L (A Child) (Parental Order: Foreign Surrogacy)*[79] illustrate that the UK legislation enables a court to make 'parental orders' (equivalent to parentage orders in the *Surrogacy Act* 2010 (NSW)) by exercising its discretion to retrospectively authorise payments. This discretion is what is missing in the *Surrogacy Act* 2010 (NSW) and other Australian surrogacy legislation.

In *Re L (A Child) (Parental Order: Foreign Surrogacy)* the parents were domiciled in the UK. They entered into a commercial surrogacy arrangement in Illinois in the USA. The arrangement was entirely legal in Illinois. The arrangement would not have been lawful in the UK since the payments the parents made to the surrogate were more than reasonable expenses. The intended parents faced immigration difficulties, although, because the child had a US passport, they were able to obtain a temporary visa. Section 54 of the *Human Fertilisation and Embryology Act* 2008 (UK) addresses parental orders. This section sets out several requirements which must be complied with to obtain parental orders but also enables the court to retrospectively authorise payments made to a surrogate even if they are in excess of reasonable expenses. Hedley J stated that s 54 weighs the balance between public policy considerations and the welfare of the child in favour of the welfare of the child. Courts will continue to scrutinise each case carefully in order to monitor public policy matters, but will only refuse a parental order in the clearest case of abuse.

Re: X & Y (Foreign Surrogacy) concerned a couple who travelled to Ukraine to enter into a commercial surrogacy arrangement. Section 27 of the *Human Fertilisation and Embryology Act* 1990 (UK)[80] provided that the woman who gave birth to the child is the mother. This is the case regardless of whether the woman is in the UK or elsewhere. Under Ukraine law the birth mother and her partner were not the parents, with the consequence that the child was parentless and stateless. DNA testing undertaken in the UK established that the intended father was the genetic father. This enabled the intended parents to apply for a parental order in the UK but that does not automatically confer citizenship.

Hedley J stated:

---

s 41; *Assisted Reproductive Treatment Act* 2008 (Vic), s 45; and *Surrogacy Act* 2008 (WA), s 10.

77 Natalie Gamble, 'The Response of United Kingdom Surrogacy Law to the Growing Surrogacy Industry' (2012) 3 *Family Law Review* 28.

78 [2008] EWHC 3030 (Fam) (9 December 2008).

79 [2011] 2 WLR 1006.

80 This Act was amended in 2008. The pre-2008 version of this Act applied in this case.

> It is clearly a policy decision that commercial surrogacy agreements should not be regarded as lawful; equally there is clearly a recognition that sometimes there may be reasons to do so. It is difficult to see what reason Parliament might have in mind other than the welfare of the child under consideration.[81]

He went on to say:

> I feel bound to observe that I find this process of authorisation most uncomfortable. What the court is required to do is to balance two competing and potentially irreconcilably conflicting concepts. Parliament is clearly entitled to legislate against commercial surrogacy and is clearly entitled to expect that the courts should implement that policy consideration in its decisions. Yet it is also recognised that as the full rigour of that policy consideration will bear on one wholly unequipped to comprehend it let alone deal with its consequences (that is, the child concerned) that rigour must be mitigated by the application of a consideration of that child's welfare. That approach is both humane and intellectually coherent. The difficulty is that it is almost impossible to imagine a set of circumstances in which by the time the case comes to court, the welfare of any child (particularly a foreign child) would not be gravely compromised (at the very least) by a refusal to make an order.[82]

Hedley J's last comment neatly sums up the problem both in the UK and Australia.[83] At least in the UK, courts can make orders conferring parentage upon intended parents whilst expressing views that do not condone commercial surrogacy. Australian courts do not have any discretion at all to take that course of action.

VI. Options for Reform

There are a number of options for reform in respect of surrogacy law in Australia and more generally, which could occur at a state, national and international level. Any international reforms will be years away because of the lack of consensus. This makes it necessary to look at what can be done more immediately at a state and federal level. The chapters by Tammy Johnson (4) and Anita Stuhmcke (5) in this volume suggest reforms at state level, and so the analysis below is limited to reforms to federal law.

It is clear, from a review of the family law cases discussed above, that the best interests of a child born as a result of surrogacy arrangement must be the

---

81 *Re: X & Y (Foreign Surrogacy)* [2008] EWHC 3030 (Fam) (9 December 2008) [20].

82 Ibid., [24].

83 For a discussion of the conflict between public policy considerations and the best interests of the child, see Mary Keyes and Richard Chisholm, 'Commercial Surrogacy – Some Troubling Family Law Issues' (2013) 27 *Australian Journal of Family Law* 105.

court's paramount consideration by virtue of the applications being parenting applications.[84] Differing concerns have been expressed by judicial officers about the reality of the child's existence and family life and how the child came to be. Regardless of how the child was conceived, by the time the intended parents apply for parenting orders, the child exists and the court will have to deal with that reality.

The first and simplest model of reform would involve amending existing sections of the *Family Law Act*. As explained in Part II above, the current provisions dealing with parentage involve a number of complex 'deeming' provisions (such as ss 60H and 60HB), a number of rebuttable parentage presumptions and a number of evidentiary provisions (for example, relating to DNA testing) and declarations of parentage. Sections 60H and 60HB and the parentage presumptions in the *Family Law Act* should be reviewed and reformed. Some of these parentage provisions were modeled on state and territory legislation that was introduced in the 1980s to provide for certainty of legal parentage for children born from assisted reproductive procedures.[85] Medical technology has greatly advanced since then, creating the possibility for a child to have up to five potential legal parents.[86] The current parentage provisions do not contemplate the different scenarios that can arise in a surrogacy arrangement. In *Re Michael*,[87] for instance, Watts J recommended that s 60H of the *Family Law Act* could be amended to make it clear that it does not apply to surrogacy arrangements.[88] If this were done, there would still be a need to clarify the law for children born from overseas surrogacy arrangements. All the provisions that could potentially apply to a range of situations need to be looked at together in order to avoid contradictory presumptions and legal uncertainty. For example, prescribed jurisdictions could be added to the *Family Law Regulations* to give effect to some foreign birth certificates by providing for a parentage presumption arising out of the information on the foreign birth certificate. Currently there are no prescribed jurisdictions for the purposes of s 69R. Prescribed jurisdictions could be limited to jurisdictions which have similar standards to the rules in Australia and could include jurisdictions that mandate pre-pregnancy counselling and legal advice, and where there have been court orders made transferring parentage. This

84 Declarations of parentage under s 69VA of the *Family Law Act* are not 'parenting orders' and therefore the best interests of the child is not the paramount consideration: *Family Law Act*, s. 64B. That is not to say that the best interests of the child are not relevant: *Ellison and Anor and Karchanit* [2012] Fam CA 602 [90]; Keyes and Chisholm, above n. 83, 123; Family Law Council, above n. 5. [2.7.2].

85 Richard Chisholm, 'Children and the Family Law Act: The 1988 Changes' (1988) *UNSW Law Journal* 153, 163.

86 For example: Two genetic parents, a surrogate, and one or more intending parents. This does not exclude the possibility of other people being parents after the birth of the child.

87 [2009] FamCA 691.

88 Ibid., [71]. The Family Law Council also made a recommendation to that effect: Family Law Council, above n. 5, 104.

would mean there had already been a level of scrutiny in the other jurisdiction and multiple sets of court proceedings could be avoided.

However, any such reform through the amendment of provisions in the *Family Law Act* would not achieve uniformity for children and parents in Australia unless Western Australia makes identical amendments to its *Family Court Act* 1997.[89] In addition, declarations of parentage made under s 69VA are only for the purposes of Commonwealth laws. State and territory laws do not automatically recognise the findings of Commonwealth courts.[90] In any event, the use of declarations of parentage in surrogacy cases is not recommended. It is inconsistent with state and territory provisions that are based on a transfer of parentage from the surrogate mother (and her partner, if any) to the intending parent/s. As Millbank has argued the use of declarations of parentage in surrogacy arrangements may have the unintended consequence that it 'sidesteps all legal safeguards concerning oversight of the validity of the surrogate's informed and continuing consent'.[91] In summary, this leads to the conclusion that a more comprehensive response is required.

Although parentage (and citizenship) can be considered separately to the regulation of the surrogacy process itself, comprehensive reform should also address surrogacy arrangements. The cases discussed above demonstrate that the laws banning commercial surrogacy are ineffective. It is also clear that many judicial officers find these decisions challenging, because some applicants are clearly circumventing state and territory laws in entering into these arrangements, so public policy issues are raised.[92] Because judges have to apply the principle that the best interests of the child is the paramount consideration, there do not appear to have been any cases, in either Australia or the UK, where a court has refused to make a parenting order in cases of children born overseas as a result of surrogacy arrangements. It is important to remember that in these cases there is no respondent seeking different orders and the child is already settled into the household of the intended parents.

Millbank has argued that a comprehensive model of reform could involve a federal regime to provide for the transfer of parentage in surrogacy arrangements.[93] A new federal regime could respond consistently to both the citizenship and parentage questions that arise for children born overseas as a result of surrogacy arrangements as well as providing for safeguards in relation to those surrogacy arrangements. It is not possible here to explore the details of Millbank's proposals, or to weigh up the competing options. As a matter of general principle though, any 'reform solution should also treat domestic and overseas arrangements with

89 The Commonwealth only has power to make laws with respect to the children of married parents in WA as that state has not referred its power to make laws with respect to ex-nuptial children to the Commonwealth.

90 See the discussion in Millbank, above n. 9, 157.

91 Ibid., 154.

92 For a recent discussion see Keyes and Chisholm, above n. 83.

93 Millbank, above n. 9, 155–6.

parity and as far as possible provide the same level of safeguards and protections to participants'.[94] As the law currently stands, children are being treated differently depending on a range of factors (place of birth, status of parents, nature of conception and birth) and this should not lead to a child having less legal protection.

The Family Law Council has recommended that the Australian Government should introduce a federal 'Status of Children Act that includes power to make orders about the status of children and legal parentage for the purposes of all Commonwealth laws'.[95] Such an Act would serve multiple purposes. It could provide a mechanism for protecting the status of children born as a result of international surrogacy arrangements, where state and territory legislation does not apply. It could also include provisions to ensure that surrogacy arrangements are consistent with international human rights obligations and enable a transfer of parentage in accordance with such guidelines. In addition, a 'stand alone' Commonwealth Act would ensure consistency in the treatment of children at least for the purposes of Commonwealth laws. It would remain the case though, that truly national consistency would require further cooperation between the Commonwealth and the states in terms of the harmonisation of laws in this area.

VII. Conclusion

The reality of commercial surrogacy cannot be ignored. Children will continue to be born as a result of surrogacy arrangements to Australian couples regardless of whether or not Australian legislation prohibits it. As a matter of the basic rights to family and identity, these children and their parents should have the reality of their family structures recognised. It does not benefit anyone for children to have legally invisible parents and for parents to have limping legal parentage. The cases analysed in this chapter illustrate the complexity and pitfalls of the current legislation in Australia. Law reform in this area is not simple. In part, this is because of our federal legal system and the fact that the states and territories are currently responsible for surrogacy. Although international solutions may be years away, reforms to the *Family Law Act* and state and territory surrogacy legislation can be made now, in order to provide better outcomes for children born as a result of surrogacy arrangements as well as their parents.

---

94 Ibid.

95 Family Law Council, above n. 5, xvi (Recommendation 6).

Chapter 9
Surrogacy in India: Strong Demand, Weak Laws

Normann Witzleb and Anurag Chawla

I. Introduction

The world looks upon surrogacy as a product of modern medical science but various incidents in Indian mythology show that the concept of surrogacy has been a part of Indian culture since the very beginning. The Bhagavata Purana, completed in the ninth century, narrates the story of Lord Balrama who was saved in his mother's womb by the act of transferring the embryo from his biological mother Devaki to a surrogate Rohini, Devaki's sister. This was done with the blessings of Vishnu, the lord of creation, to protect the child from the wrath of his maternal uncle Kansa, who had sworn to kill the child at birth.[1] In the Sanskrit epic Mahabharata, King Vichitravirja remained without heir to continue the Kuru dynasty. At the request of his mother, his half-brother Vyasa agreed to be a surrogate father and shared a bed with the two widows of Vichitravirja leading to the birth of the Princes Dhritarashtra, Pandu and Vidhur.[2] These early examples show that rather than frowning upon surrogacy, Indian mythology saw it as a way to protect or create a family in exceptional circumstances.

India has been at the forefront of modern developments of surrogacy and Assisted Reproductive Technology (ART). The world's second IVF (in vitro fertilisation) baby Kanupriya alias Durga was apparently born in Kolkata on 3 October 1978, about two months after Louise Joy Brown, the world's first IVF baby, was born in Great Britain.[3] The era of commercial surrogacy began in India

---

* This chapter was current at 15 March 2014. Some later developments have been taken into account. All websites were last accessed 15 March 2015. Mr Chawla thanks his Associate, Ms Pooja Yadav, Advocate, for her assistance in preparing this chapter.

1 See David Adams Leeming, *Creation Myths of the World: An Encyclopedia*, Volume 1 (Santa Barbara, CA: ABC-CLIO, 2011), 449.

2 See Jayatri Gosh, 'Satyavati: The Matriarch of the Mahabharata', in Mandakranta Bose (ed.), *Faces of the Feminine in Ancient, Medieval, and Modern India* (Oxford: Oxford University Press, 1999), 41.

3 Law Commission of India, *Need for Legislation to Regulate Assisted Reproductive Technology Clinics as Well as Rights and Obligations of Parties to a Surrogacy* (Report No. 228, 2009), 6. This claim is controversial: see Usha Rengachary Smerdon, 'Crossing

in 1997, when a woman reportedly agreed to act as a 'gestational carrier'[4] and used the payment she received to finance medical treatment for her paralysed husband.[5] Since then, commercial gestational surrogacy has become a feature of reproductive technology in India. While dependable statistics are hard to come by, the number of surrogacies has risen sharply over the last decade and it is now estimated that about 2,000 children are born via surrogacy in India each year.[6]

Modern medical infrastructure, low cost, favourable laws and easy availability of surrogates are the pull factors which have contributed to India becoming 'the world's top destination for commercial surrogacy'.[7] In contrast to most other jurisdictions (with the notable exceptions of Georgia, Nepal, Russia, Ukraine, and some states in the US and Mexico) India has not erected hurdles to commercial surrogacy. The practice gained validity in 2002, when the Indian Council for Medical Research issued non-binding guidelines, which envisaged that intended parents provide monetary compensation to the surrogate mother for her services.[8] Importantly, a 2008 decision of the Supreme Court of India acknowledged the legality of commercial surrogacy arrangements in India.[9]

This chapter examines the legal regulation of surrogacy in India and how it affects clinics, medical practitioners and the human rights of surrogates and intended parents, especially in cases involving foreigners. Section II begins by providing background information on modern surrogacy practice in India, while section III considers the present laws governing surrogacy in India. Section IV explores the particular problems posed by international surrogacy arrangements, and section V discusses the Draft Assisted Reproductive Technology (Regulation) Bill 2010, currently under consideration. Finally, section VI touches upon the

---

Bodies, Crossing Borders: International Surrogacy between the United States and India' (2008) 39 *Cumberland Law Review* 15, 20–21.

4 In a 'gestational carrier' arrangement, the surrogate does not have a genetic link to the embryo she carries. The embryo will be conceived through IVF, using an egg of the intending mother or a third party donor, and then be implanted into the surrogate.

5 Sandhya Srinivasan, 'Surrogacy comes out of the closet', *Sunday Times of India*, 6 July 1997.

6 Shekhar Bhatia, 'Revealed: How more and more Britons are paying Indian women to become surrogate mothers', *The Telegraph* (online), 26 May 2012, available at http://www.telegraph.co.uk/health/healthnews/9292343/Revealed-how-more-and-more-Britons-are-paying-Indian-women-to-become-surrogate-mothers.html.

7 Kari Points, 'Commercial surrogacy and fertility tourism in India: The case for Baby Manji', *The Kenan Centre for Ethics*, 3, available at http://www.duke.edu/web/kenanethics/CaseStudies/BabyManji.pdf.

8 Ministry of Health and Family Welfare (Government of India), Indian Council of Medical Research and *National Academy of Medical Sciences, National Guidelines for Accreditation, Supervision and Regulation of ART Clinics in India* (2005), [3.5.4].

9 *Baby Manji Yamada v Union of India* [2008] INSC 1656, JT 2008 (11) SC 150 (29 September 2008).

social impact, human rights and ethical implications of surrogacy in India and how they should inform the debate over future regulation.

This chapter argues that the absence of specific laws leaves surrogates and, to a lesser extent, commissioning parents open to uncertainty and potential human rights violations. Stricter regulation, aimed at protecting the rights of all participants and backed up by credible enforcement, would alleviate some of the concerns commonly held about commercial surrogacy in India. The chapter demonstrates that the international dimension of many Indian surrogacy arrangements creates further complexities that require international dialogue and the development of a coordinated approach.

II. Modern Surrogacy Practice in India

The rise of ART, including surrogacy, should be considered in the context of India's efforts to develop a thriving 'medical tourism' sector. Since 2003, the Indian Government has adopted various measures to promote the country as a 'global health destination',[10] including infrastructural improvements, special incentives for hospitals that treat foreign patients and the introduction of a medical visa scheme.[11] As a result, the number of persons coming to India for medical services increased from an estimated 180,000 in 2005 to 650,000 in 2009, and India now ranks second in the world (after Thailand) in the number of foreign patients treated.[12] During these years, the reproductive segment of the Indian cross-border medical services market also showed phenomenal growth. As a result of the immense demand for fertility services, the number of clinics providing ART treatment has grown prolifically and is now estimated to be around 500,[13] or even 1,000.[14]

Surrogates in India usually belong to the poorer sections of society and offer their services at relatively low cost, compared to elsewhere. It is reported that the fees for a surrogate in India are somewhere between US$2,500 and US$7,000,[15] generally paid in instalments over nine months, whereas the compensation for

10 Sunita Reddy and Imrana Qadeer, 'Medical Tourism in India: Progress of Predicament' (2010) 45 *Economic and Political Weekly* 69.

11 Shree Mulay and Emily Gibson, 'Marketing of Assisted Human Reproduction and the Indian State' (2006) 49 *Development* 84, 85–6.

12 Anita Medhekar, 'Indian Government Policy to Support Trade in Medical Tourism Services', in Dennis Emmett (ed.), *Proceedings of the Seventh International Conference on Healthcare Systems & Global Business Issues*, Jaipur National University, Jaipur, India (3–6 January 2013), 205, 209, available at http://jnujaipur.ac.in/.

13 International Federation of Fertility Societies, 'IFFS surveillance 2010', 7–8, available at https://iffs.site-ym.com/resource/resmgr/newsletters/iffs_surveillance_2010.pdf.

14 Bhatia, above n. 6.

15 Kalindi Vora, 'Indian Transnational Surrogacy and the Commodification of Vital Energy' (2009) 28 *Subjectivity* 266, 270.

surrogates in the US, the other major centre of commercial surrogacy, tends to be between US$14,000 and US$30,000,[16] plus significant other costs. These cost advantages, combined with the lower cost of medical treatment, have contributed to the majority of surrogacies in India now being commissioned by foreigners or non-resident Indians.[17]

Surrogacy in India is governed predominantly through private agreements between the parties, flanked by ethics rules and guidelines for ART, customary social practices within the community, and occasional judicial decisions that seek to resolve disputes by reference to principles of ordinary contract law, family law, citizenship law, as well as various forms of draft legislation and law commission reports.

Fertility clinics in India are mainly in the private sector and the increasing number of surrogacy cases provide a financial boon to these clinics and a livelihood to all those who are associated with them. However, there are concerns that the profit interests of fertility service providers have been allowed to outweigh public health interests, ethical concerns and human rights norms. Some critics oppose commercial surrogacy on principle because they view it as denigrating motherhood by transforming it into a commodity and undermining the dignity of women.[18] Other observers concede that commercial surrogacy can create a win-win situation for intended parents as well as surrogates.[19] It allows commissioning couples or individuals to enjoy the otherwise unattainable privilege of parenthood with genetic link to the child. It provides surrogate mothers with a means of lifting their families from poverty as the fee that is equivalent to 5 or even 15 times their, or their husband's, regular annual income.[20]

Those who regard commercial surrogacy as morally acceptable focus their concern on the fact that India has left it largely unregulated. This legal vacuum opens the door to exploitation of surrogates and, to a lesser degree, of prospective

16 Smerdon, above n. 3, 86; Lorraine Ali and Raina Kelley, 'The curious lives of surrogates', *Newsweek*, 7 April 2008, 47 ('$20,000–25,000'), available at http://www.newsweek.com/curious-lives-surrogates-84469.

17 Nadimpally Sarojini, Vrinda Marwah and Anjali Shenoi, 'Globalisation of Birth Markets: A Case Study of Assisted Reproductive Technologies in India' (2011) 7(27) *Globalization and Health* 4.

18 Centre for Legislative Research and Advocacy and SAMA: A Resource Group for Women and Health, Policy Brief – Assisted Reproductive Technologies (ARTs): 'Welcome Kit for Parliamentarians' 2009, 1, available at http://www.clraindia.org/include/ART.pdf; Anton Van Niekerk and Liezl Van Zyl, 'The Ethics of Surrogacy: Women's Reproductive Labour' (1995) 21 *Journal of Medical Ethics* 345; but see also Hugh V. McLachlan, 'Defending Commercial Surrogate Motherhood against Van Niekerk and Van Zyl' (1997) 23 *Journal of Medical Ethics* 344.

19 Natalie Gamble, 'Surrogacy: Creating a Sensible National and International Legal Framework' (2012) *International Family Law* 308.

20 Abigail Haworth, 'Surrogate mothers: Wombs for rent', *Marie Claire* (online), 29 July 2007, available at http://www.marieclaire.com/world-reports/news/international/surrogate-mothers-india.

parents. International surrogacy cases bring together wealthy clients from predominantly Western countries and Indian women who have often received little education and live in economic strife. Indian surrogates often hail from rural areas surrounding the major centres of surrogacy and become aware of surrogacy through word of mouth or recruitment agents.[21] They are generally married and have children of their own.[22] Their husbands are closely involved in the decision-making process because clinics require them to consent to the surrogacy.

Surrogates as well as prospective parents are likely to regard surrogacy as a 'last resort' to change their current circumstances, which makes them vulnerable and susceptible to taking risks that they may not fully appreciate. In this exceptional situation, they give themselves into the hands of ART clinics and other intermediaries who not only control the process but also pursue commercial interests of their own. The medical processes involved in surrogacy are complex and the prospects inherently uncertain, which means that there is a heightened responsibility on the clinics to explain the risks and repercussions fully and honestly. Yet, surrogates and prospective parents do not often seek independent advice, neither medical nor legal, before proceeding, and surrender themselves to intermediaries and clinics. As if this complex web of relationships, needs and interests was not fraught enough, there is of course another vulnerable group to protect: any regulation of surrogacy also needs to respect and protect the rights and welfare of the children born through surrogacy. A significant concern with Indian surrogacy practice is that it maintains the anonymity of egg and sperm donors, making it impossible for children born through surrogacy to trace their genetic heritage, which may negatively impact on their sense of identity.

Surrogacy arrangements in India have a number of features that distinguish them from the practice in other countries that allow commercial surrogacy. These include language, culture and class barriers that make it uncommon for surrogates and prospective parents, particularly in inter-country cases, to have sustained contact prior and after birth, whereas surrogates in the US and Israel often maintain various degrees of involvement in the children's lives and their families after giving birth.[23] While these barriers between prospective parents and surrogates make it difficult for participants to create a personal relationship with one another,

---

21 Amrita Pande, '"At Least I Am Not Sleeping with Anyone": Resisting the Stigma of Commercial Surrogacy in India' (2010) 36 *Feminist Studies* 292; Centre for Social Research, *Surrogate Motherhood – Ethical or Commercial* (Final Report, 2013), available at http://www.womenleadership.in/Csr/SurrogacyReport.pdf.

22 Ibid.; Sharvari Karandikar et al., 'Economic Necessity or Noble Cause? A Qualitative Study Exploring Motivations for Gestational Surrogacy in Gujarat, India' (2014) 29 *Affilia: Journal of Women and Social Work* 165.

23 See Ali and Kelley, above n. 16, 44; Elly Temen, *Birthing a Mother: The Surrogate Body and the Pregnant Self* (Berkeley, CA: California University Press, 2010); and Anthony Wood, 'Surrogacy: A Personal Perspective', Chapter 2 in this collection.

they do not make it impossible to interact with care, empathy and mutual respect.[24] Most Indian surrogates will keep the arrangement a secret from their wider family and community because they fear stigma arising out of ignorance that surrogacy does not involve sexual contact.[25] Many surrogates therefore prefer to stay in accommodation close to the clinics and away from neighbours or in-laws.[26] Living at surrogate hostels for the duration of the pregnancy is also encouraged by the clinics because it makes it easier to ensure that the surrogates have an appropriate diet, do not engage in strenuous work and are within easy reach for medical check-ups.[27] In these hostels, the women live and interact with other surrogates, and can be visited by their immediate family.

Financial reward is the primary motivation for most Indian surrogates, who often report a compelling economic need, but in some cases also a desire for a better home or better education for their children, as their aims.[28] Surrogacy in India has been analysed as a form of work,[29] yet it is an 'emotional labour' that makes unique demands, forges complex interpersonal relationships, and blends financial and altruistic considerations.[30] Despite the bond that surrogates develop with the growing foetus, instances where surrogates do not wish to part with a child they deliver for another couple are rare. This is partly due to the fact that they have no genetic link to the child they gestate and almost invariably already have a family of their own, but also that Indian law upholds clauses commonly contained in surrogacy contracts under which they relinquish any rights to the child from the outset.

---

24 Jennifer Parke, 'Care Ethics and the Global Practice of Commercial Surrogacy' (2010) 24 *Bioethics* 333; Wannes van Hoof and Guido Pennings, 'Cross-border Reproductive Care around the World: Recent Controversies', in David Botterill, Guido Pennings and Tomas Mainil (eds), *Medical Tourism and Transnational Health Care* (Basingstoke: Palgrave Macmillan, 2012), 98, 107.

25 Amrita Pande, 'Commercial Surrogacy in India: Manufacturing a Perfect Mother-Worker' (2010) 35 *Signs: Journal of Women in Culture and Society* 969; SAMA-Resource Group for Women and Health, *Birthing a Market* (New Delhi: SAMA, 2012), 120–31, available at http://www.samawomenshealth.org/downloads/Birthing%20A%20Market.pdf.

26 Pande, 'At Least I Am Not Sleeping with Anyone', above n. 21.

27 Ibid.; Karandikar, above n. 22.

28 Centre for Social Research, above n. 21, 54.

29 For a feminist enquiry into Indian surrogacy practices, see Vora, above n. 15; Pande, 'At Least I Am Not Sleeping with Anyone', above n. 21.

30 The term 'emotional labor' was coined by Arlie Hochschild, *The Managed Heart: Commercialisation of Human Feeling* (Berkeley, CA: California University Press, 1983). See also Pande, 'Commercial Surrogacy in India', above n. 25 (emphasising the significance that surrogates attach to the bond the pregnancy creates between them, the commissioning mother and child).

III. Present Laws Governing Surrogacy in India

A. National Guidelines for Accreditation, Supervision and Regulation of ART Clinics in India 2005

In 2002, the Secretary of Family Welfare released a draft of 'National Guidelines for accreditation, supervision and regulation of ART clinics in India'.[31] It was drafted by a committee formed by the Indian Council of Medical Research (ICMR) and the National Academy of Medical Sciences (NAMS). The document acknowledged that the increasing demand for ART in India had resulted in a mushrooming of fertility clinics, and that 'repulsive tales' of malpractice had emerged about some operators.[32] The guidelines aimed to fill the lacuna left by the absence of specific regulation on accreditation and supervision of fertility clinics. Following several years of discussion and debate, primarily among the ICMR, the NAMS, practitioners of ART and the Ministry of Health and Family Welfare, as well as external consultations, the 'National Guidelines for Accreditation, Supervision and Regulation of ART Clinics in India' were published in 2005 ('the 2005 Guidelines').

The 2005 Guidelines establish a procedure for state governmental bodies to oversee all matters relating to the accreditation, supervision, and regulation of ART clinics. They also lay down specific standards in relation to technical equipment and responsibilities of the clinic, the personal expertise of the clinic professionals, and the procedures and protocols to be followed. In relation to the role and responsibilities of clinics providing surrogacy services, the 2005 Guidelines provide, amongst other things that:

- Clinics are obliged to counsel the parents and the surrogate mother about the implications of surrogacy (3.4).
- There are no bars to single women or men using ART services (3.5.1).[33]
- Clinics should not advertise for surrogates. Finding a surrogate should be the responsibility of the intended parents and the semen banks (3.10.4).
- Clinics must not be a party to any commercial aspect in donor programmes or gestational surrogacy (3.5.3).

---

31 Ministry of Health and Family Welfare (India), 'ART Clinics in India' (Press Release, 4 September 2002), available at http://pib.nic.in/archieve/lreleng/lyr2002/rsep2002/04092002/r040920029.html; Nirupa Sen, 'ICMR Spurs Public Debate on Infertility Clinics' (2002) 83 *Current Science* 1185.

32 Sen, above n. 31.

33 However, foreign parents commissioning surrogacy arrangements in India are now required to obtain a medical visa and such medical visas may be issued only to a 'man and woman … duly married … at least for two years', available at http://boi.gov.in/content/surrogacy. This excludes same-sex couples and single persons from obtaining a visa for the purposes of travelling to India to commission a surrogacy arrangement.

The 2005 Guidelines also contain specific rules on the selection, screening and status of surrogate mothers, including:

- The surrogate mother must not be below 21 and over 45 years of age (3.10.5) and may not act as a surrogate more than three times in her life (3.10.8).
- A surrogate must register as a patient in her own name (3.5.4) and disclose that she is a surrogate mother and all the necessary information about the genetic parents such as names, addresses, etc.
- The surrogate must not be an oocyte donor and surrogate for the same couple (3.5.4).
- The prospective surrogate mother must be tested for HIV and disclose other risk factors such as intravenous drug use and blood transfusions (3.10.7).

The 2005 Guidelines also attempt to clarify the relationship between the surrogate mother and the intended parents by providing that:

- All the expenses of the surrogate mother during the period of pregnancy and post-natal care relating to pregnancy should be borne by the couple seeking surrogacy (3.5.4; see also 3.10.3).
- The surrogate mother 'would also be entitled to a monetary compensation from the couple for agreeing to act as a surrogate' (3.5.4). The amount should be decided between the couple and the proposed surrogate (3.5.4).

In respect of parental rights and responsibilities, the 2005 Guidelines provide as follows:

- A third-party donor and a surrogate mother must relinquish in writing all parental rights concerning the offspring and vice versa (3.5.5).
- A child born through surrogacy must be adopted by the genetic (biological) parents unless they can establish through genetic (DNA) fingerprinting that the child is theirs (3.10.1).[34]
- A child born through ART shall be presumed to be the legitimate child of the couple, and therefore have a legal right to parental support, inheritance, and all other privileges of a child born to a couple through sexual intercourse (3.12.1).
- The birth certificate of the child must bear the name of the intended parents and not the surrogate (3.5.4).
- A child will not receive information on the name and address, that is, the identity of the gamete donor or surrogacy mother. However, on reaching the age of 18, they have a right to seek other information about their genetic parent/

34 This guideline assumes that, under Indian law, legal parenthood of a commissioning parent derives from descent or adoption.

surrogate mother (3.4.8). Likewise, the clinic must keep all information about the donor, recipients and couple confidential and not disclose the identity of the donor to the parents (except when directed by a court).

These guidelines have succeeded in creating a framework for participants in surrogacy processes and assumed a crucial role in filling some of the legal void. In accordance with the guidelines, surrogacy in India will be gestational (rather than traditional), can be commercial and protects the anonymity of egg or sperm donors.

However, the 2005 Guidelines are not binding and lack clarity in many respects which reduces their potential to provide guidance and minimise conflict. They also do not state any overarching philosophical framework that would help in deciding the difficult ethical and regulatory dilemmas raised by surrogacy.[35] It has been commented that, instead of building in checks and controls, the guidelines have the effect of actually promoting surrogacy.[36] The guidelines lean too much towards protecting the interests of ART providers and prospective parents, leaving surrogate mothers vulnerable and open to exploitation. Their permissive stance is viewed quite critically, in particular by those who oppose surrogacy.[37] More generally, public health and social policy experts note that the guidelines reinforce social prejudices and stigma traditionally associated with infertility in India, rather than stressing the need for public health measures to prevent infertility or encouraging alternative ways of dealing with childlessness such as adoption and fostering.[38]

In 2006, the Indian Council of Medical Research (ICMR) released a 'Statement of Specific Principles for Assisted Reproductive Technologies'.[39] These Principles, while not containing much detail on surrogacy, largely reflect the 2005 Guidelines but, interestingly, appear to strengthen the position of the surrogate mother vis-à-vis the commissioning parents by proposing that the intended parents should have a 'preferential right to adopt the child subject to six week's postpartum delay for necessary maternal consent'.[40]

---

35 Mulay and Gibson, above n. 11, 90.

36 Jyotsna Agnihotri Gupta, 'Reproductive Biocrossings: Indian Egg Donors and Surrogates in the Globalized Fertility Market' (2012) 5 *International Journal of Feminist Approaches to Bioethics* 25, 43.

37 Ibid., 43–4.

38 Laxmi Murthy and Vani Subramanian, 'ICMR Guidelines on Assisted Reproductive Technology: Lacking in Vision, Wrapped in Red Tape' (2007) 4 *Indian Journal of Medical Ethics* 123, 124.

39 This Statement formed part of the 'Ethical Guidelines for Biomedical Research on Human Participants': see Indian Council of Medical Research, *Ethical Guidelines for Biomedical Research on Human Participants* (2006), ch. VIII, available at http://www.icmr.nic.in/ethical_guidelines.pdf.

40 Ibid., 102.

B. Surrogacy in Indian Courts: Putting General Law to Work

In the absence of specific laws on surrogacy, it has been the task of the courts to develop and apply general principles of law to decide disputes arising from surrogacy arrangements. Areas of particular concern include the enforceability of the surrogacy contract, the legitimacy of children born through surrogacy, and the relationship between surrogate mother and the intended parents.

Without binding regulation, the legal fulcrum governing surrogacy is the contract between the intended parents and the surrogate. Questions about the legality and validity of surrogacy arrangements are decided upon primarily by reference to the general provisions of the Indian *Contract Act* 1872. Section 10 of this Act provides that all agreements are contracts, if they are made by free consent of parties competent to contract, for a lawful consideration and with a lawful object, and are not expressly declared to be void. A surrogacy agreement that satisfies these conditions is, in principle, an enforceable contract and can therefore, under section 9 of the *Civil Procedure Code* 1908, be the subject of a suit before a civil court for adjudication of all disputes relating to it, and for a declaration or injunction. While section 23 of the *Contract Act* declares contracts that are immoral or opposed to public policy as unlawful and therefore void, surrogacy contracts have not been successfully challenged on that basis before Indian courts.

In the *Baby Manji* case,[41] a non-governmental organisation called Satya filed a petition before the Supreme Court of India challenging directions given by the Rajasthan High Court relating to the custody of the baby Manji Yamada. Baby Manji was conceived with the gametes of a Japanese man, Ikufumi Yamada, and an anonymous Indian egg donor. She was delivered by a gestational surrogate at an Indian fertility clinic in Anand. Before she was born, her genetic father Yamada and his wife, who had consented to the treatment, separated and the issue of who should have custody came before the courts. Satya filed a petition seeking to prevent Yamada from taking Manji to Japan. The NGO submitted that there were no laws on surrogacy in India and that it was in the public interest that the Union of India (the central government) should enforce stringent laws relating to surrogacy to curb abuses. The Supreme Court held that any complaint regarding the child's welfare would first have to be directed to the Commission for the Protection of Child Rights which had statutory powers of inquiry into child rights under the *Commissions For Protection of Child Rights Act* 2005. As no such prior complaint had been made, the Court disposed of the petition on jurisdictional grounds. In the course of its decision, however, the Supreme Court discussed the practice of surrogacy in India and effectively declared commercial surrogacy to be legal in India, when it stated, in *obiter dictum*, that:

41 *Baby Manji Yamada v Union of India* [2008] INSC 1656, JT 2008 (11) SC 150 (29 September 2008).

> 'Commercial surrogacy' is a form of surrogacy in which a gestational carrier is paid to carry a child to maturity in her womb and is usually resorted to by well off infertile couples who can afford the cost involved or people who save and borrow in order to complete their dream of being parents. This medical procedure is legal in several countries including in India where due to excellent medical infrastructure, high international demand and ready availability of poor surrogates it is reaching industry proportions.[42]

The intended parent or parents can also move an application under the *Guardians and Wards Act* 1890 seeking an order of appointment or a declaration as the guardian of the surrogate child.[43] More commonly, however, they bring a civil suit for a declaration of parentage.

Under section 112 of the *Evidence Act* 1872, birth of a child during marriage is conclusive proof of legitimacy. In cases where the surrogate mother is married, the child born to her is presumed to be the legitimate child of her and her husband. However, this presumption is rebuttable. In line with the 2005 Guidelines, surrogacy contracts often contain clauses that the surrogate mother and her husband relinquish all parental rights over the child, that the child is to be regarded the legal child of the commissioning parent or parents, and that custody of the child rests with the commissioning parents.

These clauses have been upheld by Indian courts when commissioning parents have applied for a declaratory order that the presumption in section 112 of the *Evidence Act* does not apply in their case and that they are the parents of the child born in a surrogacy arrangement.[44] In such cases, the courts have accepted the validity of contractual provisions as to parentage and custody and admitted the 2005 Guidelines and DNA reports as relevant evidence. Courts have also examined whether the birth is duly registered as required by section 17 of the *Registration of Births and Deaths Act* 1969 and the birth certificate of the child born contains the name of the intended parents. Once the court is satisfied that the agreement for surrogacy between the parties is valid, that the DNA report confirms the biological parentage of the commissioning parent or parents and that the birth certificate is compliant, courts tend to declare the commissioning parents as the legal parents under order XV of the *Code of Civil Procedure* 1908.

Such declaratory suits are usually not contested by the surrogate mother and her husband. Thus, Indian court orders declaring the parental rights of the commissioning parents are not sought in order to resolve a conflict between the

42 Ibid.

43 See also Law Commission of India, above n. 3, 21.

44 *MA & MI v SD & KS*, 20 April 2011, decided by Dr Neera Bharihoke, ADJ-V, South District, Saket Court Complex, New Delhi; *HC & BC v RS & AS*, 10 March 2011, decided by Ms Anu Aggarwal, Civil Judge-02: South, Saket Court Complex, New Delhi (anonymisation by the authors).

commissioning parents and the surrogate, but rather, because they may assist in overseas proceedings regarding parentage and custody.[45]

IV. International Surrogacies in India: Bringing Home Baby

International surrogacy cases can pose severe problems regarding citizenship and visa issues, in particular where foreign nationals use a surrogacy arrangement in India to circumvent restrictive laws in their home jurisdictions. These conflicts between the different regimes erupt when the commissioning parents intend to bring their newborn children home. The Indian authorities require a passport and visa to take their children out of India (exit visa). The destination countries likewise require that the child enter with a valid passport and the appropriate entry visa (if any).

Indian authorities will not recognise children born to foreign commissioning parents as Indian nationals. This coincides with the 2005 Guidelines, which state that a child born through ART would be the legitimate child of the parents who opted for ART (3.12.1). This means that a child born to foreign commissioning parents will generally not receive an Indian passport on which to exit India. Parents therefore need to apply to their home country to issue them with a travel document for the child. Destination countries respond to such citizenship and passport applications in different ways.[46] States which prohibit surrogacy, either in the form of commercial surrogacy or even all forms of surrogacy, generally do not recognise surrogacy arrangements as a basis for parental status decisions. In these jurisdictions, the general rules concerning legal parentage will apply to any child born through surrogacy, often regarding the surrogate as the legal mother and presuming her husband (if any) to be the legal father. This can create insurmountable hurdles for the conferral of citizenship by descent and hence for

45 On the recognition of foreign judgments on surrogate motherhood, see Daniel Gruenbaum, 'Foreign Surrogate Motherhood: mater semper certa erat' (2012) 60 *American Journal of Comparative Law* 475, 488 ff.; Normann Witzleb, 'Vater werden ist nicht schwer? – Begründung der inländischen Vaterschaft für Kinder aus ausländischer Leihmutterschaft', in Normann Witzleb et al. (eds), *Festschrift für Dieter Martiny zum 70. Geburtstag* (Tübingen: Mohr Siebeck, 2014), 231–7.

46 For details, see Hague Conference on Private International Law, *A Preliminary Report on the Issues Arising from International Surrogacy Arrangements* (Preliminary Document No. 10 of March 2012), [8]–[41]; Hague Conference on Private International Law, *A Study of Legal Parentage and the Issues Arising from International Surrogacy Arrangements* (Preliminary Document No. 3 C of March 2014); Katarina Trimmings and Paul Beaumont, 'General Report on Surrogacy', in Katarina Trimmings and Paul Beaumont (eds), *International Surrogacy Arrangements: Legal Regulation at the International Level* (Oxford and Portland, OR: Hart Publishing, 2013), 439, 443–64; Charles P. Kindregan Jr. and Danielle White, 'International Fertility Tourism: The Potential for Stateless Children in Cross-Border Commercial Surrogacy Arrangements' (2013) 36 *Suffolk Transnational Law Review* 527.

entry of the child to the parents' home country.[47] These states appear to proceed on the rationale that it would undermine their own policy choice against surrogacy if they 'rewarded' parents who present them with a *fait accompli*, the child born through surrogacy, with parental rights.

Other states respond to this circumvention of their own restrictive laws more pragmatically. They are guided by the best interests of the child and enable the new family to leave India by issuing the required travel documents to the child. Australia is among the countries belonging to this second group. It does not seek to enforce its ban on commercial surrogacy extraterritorially by denying citizenship to children born to Australians through overseas surrogacy arrangements.[48] Provided that at least one parent can establish their biological link to the child, the Australian Department of Immigration and Citizenship will grant Australian citizenship 'by descent' (based on genetic parentage) regardless of whether Australian family law recognises this parent as the 'legal' parent.

In prohibitionist countries, children face severe hurdles to leave India and to enter the home jurisdictions of their parents. The two standout cases, which made international headlines, are the *Baby Manji case* concerning a baby born to Japanese parents and the case involving the twins whose German parents had to fight for more than two years before they were allowed entry into Germany (the *Balaz Twins case*).

A. Baby Manji Case[49]

The *Baby Manji case* of 2008, referred to above, was one of the first cases to exemplify the difficulties that can arise over parental status and citizenship in international surrogacy cases.[50] Baby Manji's genetic father Yamada was caught in a harrowing limbo when neither the Indian nor the Japanese governments regarded it as their responsibility to provide him with consular assistance and to issue his baby daughter with the required travel documents to leave India and enter Japan.

The Japanese Government refused to issue a passport because Japanese law does not recognise surrogacy and regards the surrogate mother as the child's legal mother. Yamada was advised by the Japanese authorities that in order to bring the baby to Japan, he would have to adopt Manji pursuant to Japanese and Indian laws and obtain an Indian passport.

---

47 Hague Conference on International Private Law (2012), ibid., [10]–[12].

48 However, it is a criminal offence for residents of the ACT, Queensland, New South Wales to arrange a commercial surrogacy overseas. See Anita Stuhmcke, 'Extraterritoriality and Surrogacy: The Problem of State and Territory Moral Sovereignty', Chapter 5 in this collection.

49 In its description of the factual events, this section draws on Points, above n. 7; Smerdon, above n. 3.

50 *Baby Manji Yamada v Union of India* [2008] INSC 1656, JT 2008 (11) SC 150 (29 September 2008).

The 2005 Guidelines provide that in cases where a couple is not able to establish by use of genetic fingerprinting that the child is biologically connected to them, the couple has to adopt the child (3.10.1). An adoption would enable a couple (or individual) genetically unrelated to create a parental relationship and, on that basis, allow the parents to apply for an Indian exit visa, as well as possibly for entry into the country of residence or origin where surrogacy is not allowed. However, Indian adoption laws are religion-specific and pose particular hurdles to prospective parents who are non-Hindu.[51] The limitations of the Indian adoption laws meant that Yamada was ineligible to adopt his biological daughter.

The application for an Indian passport for Manji required the submission of a birth certificate. However, the Anand Municipal Registrar had doubts as to whom to name as the mother of Manji on the birth certificate: the surrogate, the egg donor or Yamada's ex-wife – and therefore refused to register the birth. Yamada then hired an Indian lawyer who appealed this decision claiming that the registration could not be refused on that basis. After receiving guidance from the Chief Registrar, Anand Municipality issued a provisional birth certificate with only Yamada's name on it. By the time the birth certificate had been secured, Yamada's Indian visa was due to expire and he needed to return to Japan. Manji remained in hospital, under the care of local friends, and Yamada's mother came to India to continue the fight with the authorities over Manji's custody and exit from India. It was when Yamada's mother applied to the Rajasthan High Court that Satya made the petition (discussed above) to prevent the child from leaving India.

The Rajasthan High Court issued notices to various Union and State authorities and required that Manji be produced in the Court within four weeks. In response Manji's grandmother filed a petition on Manji's behalf in the Supreme Court of India to grant her temporary custody. The Supreme Court made the order as requested, restrained the police from taking any steps to produce Manji before the Rajasthan High Court, and sought assistance of the Solicitor General of India to examine the surrogacy and nationality issues raised by the case. The Solicitor General advised that the issuance of a travel document would be a matter for the Union of India (the central government) and the application would be disposed of expeditiously after a complete application for travel documents for baby Manji was filed.

After the Supreme Court gave its judgment, the Jaipur passport office gave special dispensation from standard rules and issued a 'certificate of identity' to Manji. This was the first time Indian authorities issued such a travel document, which is intended for the stateless or those who cannot obtain a passport from their own country, to a child born through surrogacy. Thereafter, the Japanese Embassy in New Delhi issued Manji a one year visa on humanitarian grounds, and Manji

---

51 Anil Malhotra and Ranjit Malhotra, 'All Aboard for the Fertility Express' (2012) 38 *Commonwealth Law Bulletin* 31, 34–5. There is no overarching secular law on the topic of adoption. Non-Hindus are eligible to adopt neglected children under the *Juvenile Justice Act* 2005 but Baby Manji was not neglected. The 2005 Guidelines do not appear to have been formulated with these complexities in mind.

arrived in Japan with her grandmother in November 2008, nearly three months after her birth and after countless twists and turns in a case that had involved India's highest authorities.

B. Balaz Twins Case

The case of the Balaz twins is an even more extreme example of the current disconformity of national laws and the uncertainty this creates for all the parties involved. The result is delay in procuring necessary documents and the need to develop ad hoc solutions to resolve resulting hardship.[52] The case concerned German residents, Jan Balaz and his wife Susanne Anna Lohle, who had also entered a surrogacy arrangement with a fertility clinic in Anand. Under the agreement, they conceived children with Balaz's sperm, and eggs from an anonymous donor. The resulting twins were caught between conflicting citizenship and adoption laws of Germany and India, which left them stateless for the first two years of their lives and unable to leave India as intended by their parents.

The uncertainties in this case begun when the Anand Municipal Registrar listed the names of the commissioning parents on the children's birth certificates even though Ms Lohle was not genetically related to the children and the birth register maintained by the hospital recorded the surrogate as the mother of the twins. The German Consulate did not accept the birth certificate as reflecting the twins' legal parentage, as surrogacy is not legally recognised in Germany. German law regarded the surrogate as the twins' mother and presumed that her husband was their father.[53] The commissioning parents were therefore unable to pass on their German citizenship to the twins and the German authorities steadfastly refused to issue German passports to them. Likewise, India was unable to grant citizenship to the twins born through surrogacy. The acquisition of citizenship by birth under the *Indian Citizenship Act* 1955 requires either one or both of the parents of the child to be Indian citizens at the time of birth of the child. The twins did not have a parent who was an Indian national, despite being born by an Indian surrogate mother, because they were commissioned by a foreign couple. Unlike other jurisdictions, including Germany and the UK, India has no law that declares the woman who gives birth to a child to be his or her legal mother.

52 For a detailed discussion, see Smerdon, above n. 3, 62–5; Yasmine Ergas, 'Babies without Borders: Human Rights, Human Dignity and the Regulation of International Commercial Surrogacy' (2013) 27 *Emory International Law Review* 117; Usha Rengachary Smerdon, 'Birth Registration and Citizenship Rights of Surrogate Babies Born in India' (2012) 20 *Contemporary South Asia* 341, 342–3.

53 See, with more detail, Susanne S. Gössl, 'Germany', in Katarina Trimmings and Paul Beaumont (eds), *International Surrogacy Arrangements: Legal Regulation at the International Level* (Oxford and Portland, OR: Hart Publishing, 2013) 131; Witzleb, above n. 45.

Despite this, the High Court of Gujarat directed that the birth certificate be corrected so as to record the name of the surrogate as the mother of the children. The Court also accepted the contention of the German couple that the children, born to an Indian surrogate mother using the gamete of an Indian anonymous egg donor, were therefore Indian nationals. On that basis, Indian passports were issued for the twins. Shortly afterwards, Balaz received a notice to surrender the passports again because the Union of India had continuing doubts that there was a sufficient legal basis for issuing the travel documents. The Indian Government then brought an appeal against the decision of the High Court of Gujarat. In the Supreme Court of India, the Solicitor General argued that children born to a surrogate mother cannot be provided with Indian citizenship. At the same time, the Indian Government engaged in behind-the-scenes negotiations with the German authorities to resolve the impasse. The German authorities were anxious not to set a precedent of granting entry to children born overseas through surrogacy. However, after months of negotiations the German authorities seemed to be willing to consider a solution via the inter-country adoption process. The problem with this avenue was that the adoption of the twins by the German couple would have required the bending of several rules of Indian domestic and international adoption law. Apart from the restrictions applying to non-Hindu prospective parents, adoption is limited to children who are 'orphan, abandoned or surrendered',[54] whereas, from an Indian perspective, the twins had a parent willing to exercise custody, viz. their biological father, Jan Balaz. The Hague Convention on Intercountry Adoption,[55] of which India is a signatory, also requires that the adopting parents do not have prior contact with the birth mother and a certificate that no adequate national placement is possible. Despite these difficulties, the Supreme Court directed the Indian Government to explore this solution further, mainly for compassionate reasons and with the acknowledgment that this would be a 'special case' that should not set a precedent.

More than two years after the birth of the children, both governments finally relented to the mounting concerns for the welfare of the twins and their commissioning parents: India issued certificates of identity to the twins and the German Government finally granted visas. While the twins were eventually able to enter Germany, their status under German law continued to be problematic. In delaying their entry for such an agonisingly long period, the German Government had also succeeded in sending a message of deterrence to other Germans considering surrogacy abroad.

---

54 Guidelines Governing the Adoption of Children 2011, s 4, issued under the *Juvenile Justice (Care and Protection of Children) Act* 2000, available at http://adoptionindia.nic.in/guideline-family/Overwiew.html.

55 Hague Convention of 29 May 1993 on Protection of Children and Cooperation in respect of Intercountry Adoption (entered into force 1 May 1955).

C. International Surrogacy: The Road Ahead

The cases of *Baby Manji* and the *Balaz Twins* exposed the perils of engaging in international surrogacy where the countries involved have strikingly different legal regimes regarding surrogacy. They serve as a warning to prospective parents to obtain comprehensive legal advice before embarking on international surrogacy and not to expect that any legal difficulties that may arise will be handled with the goodwill of the state parties concerned. They are, however, only the most publicised Indian examples of a problem that has started to command worldwide attention. The Permanent Bureau of the Hague Conference on Private International Law currently charts the issues arising from international surrogacy arrangements and explores the feasibility of drawing up a multilateral instrument in this area.[56] Finding a consensus on a suitable legal framework will be difficult as long as countries adopt policy choices on surrogacy that are fundamentally opposed to one another.

Moving forward, it needs to be acknowledged that the disparity in national laws not only creates many of the legal difficulties described but is also the reason why the demand for international surrogacy arises in the first place. To the extent possible, international solutions need to find a middle ground between the permissive laws of countries such as India and the US and the prohibitive stance taken by countries such as Japan, Germany and many others. While some propose a global ban on surrogacies,[57] others fear that this may only drive the practice underground and further impact on the best interests of the children, surrogates and intended parents.[58] The ideal, yet perhaps unattainable, solution would be an international treaty creating a coherent system for ethical international surrogacy that addresses children's rights, parental rights and citizenship issues.[59] For the time being, the most realistic solution appears to lie in a 'coordinated approach' under which countries allowing commercial surrogacy erect hurdles against international arrangements if the destination country is likely to deny parental recognition to the prospective parents, and destination countries grant parental recognition to children born as a result of overseas surrogacy provided certain minimum standards of protection have been met.[60]

---

56 Hague Conference on Private International Law, 'The Desirability and Feasibility of Further Work on the Parentage/ Surrogacy' (Preliminary Document No. 3 C of March 2014); see also Hague Conference, above n. 46.

57 Gupta, above n. 36; Smerdon, 'Crossing Bodies, Crossing Borders', above n. 3.

58 Katarina Trimmings and Paul Beaumont, 'International Surrogacy Arrangements: An Urgent Need for Legal Regulation at the International Level' (2011) 7 *Journal of Private International Law* 627, 647.

59 Ibid.; Casey Humbyrd, 'Fair Trade International Surrogacy' (2009) 9 *Developing World Bioethics* 111; Kristiana Brugger, 'International Law in the Gestational Surrogacy Debate' (2012) 35 *Fordham International Law Journal* 665, 680.

60 See also Erin Nelson, 'Global Trade and Assisted Reproductive Technologies: Regulatory Challenges in International Surrogacy' (2013) 41 *Journal of Law, Medicine and Ethics* 240, 248.

Recent measures of the Indian Government, including the Draft Assisted Reproductive Technology (Regulation) Bill 2013 and new visa rules, are a step in this direction. They are considered in the next section.

V. The Draft Assisted Reproductive Technology (Regulation) Bill 2010

The problems arising from a lack of regulation prompted the Indian Government to commit to introducing legislation that will define the rights of all parties involved in surrogacy agreements. In 2008, an early version of an Assisted Reproductive Technology (Regulation) Bill,[61] drafted by a 12-member committee of experts drawn primarily from the medical profession and government, was made available for public response. It was then updated in 2010, and after some further amendments in 2013, the Ministry of Health and Family Welfare is currently preparing a final version of the Bill for introduction to the Indian Parliament.[62] The ambit of the Bill goes beyond surrogacy, and aims to introduce a comprehensive regulatory framework for the booming ART industry. The Bill will introduce a requirement that all clinics providing ART services must be registered in a new National Registry of ART clinics, and clinics will only be allowed to operate after an expert committee has determined that they comply with stipulated minimum requirements.

ART service providers, civil society groups and law reformers have welcomed the fact that the Indian Government has finally embarked on regulating this area.[63] Yet, as far as surrogacy is concerned, it is evident that the Bill is largely modelled on the 2005 Guidelines. Thus, the proposed legislation will not impact greatly on surrogacy providers who already follow the existing guidelines. However, it is likely to increase protection against unethical operators and allow for enforcement action in cases of non-compliance. Yet, it is open to question how the provisions will be enforced in a legal system that is plagued with delays and inefficiencies and in which many surrogates lack the financial capacity or education to defend their rights.

The Bill proposes that:

- Surrogacy agreements between a surrogate and the couple or individual seeking surrogacy be legally enforceable: cl 34(1).
- All expenses incurred by the surrogate relating to the pregnancy shall be borne by the couple or individual seeking surrogacy: cl 34(2).
- The surrogate may also receive monetary compensation for agreeing to act as a surrogate: cl 34(3).
- A surrogate shall relinquish all parental rights over the child: cl 34(4).

61 Available at http://icmr.nic.in/guide/ART%20REGULATION%20Draft%20Bill1.pdf.

62 At the time of writing, the 2013 version of the Bill has not been made public.

63 Gupta, above n. 36.

- A woman acting as a surrogate in India must not be less than 21 years or over 35 years old: cl 34 (5).

The Bill also continues to allow foreigners to avail themselves of surrogacy services but does not resile from the position that children born to foreigners in India do not become Indian citizens (cl 35(8)). The Bill does, however, take precautions intended to address some of the difficulties that have arisen with international surrogacies. Under the proposed provisions, non-resident commissioning parents (whether foreigners or Indian):

- Must appoint a local guardian who will take care of the interests of the surrogate during the pregnancy as well as after the delivery until the baby is handed over to the commissioning parents: cl 34(19).
- Must establish to the ART clinic through proper documentation (a letter from either the embassy of the country in India or from the foreign ministry of that country) that their country of origin or residence permits surrogacy and that the child born through surrogacy in India will be permitted entry in that country as a biological child of the commissioning couple/individual.

If enacted, the provisions relating to international surrogacy would help to eliminate the resurgence of cases such as *Baby Manji* and the *Balaz Twins*, in which mismatched domestic laws left children marooned and stateless in India and with 'limping' parentage because of conflicting private international laws.

The ART (Regulation) Bill aims to create more legal certainty for surrogacy arrangements and to define the rights of the parties involved in the surrogacy process. However, critics of the Bill comment that the bias towards the interests of the ART clinics and the commissioning parents has been retained.[64] For example, the Bill states that a woman shall not act as a surrogate for more than five successful births in her lifetime, including her own children,[65] and not undergo more than three embryo transfers for the same couple.[66] This would take the maximum number of times she can undergo IVF cycles to a figure that may jeopardise her physical and mental health. Following the recommendation of the Law Commission Report, the Bill also imposes the requirement for the surrogate mother to relinquish all parental rights in favour of the commissioning parents.

Despite the many years that this Bill was under discussion, it is not comprehensive and there remain issues with the clarity of the provisions.[67] For

64 Imrana Qadeer, 'New reproductive technologies and health care in neo-liberal India: Essays' (Centre for Women's Development Studies, 2010), 41–2, available at www.cwds.ac.in/OCPaper/Monograph-Imrana.pdf.

65 The Assisted Reproductive Technologies (Regulation) Bill 2010 (Draft), cl 34(5).

66 Ibid., cl 34(9).

67 See Law Commission, above n. 3, 19–21; Jwala D. Thapa, 'Analysing the status of the surrogate mother under The Assisted Reproductive Technologies (Regulation)

example, cl 34(24) states that 'commissioning parent(s) shall ensure that the surrogate mother and the child she delivers are appropriately insured until the time the child is handed over'. However, it remains unclear what would qualify as an 'appropriate insurance', in particular, whether this refers to health insurance only or also includes life insurance to cover the unlikely, but real,[68] risk of death caused from pregnancy complications. These doubts are also not eliminated by cl 34(2), which creates the obligation to pay '[a]ll expenses, including those related to insurance if available' because this provision seems to envisage that there may be surrogacy arrangements for which insurance cannot be taken out. The need for further clarification also arises in the consent provisions. Clause 24(1) provides for a requirement of written consent to all ART procedures and the appendix to the Bill provides consent forms in English but many of the surrogates are illiterate and only speak Hindi, Gujarati or local dialects. The Bill is silent regarding how ART clinics can ensure, and document, free and fully informed consent in these very common scenarios. As a result of patriarchal family structures, there is also a real risk that a woman's husband or his family might pressure her into agreeing to become a surrogate. A requirement for independent counselling about the considerable health and emotional risks and consequences of surrogacy procedures would be a possible measure to counteract such coercion and duress.[69]

These and other examples raise doubt that the Bill goes far enough to clarify the law and, more particularly, to improve the protections for surrogates. Despite these inadequacies, it would be significant progress if the Bill were enacted because it lays down rules that bind all participants, including those that do not currently adhere to the guidelines.

Even before the Bill has been enacted by Parliament, the Indian Government tightened up the visa rules for foreign nationals who seek to enter India for the purposes of entering into a surrogacy arrangement. Without prior notice or consultation with ART clinics, the Indian Ministry of Home Affairs instructed the Indian Ministry of External Affairs, in late 2012, that intending parents must enter India on a medical visa, rather than a tourist visa.[70] In line with the rationale of the draft Bill to prevent limping parentage and unresolved citizenship issues, intending parents must now submit a letter issued by their national authorities that

---

Bill 2010' (NUJS Working Paper Series, WP 2012/01), available at http://www.nujs.edu/workingpapers/analysing-the-status-of-the-surrogate-mother-under-the-assisted-reproductive-technologies-regulation-bill2010.pdf.

68 Article, 'Surrogate mother dies of complications', *The Times of India* (online), 17 May 2012, available at http://articles.timesofindia.indiatimes.com/2012-05-17/ahmedabad/31748277_1_surrogate-mother-surrogacy-couples.

69 See also George Palattiyil et al., 'Globalization and Cross-Border Reproductive Services: Ethical Implications of Surrogacy in India for Social Work' (2010) 53 *International Social Work* 686, 694.

70 Ministry of External Affairs, letters ref F. No.25022/74/2011-F.I, dated 9 July 2012 and 7 March 2013.

their country allows surrogacy and permits children born through Indian surrogacy to enter the parents' home country. Unexpectedly, the new visa rules also state that surrogacy visas will only be granted to heterosexual intending parents who have been married for a minimum of two years. This has effectively excluded same-sex couples, singles, and heterosexual de facto couples from seeking surrogacy in India. The full impact of the new visa rules on other intending parents and the inter-relationship of the visa rules with any future surrogacy laws remain in some doubt. Much will depend on whether intending parents will be able to obtain documentation from their home countries that will satisfy the Indian visa authorities,[71] and in what form India will coordinate its visa requirements and surrogacy laws.

VI. Social Impact and Ethical Implications of Surrogacy in India

The laissez-faire approach to surrogacy in India raises questions about its impact on participants in surrogacy and the wider community. Surrogacy in India has been the subject of increasing attention by experts from a variety of disciplines, including health policy,[72] social work,[73] feminist ethnography,[74] and bioethics.[75] As clinics and agents are under few constraints with regard to the processes they adopt, fieldwork in clinics and surrogacy hostels provides important insights into the actual practice of surrogacy. Ethnographic enquiries into the surrogacy workers' stories also instil caution against the uncritical use of Western categories of morality, autonomy, and well-being. The biographies, beliefs and experiences of surrogates may bear little resemblance to those of Western observers and, in any event, are so varied that categorical judgments are best avoided.

---

71 The Australian Government provides a letter that contains general information on the legal regulation of surrogacy in Australia and the requirements of Australian citizenship laws; see available at http://www.india.highcommission.gov.au/files/ndli/Letter.pdf.

72 See, for example, Andrea Whittaker, 'Challenges of Medical Travel to Global Regulation: A Case Study of Reproductive Travel in Asia' (2010) 10 *Global Social Policy* 396, 403 ff.

73 Palattiyil, above n. 69; Karandikar, above n. 22. For a multidisciplinary perspective, see also Sayantani DasGupta and Shamita Das Dasgupta (eds), *Globalization and Transnational Surrogacy in India: Outsourcing Life* (Plymouth: Lexington, 2014).

74 See, for example, Aditya Bharadwaj, 'The Other Mother: Supplementary Wombs, Surrogate State and ARTs in India', in Stefan Beck, Maren Klotz and Michi Knech (eds), *Reproductive Technologies as Global Form: Ethnographies of Knowledge* (Chicago, IL: University of Chicago Press, 2012) 139; Pande, 'Commercial Surrogacy in India', above n. 25; Vora, above n. 15.

75 See, for example, Gupta, above n. 36; Maya Unnithan, 'Infertility and Assisted Reproductive Technologies (ARTs) in a Globalising India: Ethics, Medicalisation and Agency' (2010) 2 *Asian Bioethics Review* 3, 13; Raywat Deonandan, Samantha Green and Amanda van Beinum, 'Ethical Concerns for Maternal Surrogacy and Reproductive Tourism' (2012) 38 *Journal of Medical Ethics* 742.

When childbearing for financial compensation strikes critics as demeaning or exploitative, it needs to be considered that surrogacy allows some Indian women to avoid other occupations that they regard as more degrading. As one 35-year-old woman described her motivation to become a surrogate: 'This is not exploitation. Crushing glass for 15 hours a day is exploitation. The baby's parents have given me a chance to make good marriages for my daughters. That's a big weight off my mind.'[76] As long as potential surrogates regard surrogacy as less harmful than other available employment, the possibility of exploitation is a weak argument for the complete prohibition of commercial surrogacy.

While it would undoubtedly be preferable if women did not to have to make such trade-offs, it should not be presumed that underprivileged women lack the capacity to make valid decisions on how to improve their lives. The surrogacy fee is often sufficient to buy a house, start a business or secure their children's education. In an unjust world, surrogacy provides these women with the prospect of earning a life-transforming sum of money that would otherwise be completely unattainable for them. Adopting a Western moral framework that only allows for 'the competing characterizations of contract pregnancy as a free choice with a win-win outcome, and an exploitive practice from which Indian women must be rescued'[77] belies the complexity of how poor Indian women live, perceive and negotiate their surrogacy work. It is also unlikely to address the underlying conditions of disadvantage and economic need.

The largely unbridled growth of reproductive medicine also has implications for the wider community. Considering the general public health situation in India, the current significance attached to ART has been said to deflect attention from improving health outcomes for the poorer sections of society, and that priority should be given to preventing infertility and improving public health outcomes.[78] There is a concern that the unregulated ART industry 'gives primacy to profits rather than the epidemiological needs of the majority in India'.[79] However, commercial surrogacy, and the provision of reproductive services to foreigners, form part of a much wider policy debate on the appropriate relationship between private health services and public health in India.[80]

The surrogacy industry that has developed in India raises a gamut of issues that go far beyond a perceived conflict between individual reproductive autonomy and uncaring commodification of motherhood and children. Its regulation requires cultural and ethical sensitivity towards conflicting perceptions of childlessness,

---

76 Haworth, above n. 20.

77 Alison Bailey, 'Reconceiving Surrogacy: Toward a Reproductive Justice Account of Indian Surrogacy' (2011) 26 *Hypatia* 715, 724.

78 Cf. Andrea Whittaker, 'Cross-border Assisted Reproduction Care in Asia: Implications for Access, Equity and Regulations' (2011) 37 *Reproductive Health Matters* 107.

79 Qadeer, above n. 64, 28.

80 See, for example, Amit Sengupta, 'Medical Tourism: A Reverse Subsidy for the Elite' (2011) 36 Signs: *Journal of Women in Culture and Society* 312; Palattiyil, above n. 69.

dignity, equality and autonomy. It is charged with issues of gender, class, race and human development in a globalising world. There can be little doubt that it is inadequate to leave the difficult issues raised by surrogate arrangements to market forces as long as participants do not meet one another on equal footing and, in any event, may not prioritise the best interests of the children conceived in these arrangements. Lack of awareness of the health and psychological risks involved, the potential harm resulting from community disapproval, and legal arrangements that structurally disadvantage surrogates remain real concerns. Regulation of commercial surrogacy should aim to protect the vulnerable and empower prospective parents, surrogates, and gamete donors to make free, fully informed and responsible decisions that have due regard to the well-being and human rights of all participants. At the very least, it needs to ensure that the needs of surrogates are properly taken care of prior, during and after the pregnancy. This includes individualised counselling, health and life insurance, adequate compensation and guaranteed access to quality medical care and legal representation. While the Draft Bill is a step in this direction, clearly more work remains to be done.

VII. Conclusion

India has emerged as a major destination internationally for cross-border reproductive care, and for commercial surrogacy in particular. A highly developed and rapidly growing ART industry offers the promise of well-trained professionals and state-of-the-art procedures at comparatively low cost, earning India the title of the 'surrogacy outsourcing capital of the world'.[81] A permissive legal environment favours the interests of commissioning parents and ART service providers. Nonetheless, there is no shortage of surrogates because many Indian women live in such dire economic conditions that the fee they can command for a contract pregnancy provides a life-changing boost to the family fortunes.

The lack of government oversight makes it paramount for surrogates and commissioning parents alike that the chosen ART provider, and any agents or intermediaries, are reputable and comply with the ethical guidelines that currently regulate the industry.

India's legal system enforces commercial surrogacy contracts, including prenatal agreements on parental rights and custody, yet denies children born of surrogacy Indian citizenship if the commissioning parents are non-Indian. This has created severe problems in some cases in which the home country of the commissioning parents refused to recognise the parental relationship between the commissioning parents and their offspring, and denied them citizenship, a passport or a visa. Yet, cases like *Baby Manji* and the *Balaz Twins* also show that restrictive laws do not deter all intending parents from entering surrogacy arrangements and that, once children are born, unsympathetic handling of surrogacy cases by

81 Sarojini, Marwah and Shenoi, above n. 17.

the parents' national authorities may violate the human rights of the children concerned and cause great harm to them.

It is a welcome development that India now seeks to prevent cases like *Baby Manji* and the *Balaz Twins* from arising in the future. New visa rules in India provide that no visa for surrogacy treatments will be granted unless the intending parents satisfy the Indian authorities that their home country will permit entry to children born through a surrogacy arrangement. This requirement (and a similar provision in the draft ART (Regulation) Bill has the potential to address some of the difficulties of citizenship and parenthood that may arise in international surrogacy cases, but it remains to be seen how these rules will operate in practice. Until further regulation is in place, prospective parents must remain particularly vigilant about the laws in their home country, as well as India, before embarking on surrogacy. They need to take great care in selecting clinics with a proven track record of successful treatment and respecting the rights of surrogates and donors. The existing legal vacuum heightens their ethical responsibilities to look after the interests of these vulnerable parties. Talking to past commissioning parents will provide important information and guidance to prospective parents on how to proceed. Intending parents would be well advised to segregate their relationships with the clinic, the surrogate, the donor and intermediaries rather than interact with a single entity that will handle everything for them. Ideally, contracts should be entered into only after each party has received independent professional advice and parents should maintain oversight of funds distributed in their names so that they can feel confident that fees reach surrogates and donors as agreed.

A proposed law to regulate the ART industry would provide more legal certainty to participants in surrogacy, yet it has been in draft stages for many years without gaining parliamentary approval. The draft Bill largely sanctions the practices envisaged by the current ethical guidelines and would therefore enshrine one of the most liberal surrogacy regimes in the world. Yet, if properly enforced, it would provide some measure of protection and a platform to act against unethical and sub-standard operators. Better regulation would also promote the interests of those who would like the ART industry to continue to flourish. It appears that, at least for the time being, the Indian Government values the benefits that can arise from allowing surrogacy arrangements, including those of a commercial character, more than the concerns voiced by those who oppose the practice from a feminist, bioethics or child rights perspective. This is also an important point to note for the work of the Hague Conference on a possible international agreement on surrogacy,[82] because any international framework would be seriously compromised if it failed to fully engage India.

---

82 This ongoing work is gaining increasing international traction: see Hague Conference on Private International Law, 'The Parentage/Surrogacy Project: an updating note' (Prel. Doc. No 3 A of February 2015), available at http://www.hcch.net/upload/wop/gap2015pd03a_en.pdf.

The debate surrounding Indian commercial surrogacy in the Western media has a tendency to sensationalise the practice and to adopt a moral high ground. While it cannot be denied that the lack of regulation provides fertile ground for human rights abuses, close observation of surrogacy in India paints a much more complex picture. Sensible regulation can have no better starting point than listening carefully to the stories of surrogates, egg or sperm donors, commissioning parents – and, as time passes, increasingly to the thousands of children who have been born through surrogacy in India.

Chapter 10
Surrogacy: American Style

Richard F. Storrow

I. Introduction

In a classification of countries as liberal, prohibitive or cautious toward assisted reproduction, from an outsider's perspective the United States might well rank as 'laissez-faire', a classification reserved for countries with almost no regulation.[1] But in actuality, at least as regards surrogacy, the form of assisted reproduction in which a woman agrees to gestate an embryo and give birth to a child for another person or couple, the regulatory situation is somewhat more complex. It is true that no federal law addresses surrogacy, but this is partly a function of the fact that legislative competence in the areas of access to surrogacy and the legal parentage determinations that flow from it currently lies with the states by virtue of the Tenth Amendment to the United States Constitution.[2] In a union made up of 50 states,[3] we find a wide variety of surrogacy regulation, ranging from prohibitive to permissive. This wide-ranging regulation reflects the fact that Americans have never been of one mind about surrogacy, whether commercial or altruistic, traditional or gestational. Viewing the regulation of surrogacy in the United States from this perspective reveals that, instead of being monolithically laissez-faire, the United States stands as a microcosm of the rest of the world, with the whole range of global attitudes towards surrogacy subsumed within its borders.

This chapter is presented in eight parts. Parts II and III provide a legal and historical backdrop to the regulation of surrogacy in the United States. Parts IV, V and VI explore how surrogacy is regulated according to different models running along the continuum from prohibitive to permissive. These parts cover both the regulation of who may have access to surrogacy, the parentage ramifications

---

* Professor of Law, City University of New York School of Law.

1 Linda Nielsen, 'Legal Consensus and Divergence in Europe in the Area of Assisted Conception – Room for Harmonisation?', in Donald Evans (ed.), *Creating the Child: The Ethics, Law and Practice of Assisted Procreation* (London: Martinus Nijhoff, 1996), 305, 306.

2 'The powers not delegated to the United States by the Constitution, nor prohibited by it to the States, are reserved to the States respectively, or to the people.'

3 The United States also possesses five territories: American Samoa, Guam, the Northern Mariana Islands, Puerto Rico and the United States Virgin Islands. Surrogacy is not currently regulated in these jurisdictions.

flowing from surrogacy arrangements, and financial matters such as taxation, insurance and consumer credit. Part VII trains a normative lens on the practice of surrogacy with a special emphasis on recent empirical work and a call for the dismantling of discriminatory barriers to the creation of families through surrogacy. Part VIII consists of a brief conclusion.

II. Surrogacy Regulation in the United States

Regulation of surrogacy in the United States runs the gamut from laws that impose criminal sanctions or prohibit enforcement of surrogacy contracts to laws that permit surrogacy within limits. In 2015, nearly half of the states have some legislation relating to surrogacy,[4] with the most recent legislative enactments having explicitly permitted the practice. Some jurisdictions have only case law governing surrogacy contracts,[5] and some states have no binding regulation at all.[6] Model laws on the subject, drafted to bring some legal uniformity to the area, have had limited success.[7]

The laws that exist seek to answer two primary questions: first, whether surrogacy should be permitted at all and, second, if permitted, within what limits. In contrast to Australia, laws imposing criminal sanctions for violations of restrictions on surrogacy are quite rare in the United States. States that discourage surrogacy generally have a statute declaring surrogacy contracts void and unenforceable. Such statutes make it difficult for the parties to a surrogacy agreement to achieve their aim without resorting to an adoption, but do not ban surrogacy per se. States that permit surrogacy determine whether the surrogate may be 'compensated,' meaning paid a fee beyond the reimbursement of her expenses.[8] Permissive states may also impose specific restrictions on access to surrogacy and regulate its parentage ramifications.[9]

4 Diane S. Hinson and Maureen McBrien, 'Surrogacy across America' (2011) *Family Advocate* 32.

5 See, for example, *SN v MB*, 935 NE2d 463 (Ohio Ct App, 2010).

6 See, for example, *ALS v EAG*, 2010 WL 4181449 (Minn Ct App, 2010) (unpublished).

7 See, for example, *Uniform Parentage Act*, available at http://www.uniformlaws.org/shared/docs/parentage/upa_final_2002.pdf; 'American Bar Association Model Act Governing Assisted Reproductive Technology' (2008) 42(2) *Family Law Quarterly* 171; American Bar Association Section of Family Law, Adoption Committee and Ad Hoc Surrogacy Committee, 'Draft ABA Model Surrogacy Act' (1988) 22(2) *Family Law Quarterly* 123.

8 See, for example, Wash Rev Code § 26.26.210(1).

9 See, for example, Utah Code Ann § 78B-15–807.

III. Historical Context

No discussion of surrogacy regulation in the United States is possible without reference to America's most notorious surrogacy case, *In re Baby M.* This New Jersey traditional-surrogacy dispute arose between a professional couple, Bill and Elizabeth Stern, and a working-class married surrogate with two children, Mary Beth Whitehead, who agreed to submit to artificial insemination and surrender the baby to the Sterns for $10,000. Whitehead, desiring to retain custody of Baby M., was sued by the Sterns, who prevailed at the trial court level.[10] In a breathtaking decision that described Mary Beth Whitehead as emotionally unstable,[11] the Sterns as devoted parents,[12] and surrogacy as a fundamental constitutional right,[13] Judge Harvey Sorkow declared that the contract would be specifically enforced via the termination of Whitehead's parental rights[14] and the grant of Elizabeth Stern's petition to adopt the child.[15]

The Supreme Court of New Jersey reversed on the question of the surrogacy contract's validity. The court viewed the case not as one of disputed parentage, since Whitehead and Bill Stern were indisputably Baby M.'s progenitors, but of disputed custody.[16] In the course of its unanimous and lengthy decision, the court reflected on the similarity between surrogacy and adoption. Because of the similarity, the court was unwilling to countenance, in contravention of adoption law, paying for the irrevocable consent to relinquish a child. The court objected as well to the attempted usurpation of the judiciary's *parens patriae* authority via a contract purporting to name the custodian of a child in advance of its birth. The court did agree with Judge Sorkow's custody analysis, however. Bill Stern was granted custody, and the case was remanded for a determination of Whitehead's visitation rights.[17]

The question of procreative liberty seemed a simpler matter. To Bill Stern's insistence on his constitutional procreative freedom, the court responded that whatever procreative liberty was involved had not been infringed. After all, Stern had had a child with Whitehead. If by raising procreative liberty Stern was trying to argue that he was the child's father but Whitehead was not the child's mother, he, quite simply, had it wrong. 'The custody, care, companionship, and nurturing that follow birth', asserted the court, 'are not parts of the right of procreation'.[18] In other words, exercises of procreative liberty do not resolve parentage questions, which require the evaluation of 'different interests' than the 'essentials' of

10 *In re Baby M*, 525 A2d 1128 (NJ Super, 1987).
11 Ibid., 1167–70.
12 Ibid.
13 Ibid., 1163–66.
14 Ibid., 1159–63.
15 *In re Baby M*, 537 A2d 1227 (NJ, 1988), 1238.
16 Ibid.
17 Ibid., 1234–35.
18 Ibid., 1254.

procreative freedom. Those different interests, it turns out, are the state's interest in the protection of children, an interest that for parentage matters requires an assessment of which one of the disputants has 'demonstrated commitment to the responsibilities of parenthood'.[19]

Baby M. was, in Carol Sanger's estimation, 'the custody trial of the twentieth century'.[20] It ignited a firestorm of controversy while it was being litigated, briefly made allies of feminists and conservative Catholics, and triggered a spate of criticism characterising surrogacy as exploitative and violative of prohibitions on baby selling.[21] On the policymaking level, there is no mistaking that the 'moral panic'[22] engendered by *Baby M.* was the catalyst for three bills at the federal level[23] and restrictions on surrogacy in several states, which, like the court in *Baby M.*, declared themselves unwilling to carry out the terms of contracts governing the bringing into existence of a child 'by conscious pre-arrangement'.[24] In spite of the sentiments that inspired them, though, these provisions did not uniformly criminalise or otherwise outlaw surrogacy. At least one other state supreme court had at the time of the decision in *Baby M.* made a convincing distinction between surrogacy and adoption,[25] and the *Baby M.* court itself similarly did not altogether disapprove of surrogacy, at least where it was unpaid and where the surrogate was not bound to an agreement to surrender the child.[26] These understandings of how surrogacy would best work may have been drowned out by the anti-surrogacy turmoil that arose from *Baby M.*, but they did resurface after the dust settled around 1992, the year Elizabeth Scott describes as 'the political high water mark of the anti-surrogacy movement'.[27]

Baby M. is remembered by many as a case that forced the tide of opinion against surrogacy. The jurisdictions that enacted statutes disapproving of surrogacy

---

19 Ibid., 1255 n.14.

20 Carol Sanger, 'Developing Markets in Baby-Making: *In the Matter of Baby M*' (2007) 30(1) *Harvard Journal of Law and Gender* 67, 69.

21 See, for example, Phyllis Chesler, *Sacred Bond: The Legacy of* Baby M (New York: Times Books, 1988).

22 Elizabeth S. Scott, 'Surrogacy and the Politics of Commodification' (2009) 72(3) *Law and Contemporary Problems* 109, 145. This is not unlike the background behind the passage of the *Surrogacy Arrangements Act* 1985 in Britain. Edward Yoxen, 'Conflicting Concerns: The Political Context of Recent Embryo Research Policy in Britain', in Maureen McNeil, Ian Varcoe et al. (eds), *The New Reproductive Technologies* (New York: St Martin's Press, 1990) 173, 193 (describing the 'moral panic' that influenced the passage of the law).

23 *Surrogacy Arrangements Act of 1987*, HR 2433, 100th Congress (1987); *Anti-Surrogate Mother Act of 1987*, HR 3264, 100th Congress (1987); *Anti-Surrogate Mother Act of 1989*, HR 576, 101st Congress (1989).

24 *In re Baby M*, 525 A2d 1128 (NJ Super, 1987), 1157.

25 *Surrogate Parenting Associates, Inc v Commonwealth*, 704 SW2d 209 (Ky, 1986).

26 *In re Baby M*, 525 A2d 1128, 1235 (NJ Super, 1987), 1264.

27 Scott, above n. 22.

in the wake of *Baby M.* included Arizona,[28] Louisiana,[29] Michigan,[30] New York,[31] Utah, and the District of Columbia.[32] These early anti-surrogacy provisions have undergone challenges and changes in the intervening years. The Arizona law has since been declared unconstitutional as applied to deny a genetic mother an opportunity to prove her maternity but otherwise remains in force.[33] Utah has since legalised compensated gestational surrogacy,[34] and bills to relax restrictions on surrogacy are currently pending in New York and the District of Columbia.[35] Despite these legal developments, *Baby M.* is far from a relic. It remains controlling law in New Jersey, where it was decided and where it was judicially clarified several years later as extending to gestational surrogacy.[36] It was the template for a more recent case involving a gay male couple and a surrogate who conceived using the egg of a donor.[37] A New Jersey court decided another gestational surrogacy case similarly in 2009, finding the intent of the parties in entering into the arrangement and the lack of genetic connection between the surrogate mother and the child to be 'distinctions without a difference' to the larger considerations in play.[38] This sense that there is no difference between traditional and gestational surrogacy may well have influenced Governor Christie's veto of legislation that would have created a regulatory framework for gestational surrogacy arrangements in New Jersey.[39]

What might seem remarkable, given what seem to be its powerful anti-surrogacy sentiments, is that New Jersey, in the aftermath of *Baby M.*, did *not* outlaw surrogacy. Today, the objectives of a surrogacy arrangement may be realized within an adoption framework. The bill vetoed by Governor Christie would have permitted

---

28 Ariz Rev Stat § 25–218.

29 La Rev Stat § 9: 2713.

30 Mich Comp Laws § 722.855. A constitutional challenge to the statute, based on the principle of procreative liberty, failed; *Doe v Attorney General*, 487 NW2d 484 (Mich Ct App, 1992).

31 NY Dom Rel Law § 122.

32 DC Code § 16–402(a).

33 *Soos v Superior Court*, 897 P2d 1356 (Ariz Ct App, 1994), 1360–61.

34 Utah Code Ann § 78B-15–801.

35 Assembly Bill 4319, Senate Bill 2765 (2015–16 Legislative Session), available at http://assembly.state.ny.us/leg/?bn=A04319&term=2015, accessed 10 March 2015; *Collaborative Reproduction Amendment Act of 2015*, DC B21-0016, 21st Council (2015-16), available at https://legiscan.com/DC/bill/B21-0016/2015.

36 *AHW v GHB*, 772 A2d 948 (NJ Super, 2000).

37 'Gay couple gets custody of surrogate twins' *UPI*, 20 December 2011, available at http://www.upi.com/Top_News/US/2011/12/20/Gay-couple-gets-custody-of-surrogate-twins/UPI-79671324416518/, accessed 16 June 2014.

38 *AGR v DRH*, FD-09-001838-07 (NJ Super, 23 December 2009).

39 Susan K. Livio, 'Christie vetoes bill that would have eased tough rules for gestational surrogates', *Star-Ledger*, 8 August 2012, available at http://www.nj.com/politics/index.ssf/2012/08/christie_vetoes_bill_that_woul.html, accessed 16 June 2014.

the automatic recognition of intended parents in gestational surrogacy cases. In a related development, an equally divided New Jersey Supreme Court, in a decision that surprised many, approved the state's refusal to place the intended mother's name on the child's birth certificate, where neither the surrogate nor the intended mother had a genetic connection to the child.[40] For the time being, at least, adoption law will remain the governing legal framework for surrogacy in New Jersey.

There are also shades of *Baby M.* in other jurisdictions. The availability of gestational surrogacy, discussed in Part V, has been influential in winning converts to surrogacy, but discomfort with traditional surrogacy continues to be reflected in the laws of several states where gestational surrogacy is permitted but traditional surrogacy is not.[41] In still other states, courts have treated the controlling issue in traditional surrogacy matters as being custody rather than parentage.[42]

Today there is very little legislative activity aimed at prohibiting surrogacy. The legislative trend, if there is one, is toward legalising surrogacy where it has been illegal,[43] or providing a statutory framework for it where it has been practised with minimal legislative guidance.[44] Recent attempts to enact prohibitions on surrogacy or to limit it to altruistic arrangements, both of which are reflected in the laws of many other countries, have met with little success. A recent proposal in South Dakota, for example, would have vested parental rights in any surrogate mother, whether gestational or traditional and whether or not she received compensation. Harold Cassidy, the lawyer who represented Mary Beth Whitehead in *Baby M.*, testified in favour of the measure, which ultimately was voted down in committee.[45] A similar fate befell a bill brought in Kansas to criminalise paid surrogacy. After overwhelming testimony in opposition to the measure and statements by the senate leadership to the effect that there was little support for it, the sponsoring senator withdrew the bill.[46]

---

40 *In re TJS*, 54 A3d 263 (NJ, 2012).

41 See, for example, ND Cent Code § 14–18–05; Tex Fam Code § 160.754(4)(c).

42 See, for example, *ALS v EAG*, 2010 WL 4181449 (Minn Ct App, 2010) (unpublished); *RR v MH*, 689 NE2d 790 (Mass, 1998).

43 See, for example,

Assembly Bill 4319, Senate Bill 2765 (2015–16 Legislative Session), available at http://assembly.state.ny.us/leg/?bn=A04319&term=2015, accessed 10 March 2015; *Collaborative Reproduction Amendment Act of 2015*, DC B21-0016, 21st Council (2015-16), available at https://legiscan.com/DC/bill/B21-0016/2015.

44 See, for example, Nev Rev Stat §§ 126.710-.810.

45 Chet Brokaw, 'South Dakota lawmakers reject anti-surrogacy bill', *Seattle Times*, 14 February 2011, available at http://seattletimes.com/html/nationworld/2014222660_apsdxgrsurrogacy.html, accessed 16 June 2014.

46 Patricia J. Williams, 'Worlds, and Wombs, Collide in Kansas Bill Criminalizing Surrogate Pregnancy Contracts' (2014) 298(8) *Nation* 10.

IV. 'Bans' on Surrogacy

A true ban or prohibition on surrogacy makes surrogacy illegal by either declaring it to be prohibited or imposing penalties upon those who would enter into or assist with such arrangements.[47] Banning surrogacy whether or not compensation changes hands, however, is not by and large the regulatory stance that states discouraging surrogacy have taken. Some of these jurisdictions have affirmatively banned compensated surrogacy,[48] but what is more common is legislation that may appear to be a prohibition of surrogacy but is in fact merely a declaration that surrogacy contracts are void and unenforceable.[49] This 'passive resistance', as Radhika Rao describes it,[50] applies in some states only to traditional surrogacy or to compensated traditional surrogacy.[51] Such laws are not bans in the true sense, since they merely force the parties to resort to an adoption to finalise the parentage designations they desire. As a practical matter, parties remain free under such laws to pre-arrange the creation of a child in precisely the way surrogacy contemplates, but adoption law does not. And though a court will refuse to enforce any provision of the contract if a dispute arises, as long as the parties continue to agree, they can invoke adoption law to help them fulfil their aims.

This 'adoption model' of surrogacy prohibits paying the birth mother compensation for her inconvenience and amounts in excess of her expenses and gives her an opportunity to keep the child. It asks that we remove the taint of payment for the surrender of a child from the arrangement, not that we disallow the arrangement entirely. This model appears particularly appropriate for traditional surrogacy cases and has been embraced by some states. Florida, for example, has a statute regulating 'pre-planned adoption contracts' in precisely this fashion.[52] New Hampshire's statute employs an adoption model for all surrogacy cases, allowing the surrogate to keep the child if she chooses to do so within 72 hours after the birth of the child.[53] A New York court, before the legislature enacted a ban on surrogacy, required the surrogate to testify under oath that she would not accept compensation beyond expenses, given the prohibition on compensation for adoption.[54]

Intended parents admittedly do not expect to have to adopt the child when they enter a surrogacy arrangement. They want the assurance that they will be

---

47 See, for example, DC Code §§ 16-402(a)-(b); Ariz Rev Stat § 25-218(A).

48 See, for example, Mich Comp Laws § 722.859; NY Dom Rel Law § 123(1).

49 See, for example, Ind Code § 31-20-1-2; Mich Comp Laws § 722.855; NY Dom Rel Law § 122; Neb Rev Stat § 25-1,200(1).

50 Radhika Rao, 'Surrogacy Law in the United States: The Outcome of Ambivalence', in Rachel Cook, Shelley Day Sclater and Felicity Kangas (eds), *Surrogate Motherhood: International Perspectives* (Oxford: Hart Publishing, 2003) 23, 31.

51 See, for example, Ky Rev Stat Ann § 199.590(4); La Rev Stat Ann § 9: 2713.

52 Fla Stat § 63.213.

53 NH Rev Stat Ann § 168-B: 25 (IV).

54 *In re Paul*, 550 NYS2d 815 (Fam Ct, 1990), 819.

legally recognised as the child's sole parents immediately upon its birth and not after the birth mother has made up her mind not to keep the child. Nonetheless, adoption law has been looked to in both anti- and pro-surrogacy jurisdictions as an important set of default principles either for justifying a ban or for shaping the regulation of surrogacy. It is apparent that adoption law has had an important influence on the development of laws regulating surrogacy in the United States, even as American attitudes toward surrogacy have softened.

V. Regulating Access

The national tone in the United States has changed since *Baby M.*,[55] and so has the practice of surrogacy. Today, gestational surrogacy is strongly preferred over traditional surrogacy, in part because the lack of any genetic connection to the child appears to ease a gestational surrogate's post-birth separation.[56] There is also less of a sense that a gestational surrogate is receiving money to relinquish *her* child but is instead providing gestational services for an infertile couple.[57] Finally, testimonials and studies have helped underscore that surrogates are not, as a class, poverty-stricken women forced against their will to participate in an exploitative transaction. There is, thus, a greater level of comfort with gestational surrogacy among intended parents and surrogates alike. By one estimation, 95 per cent of all surrogacies that take place in the United States are gestational.[58] These developments have led to hybrid legislation, where a state chooses to ban traditional surrogacy but to permit gestational surrogacy.[59]

The greater level of comfort Americans feel toward surrogacy has influenced the law in the direction of bestowing legal recognition upon the intended parents without the necessity of adoption. This approach makes sense in gestational surrogacy where the surrogate, lacking a genetic connection to the child, is not legally recognised as the mother.[60] Some courts will even issue a pre-birth judgment of parentage to this effect, which helps ensure that the intended parents' names will

55 Jane E. Brody, 'Much has changed in surrogate pregnancies', *NY Times*, 21 July 2009, available at http://www.nytimes.com/2009/07/21/health/21brod.html?pagewanted=1&partner=rss&emc=rss, accessed 16 June 2014.

56 *See Uniform Parentage Act*, above n. 7, art 8 cmt, 9B ULA 361 (2001) ('The practice of having a woman perform both functions is generally strongly disfavoured by the assisted reproduction community. Experience has shown that the gestational mother's link to the child sometimes creates additional emotional and psychological problems in enforcing a gestational agreement.').

57 *Surrogate Parenting Associates, Inc v Commonwealth*, 704 SW2d 209 (Ky, 1986); *In re LJ*, 505 NYS2d 813, 818 (Fam Ct, 1986).

58 Hinson and McBrien, above n. 4, 34.

59 See, for example, ND Cent Code § 14-18-05; Tex Fam Code § 160.754(4)(c).

60 See, for example, Nolan v LaBree, 52 A3d 923 (Me 2012).

appear on the child's birth certificate in the first instance.[61] This approach might be taken as well in states that allow traditional surrogacy. The procedure by which this result is achieved is not necessarily straightforward and may entail considerable governmental oversight in the form of limitations on access to surrogacy. The following 25 examples have been compiled from a review of various jurisdictions, and are typical of the requirements imposed on surrogacy arrangements:

1. Agreements must be judicially pre-approved.[62] A guardian ad litem must be appointed for any resulting child prior to the hearing on judicial pre-approval.[63]
2. Agreements must be in writing and signed by all parties.[64]
3. Agreements do not apply to pregnancies brought about by sexual intercourse.[65]
4. Only gestational surrogacy is permitted.[66] The surrogate's husband may not contribute his sperm.[67]
5. Compensation of the surrogate is either prohibited,[68] or must be deemed reasonable or in good faith.[69] The contract must provide for adequate healthcare expenses for the surrogate.[70] No fees or commissions are permitted for brokering a surrogacy arrangement.[71] A client's funds paid to a broker must be held in escrow or in a trust account maintained by an attorney.[72]

---

61 See, for example, Cal Fam Code § 7962(e); *Kristine H v Lisa R*, 117 P3d 690 (Cal, 2005); *Raftopol v. Ramey*, 12 A3d 783 (Conn, 2011); *Culliton v Beth Israel Deaconess Med Ctr*, 756 NE2d 1133 (Mass, 2001); *Doe v NY City Bd of Health*, 782 NYS2d 180 (Sup Ct, 2004). Connecticut now has a 'law allowing same-sex couples to be named as parents on the birth certificates of children born to surrogates'. Kate Zernike, 'Court's split helps provide little clarity on surrogacy', *NY Times*, 25 October 2012.

62 See, for example, Fla Stat § 63.212(1)(i); NH Rev Stat Ann §§ 168-B: 16(I)(a), 168-B: 23; Tex Fam Code §§ 160.751 to .763; Utah Code Ann §§ 78-45g-801 to -809; Va Code Ann §§ 20-159(B), 160(A); *Uniform Parentage Act*, above n. 7, § 803, 9B ULA 364 (2001) (model law explaining requirements for judicial pre-approval of gestational agreements).

63 See, for example, Va Code Ann § 20-160(A).

64 See, for example, Nev Rev Stat §§ 126.750(3)(a), (c).

65 See, for example, Tex Fam Code § 160.754(f); Utah Code Ann § 78B-15-801(5).

66 See, for example, 750 Ill Comp Stat 45/6(1)(A), 47/10-47/70; Nev Rev Stat § 126.740(c); Utah Code Ann §§ 78B-15-801(7).

67 See, for example, Utah Code Ann §§ 78B-15-801(7), (8).

68 See, for example, Fla Stat § 742.15(4); Va Code Ann § 20-160(B)(4); Wash Rev Code § 26.26.230.

69 See, for example, Nev Rev Stat § 126.810; Utah Code Ann § 78B-15-803(2)(h).

70 See, for example, Utah Code Ann § 78B-15-803(2)(g).

71 See, for example, NH Rev Stat Ann § 168-B: 16(IV).

72 See, for example, Cal Fam Code §§ 7961(a)(1)-(2); 750 Ill Comp Stat 47/25(b)(4).

6. The surrogate must have had one previous pregnancy resulting in a live birth or delivery.[73]
7. If she is married, the surrogate's husband must expressly agree to the terms of the contract.[74]
8. The surrogate (or all parties) must undergo psychological counselling.[75]
9. The surrogate must have legal counselling and must document her receipt of information regarding the ramifications of the contract.[76] The intended parents must have legal counselling and must document their receipt of information regarding the ramifications of the contract.[77] The surrogate's counsel must be separate and independent from the intended parents'.[78]
10. The surrogate must not be receiving state assistance.[79]
11. The surrogate's husband must be a party to the contract/must join in the petition to obtain judicial validation of the agreement.[80]
12. Either the surrogate or the intended parents must reside in the state.[81]
13. The surrogate and the intended parents must be 18[82] or 21.[83] If a minor, the surrogate must be emancipated.[84]
14. The surrogate and the intended parents must have psychological evaluations.[85] Surrogates and intended parents must have medical examinations.[86] The surrogate and the intended parents must receive genetic counselling if the surrogate is over the age of 35.[87]

73 See, for example, 750 Ill Comp Stat 47/20(a)(2); NH Rev Stat Ann § 168-B: 17(V); Utah Code Ann § 78B-15-803(2)(f); Va Code Ann § 20-160(B)(6).

74 See, for example, 750 Ill Comp Stat 47/25(c)(2). A Nevada statute states that the consent of the legal spouse or domestic partner of the surrogate is not required and nor will the spouse or partner be a presumed parent. Nev Rev Stat §§ 126.770(1)-(2).

75 See, for example, Utah Code Ann § 78B-15-803(2)(d).

76 See, for example, 750 Ill Comp Stat 47/20(5), 47/25(b)(3.5); Nev Rev Stat §§ 126.740(b), 126.750(2)(d).

77 See, for example, 750 Ill Comp Stat 47/20(b)(4), 47/25(b)(3.5).

78 See, for example, Cal Fam Code § 7962(b); 750 Ill Comp Stat 47/25(b)(3); Nev Rev Stat § 126.750(2).

79 See, for example, Utah Code Ann § 78B-15-801(2).

80 See, for example, Utah Code Ann § 78B-15-802(3).

81 See, for example, Tex Fam Code § 160.755(b)(1); Utah Code Ann § 78B-15-802(2).

82 See, for example, Fla Stat § 742.15(1).

83 See, for example, NH Rev Stat Ann § 168-B: 17(I); Utah Code Ann § 78B-15-801(6).

84 See, for example, Wash Rev Code § 26.26.220.

85 See, for example, 750 Ill Comp Stat 47/20(b)(3); NH Rev Stat Ann § 168-B: 18(I).

86 See, for example, Nev Rev Stat § 126.740(a); NH Rev Stat Ann §§ 168-B: 16(III), 168-B: 19(I); Va Code Ann § 20-160(B)(7).

87 See, for example, NH Rev Stat Ann § 168-B: 19(II).

15. The surrogate mother must not have a diagnosed intellectual, mental, or developmental disability.[88] She must be in good health without conditions that could affect her pregnancy.[89]
16. The surrogate mother must have health insurance that will cover the period of her pregnancy and eight weeks postpartum.[90]
17. The intended mother must be incapable of gestating a child or not without unreasonable risk to her physical and mental health or that of the child.[91]
18. At least one of the intended parents (or both of them) must contribute her gametes.[92] Either the surrogate or the intended mother must provide the ovum.[93]
19. The intended parents must be married.[94]
20. The intended parents must meet the standards of parental fitness employed in adoption proceedings[95] or must be determined to be suitable parents.[96] The surrogate and her husband must meet the standards of fitness required of adoptive parents.[97]
21. The intended parents must submit to a home study.[98] The surrogate and her husband must submit to a home study.[99]
22. The physician must provide the parties with certain specified pieces of information in order that the parties be capable of giving informed consent.[100] Informed consent must be documented.[101]
23. The contract may not deny the surrogate the right to make decisions to safeguard her health or the health of the foetus she is carrying.[102]

---

88 See, for example, Wash Rev Code § 26.26.220.

89 See, for example, NH Rev Stat Ann § 168-B: 17(V).

90 See, for example, 750 Ill Comp Stat 47/20(a)(6).

91 See, for example, Fla Stat § 742.15(2)(a); NH Rev Stat Ann § 168-B: 17(II); Utah Code Ann § 78B-15-803(2)(b); Va Code Ann § 20-160(B)(8).

92 See, for example, 750 Ill Comp Stat 47/20(b)(1); NH Rev Stat Ann § 168-B: 17(III); Tenn Code Ann § 36–1-102(48)(A); Va Code Ann § 20-160(B)(9).

93 See, for example, NH Rev Stat Ann § 168-B: 17(IV); Tenn Code Ann § 36-1-102(48)(A).

94 See, for example, Fla Stat § 742.15(1); Tenn Code Ann § 36-1-102(48)(A); Tex Fam Code § 160.754(b); Utah Code Ann § 78B-15-801(3); Va Code Ann § 20-156.

95 Utah Code Ann § 78B-15-803(2)(c); Va Code Ann § 20-160(B)(3).

96 See, for example, NH Rev Stat Ann § 168-B: 18(II).

97 See, for example, Va Code Ann § 20-160(B)(3).

98 See, for example, Utah Code Ann § 78B-15-803(2)(c); Va Code Ann § 20-160(A).

99 See, for example, NH Rev Stat Ann § 168-B: 18(III); Va Code Ann § 20-160(B)(2).

100 See, for example, Tex Fam Code § 160.754(d).

101 See, for example, NH Rev Stat Ann § 168-B: 16(I)(c).

102 See, for example, Fla Stat §§ 63.212(1)(i)(3)(b), 742.15(3)(a); NH Rev Stat § 168-B: 6; Tex Fam Code § 160.754(g); Va Code Ann § 20-163A; *Uniform Parentage Act*, above n. 7, § 801(f).

24. The intended parents must agree to accept custody of the child immediately upon his or her birth and to assume sole responsibility for him or her[103] regardless of the condition, gender or number of the children.[104]
25. The contract must be witnessed by two competent adults.[105] The contract must be notarised.[106]

Despite what appears to be a tidy list of requirements, there is, in actuality, a great deal of variation among the states. Some states, for example, friendly though they are to surrogacy contracts, do not permit compensation over and above medical and other expenses related to the pregnancy.[107] Some states allow commissioning parents to be unmarried or single.[108] In some jurisdictions only gestational surrogacy is permitted,[109] making it less likely that the surrogate will refuse to relinquish the child.[110] Making counselling and psychological evaluation available to surrogates before they embark on the journey is commonly recommended (and in some jurisdictions, required),[111] as is the mandate that the surrogate have experienced at least one pregnancy.[112]

The most salient feature of this regulatory approach to surrogacy is that it bars some individuals from becoming parents with the help of surrogates and bars some women from becoming surrogates. It thus sends a clear message about who is deserving of the right to resort to surrogacy. It also fixes the terms of the agreement, eliminating any sense that there is a free market for surrogacy in which freedom of contract reigns. Finally, it installs the state as a gatekeeper and arbiter of the agreement from its very inception. Recent legislation on surrogacy in the

103 See, for example, 750 Ill Comp Stat 47/25(c)(4).

104 See, for example, Nev Rev Stat § 126.750(4)(d)(1).

105 See, for example, 750 Ill Comp Stat 47/25(b)(5).

106 See, for example, Nev Rev Stat § 126.750(2)(c); Va Code Ann § 29-160(A); compare Cal Fam Code § 7962(c) (requiring notarisation or witnessing in accordance with the requirements of the jurisdiction where the contract is executed).

107 See, for example, Fla Stat §§ 63.212-.213, 742.15-.16; Nev Rev Stat § 126.045; NH Rev Stat Ann § 168-B: 25; Utah Code Ann § 78B-15–803; Wash Rev Code §26.26.

108 See, for example, Wash Rev Code § 26.26.210.

109 See, for example, 750 Ill Comp Stat Ann 45/6(1)(A), 47/10-47/70; Nev Rev Stat § 126.740(c); Utah Code Ann §§ 78B-15-801(7).

110 See *Uniform Parentage Act*, above n. 7, art 8 cmt, 9B ULA 361 (2001) ('The practice of having a woman perform both functions is generally strongly disfavored by the assisted reproduction community. Experience has shown that the gestational mother's link to the child sometimes creates additional emotional and psychological problems in enforcing a gestational agreement.').

111 See, for example, NH Rev Stat Ann §§ 168-B: 1-B: 32; Utah Code Ann § 78B-15-803(2)(d); Va Code Ann § 20-156-65.

112 See, for example, NH Rev Stat Ann § 168-B: 17; Tex Fam Code § 160.756; Va Code Ann § 20-160.

United States follows this model, but does not uniformly retain the judicial pre-approval requirement.

The oversight model of surrogacy regulation dates from the 1980s, when the National Conference of Commissioners on Uniform State Laws (NCCUSL) promulgated the *Uniform Status of Children of Assisted Conception Act* ('USCACA'). The USCACA embodied two options relating to surrogacy:

> *Option A*, permitting surrogacy, but closely regulating it; and
> *Option B*, outlawing surrogacy.

The Act was largely unsuccessful and was repealed in the 2000 when its provisions relating to surrogacy, save for Option B, were embodied in the new Article 8 of the *Uniform Parentage Act* (UPA).

Dating from 1973, the *Uniform Parentage Act* was promulgated primarily to eliminate the differential treatment of marital and non-marital children. In its first iteration, the Act contained a section addressing the use of artificial insemination by married couples. In the 2000 overhaul of the UPA, NCCUSL added Article 8 to govern the ability of married couples to commission gestational or traditional surrogates and to establish parentage in such matters. The UPA contains a judicial pre-approval requirement, but it does not require that at least one of the intended parents be a genetic parent of the child. In the course of the judicial validation procedure, the court will verify the voluntariness of the entry of the parties into the agreement and whether they understand its terms.[113] Those terms must make clear 'which party is responsible for all reasonable health care expenses associated with the pregnancy' even if the agreement is eventually rescinded by either party.[114] The agreement is revocable until the gestational carrier actually becomes pregnant.[115] After the child's birth, upon confirmation of the parentage of the intended parents, 'a birth certificate naming the intended parents as the child's parents' issues.[116]

In 2002, NCCUSL revamped Article 8 to eliminate the limitation on the use of surrogacy to married couples. The change was motivated by the necessity of aligning Article 8 with the original spirit of the UPA. Like the USCACA, the UPA's Article 8, in either its former or new and improved form, has been of little interest to state legislatures. Only two states, Virginia and North Dakota, made use of the USCACA, and only Texas and Utah, the home states of the reporters of the new UPA, enacted the 2000 form of Article 8, albeit with some revisions.[117]

Several financial issues in connection with access to surrogacy deserve mention, only some of which are alluded to in the list of requirements for surrogacy contracts. First, when we think of commercial surrogacy, we tend to

113 Tex Fam Code § 160.756(b)(4).
114 Tex Fam Code § 160.756(b)(6).
115 Tex Fam Code § 160.759(a).
116 Tex Fam Code § 160.760(b)(3).
117 Tex Fam Code § 160.754; Utah Code Ann §§ 78B-15-801 et seq.

understand that this type of surrogacy entails compensation or payment in addition to the reimbursement of expenses. But there is an unfortunate lack of uniformity in the use of the words compensation, reimbursement, and payment in this context. For example, some states make clear that surrogacy is not like adoption, so that compensation is permitted. Other states provide that compensation may consist only of reimbursable expenses. Some jurisdictions prohibit paid surrogacy; others allow it so long as the payment does not induce the surrogate to relinquish the child. Still other states limit payment to what is reasonable. Payments beyond expenses are not what we associate with altruistic or compassionate surrogacy, which is understood to allow reimbursement to the surrogate of her expenses, but no more. A Nebraska statute implies that an arrangement will not be considered surrogacy *unless* compensation is involved.[118] New Jersey, Nevada and Virginia say variously that the surrogate must not be compensated or must be 'unpaid'. Despite the lack of uniformity in the usage of terms relating to compensation, it is reasonable to think that in any surrogacy, whether compensated or 'for free', some money will change hands.

Surrogates who are compensated or even reimbursed for their work can expect to report the income on their income tax returns at both the federal and state levels.[119] The surrogate may be permitted to deduct from this income the ordinary and necessary expenses she incurred to generate the income.[120] The primary issue in this context is not liability for reporting but compliance.[121] In the absence of clear Internal Revenue Service guidance on this question, it is safe to assume that compliance will be low.[122]

Whether the costs of surrogacy incurred by the intended parents may be deducted as medical expenses is a different question. Expenses to treat infertility are understood to be properly deductible and were ruled to be so in a case involving a woman who paid a third party for her egg in order to achieve a pregnancy. But the Internal Revenue Service disallowed deductions in the case of a single man who engaged surrogate mothers to assist him in having two children. An appeals court agreed that the expenses had not been incurred to treat the medical condition of infertility.[123] The United States Supreme Court declined to review the matter.

Insurance for surrogacy is another area of interest. Although insurance for infertility treatment is an important current issue in the United States, there appears to be little support behind calls for the insurance industry to provide

118 Neb Rev Stat § 25-1,200(1).

119 Bridget J. Crawford, 'Taxation, Pregnancy and Privacy' (2010) 16(2) *William and Mary Journal of Women and the Law* 327.

120 Ibid.; Morgan Holcomb and Mary Patricia Byrn, 'When Your Body Is Your Business' (2010) 85(4) *Washington Law Review* 647, 675, 680.

121 Ibid.

122 Ibid.

123 *Magdalin v Commissioner of Internal Revenue*, No. 09-1153, 2009 WL 5557509 (1st Cir, 17 December 2009).

coverage for the costs incurred by intended parents when they engage a surrogate. Indeed, insurance companies sometimes specifically exclude surrogacy from coverage under their policies. Some states, though, have disallowed carriers from denying surrogate mothers coverage for pregnancy services when claimed under their own health insurance policies. Insurance for the child will depend upon the child's legal parentage, another reason why intended parents may desire a pre-birth order of parentage.[124]

Finally, as consumer credit has tightened, infertility clinics and brokers have begun to develop their own financing products or to partner with third-party lenders.[125] The business of lending money for infertility treatment and assisted reproduction is deemed 'recession-proof', since often patients are so determined to have a child that they will willingly incur further debt despite whatever financial plan they had in place before they began treatment.[126]

VI. Regulating Parentage

The second main area of surrogacy regulation in the United States relates to parentage. The issue at this point in the surrogacy journey is whether the law will recognise that the surrogate is *not* the legal mother, even though she gestated the child and may be its genetic progenitor. The rules in this area are equally concerned with the status of the intended parents and whether they, even if not genetically related to the child, may be deemed the child's legal parents from the moment of the child's birth. As noted in Part V above, statutes often do the good work of ensuring this result, but many states lack laws on surrogacy. Courts in such jurisdictions will, of necessity, rely on well-established parentage principles to resolve disputed surrogacy arrangements.

This leads to the second most well-known surrogacy dispute in the United States, a case that was being litigated in the lower courts in California during the period when the United States saw the most anti-surrogacy-inspired legislative activity. In *Johnson v. Calvert*,[127] Anna Johnson agreed to gestate an embryo created using the gametes of Mark and Crispina Calvert. Upon reaching the

---

124 Charles P. Kindregan, Jr and Maureen McBrien, *Assisted Reproductive Technology: A Lawyer's Guide to Emerging Law and Science* (Chicago, IL: American Bar Association, 2011), 361 n. 125.

125 See, for example, The Center for Surrogate Parenting, *Financial Options*, available at http://www.creatingfamilies.com/IP/IP_Info.aspx?ID=247; Surrogacy Financial Program & Cost Information, The Select Surrogate, at available at http://www.selectsurrogate.com/surrogacy-cost-info.html.

126 Susan Johnston, 'Can you afford fertility treatment?', *USA Today*, 20 August 2012, available at http://money.usnews.com/money/personal-finance/articles/2012/08/20/can-you-afford-fertility-treatments, accessed 16 June 2014.

127 851 P2d 776 (Cal, 1993).

seventh month of her pregnancy, Johnson demanded full payment for her services and threatened to keep the child if payment was not forthcoming. In response, the Calverts sued to establish their rights to the child. At a trial held after the child's birth, the court named the Calverts the parents of the child based on the genetic relationship between them, declared the contract enforceable, and terminated the visitation rights Johnson had been granted pending the outcome of the trial.

Johnson appealed, first to the California Court of Appeals and then to the California Supreme Court, both of which affirmed the trial court's ruling. The Supreme Court asserted that either a genetic contribution or a gestational contribution could support a declaration of maternity under California law and could find no legislative preference for either one. Faced with two equally viable claims to maternity, the court, with the aid of scholarly opinion, decided to use intention, as manifested in the surrogacy agreement, to break the tie. Absent the Calverts' intent, declared the court, the child would never have existed. Under this analysis, Johnson became a mere facilitator of the Calverts' intent; any intention she had had in asserting parentage was subordinate to theirs, it being clear that had she asserted these same intentions before entering into the agreement, the Calverts would most assuredly have withdrawn from the project.

Testing the new approach in other surrogacy disputes, the California Court of Appeals decided a case the following year that, in contrast to *Johnson*, involved traditional surrogacy. Finding no doubt as to the identity of the biological mother in such cases, in short, 'no 'tie' to break',[128] the Court declined to enforce the surrogacy contract, deeming it incompatible with parentage and adoption principles.

Finally, with *Johnson* and *Moschetta* as precedents, the California Court of Appeals, in *Buzzanca v. Buzzanca*, again scrutinised parentage in the context of gestational surrogacy. In that case, married couple Luanne and John Buzzanca contracted with a surrogate to gestate an embryo they had acquired but to which neither had contributed genetic material.[129] The couple separated, and Luanne petitioned to be named baby Jaycee's mother. The identities of the genetic contributors were not known, and the surrogate made no claim to Jaycee. On these facts, the trial court ruled that Jaycee had no legal parent. Since as in *Moschetta* there was no tie to break, the Court of Appeals instead drew an analogy to California's artificial insemination law, which bestows paternity upon a husband who consents to the artificial insemination of his wife with the sperm of a donor and declares the donor not to be a father. Since Luanne had arranged for a medical procedure to be performed on the surrogate that resulted in her pregnancy and the eventual birth of a child, the surrogate in essence gave birth to the child on Luanne's behalf. Luanne's intentional act determined her legal motherhood, just as a husband's act of consenting to artificial insemination of his wife would determine his legal fatherhood. To resort to adoption law in this context, the court

128 *In re Moschetta*, 30 Cal Rptr 2d 893 (Ct App, 1994), 895.

129 *Buzzanca v. Buzzanca*, 72 Cal Rptr 2d 280 (Ct App, 1998), 282, 283.

reasoned, would be 'an exercise in circular reasoning, because it assumes the idea that it seeks to prove; namely, that a child who is born as the result of artificial reproduction is somebody else's child from the beginning'.[130] The court described this view of intentional parenthood as applicable 'to any situation where a child would not have been born but for the efforts of the intended parents'.[131] Several states now have statutes that explicitly define an 'intended parent' as one whose intent is to become the legal parent of a child born of assisted reproduction or gestational surrogacy.[132] To be an intended parent does not require that one have a genetic relationship to the child.[133]

Unlike any other form of assisted reproduction, surrogacy demonstrates the fragmentation of parentage into genetic, gestational and intentional components, but the approach taken by California has not been uniformly embraced. A decision by an Ohio court did not place gestation on an equal footing with genetics but instead considered the 'genetic imprint' to be superior.[134] A Utah court even deemed it unconstitutional for the state to conclusively presume that a gestational surrogate is the legal mother.[135] But in neither of those cases was the gestational surrogate making a bid for maternity, so no tie-breaking was required. In a case where the genetic and gestational mother were in a same-sex relationship and wanted to raise the child together, the court saw no impediment to the recognition of two mothers. The court left open the question of whether intent was relevant or determinative of legal parentage.[136]

The role of intention in parentage determination has been of interest to scholars of family law. Janet Dolgin sees two paradigms at work in surrogacy jurisprudence, a biological-parentage paradigm in traditional surrogacy cases and a presumptive-parentage paradigm in gestational surrogacy cases. She argues that, in gestational surrogacy cases, courts feel freer to reject an adoption default model and to give legal weight to intention than they do in traditional surrogacy cases where genetics and gestation are joined.[137] While Dolgin's analysis is primarily descriptive, Marsha Garrison assumes a more normative stance. Garrison believes creating different parentage rules for assisted reproduction cases is a bad idea in general and, more specifically, that any emphasis on intention in determining parentage in such cases is unnecessary and even dangerous. According to Garrison, the

---

130 Ibid., 291.

131 Ibid.

132 See, for example, Cal Fam Code § 7960(c); Conn Gen Stat § 7-36(17); 750 Ill Comp Stat 47/10; Minn Stat § 524.1-201(31); Tex Fam Code § 160.102(9).

133 Ala Code § 26-17-102(12); Conn Gen Stat § 7-36(17); Tex Fam Code § 160.102(9); Va Code Ann § 20-156.

134 *Belsito v Clark*, 644 NE2d 760 (Ohio Misc, 1994).

135 *J.R. v Utah*, 261 F Supp 2d 1268 (D Utah, 2003).

136 *In re Sebastian*, 879 NYS2d 677 (Surr Ct, 2009) 685 n.27.

137 Janet L. Dolgin, *Defining the Family: Law, Technology, and Reproduction in an Uneasy Age* (New York: New York University Press, 1997), 62.

danger lies in ignoring important facts: the law has never recognised intentional parenthood, and technological reproduction does not create genuinely new or different family forms. Garrison urges courts to apply well-established, traditional methods of determining parentage in these cases and, in the interest of fairness, to reject special theories applicable only to technological families.[138]

Although Dolgin is certainly correct in asserting that there has been a tendency to distinguish between traditional and gestational surrogacy in both public opinion and law, no true consensus has emerged that the two types of surrogacy require different legal treatment. It is enough to say that traditional surrogacy is treated as legally distinct from gestational surrogacy in some American jurisdictions but not in others. Rather than exhibiting a consensus, this state of affairs more genuinely signals that the uncertainty of a surrogacy arrangement is greater in jurisdictions that have no legislation to govern it[139] than it is where a statute dictates that traditional surrogacy requires an adoption or establishes that traditional and gestational surrogacy are permitted on equivalent terms. As for Garrison, of course there is much to be said for consistency in the law. The important point about surrogacy, though, is that many jurisdictions, like California, are extending themselves strenuously in the direction of according legal recognition to 'technological' families and are doing so using legal principles based on family building realities that have emerged only because technological families are now possible. Californian law-makers quite likely perceive that there is little danger in doing so and that there is a need to have laws that respond flexibly to the new ways its residents are choosing to form their families.

Access to surrogacy in States like California brings with it heightened awareness of the importance of intention in parentage determination. But within the United States, cross-border issues can arise when the parties are residents of different states and the birth may take place in a third. Restrictive jurisdictions may border permissive ones (Texas and Louisiana, for example), so that the birth of the child in the permissive jurisdiction may not seamlessly result in the recognition of the intended parentage in the more restrictive state. Another danger is that the birth of the child in a restrictive jurisdiction may cause the surrogacy agreement to unravel. In one case, commissioning parents asked that their surrogate abort the foetus in keeping with the terms of the agreement when multiple defects were discovered. The surrogate refused, even after the intended parents offered her $10,000 to terminate the pregnancy. Connecticut, where the arrangement was made, recognises the intended parents as the parents. The surrogate thus elected to give birth in Michigan, where she would be recognised as the mother of the child.[140] Some states with disapproving statutory regimes make it clear that, in a battle for

138 Marsha Garrison, 'Law Making for Baby Making: An Interpretive Approach to the Determination of Legal Parentage' (2000) 113 *Harvard Law Review* 835, 882.

139 Mark Hansen, 'And Baby Makes Litigation: As Surrogacy Becomes More Popular, Legal Problems Proliferate' (2011) 97(3) *American Bar Association Journal* 52, 53.

140 Erik Ortiz, 'Surrogate mom offered $10K to abort baby after parents discover she would be born with disabilities', *New York Daily News*, 5 March 2013, available at

parentage, the fact that the surrogate agreed to the arrangement will not be held against her in evaluating the best interests of the child.[141]

Some states' parentage statutes do not address surrogacy arrangements at all, leaving the parentage ramifications that flow from such arrangements in question.[142] In such states, individual courts may be willing to issue pre-birth judgments of parentage ordering the issuance of birth certificates bearing the names of the intended parents.[143] But more than likely, the default approach in such cases will be to resolve them with adoption principles, as Arkansas's courts did in two cases involving cross-border surrogacy.[144] Washington, which prohibits commercial surrogacy within its borders, takes an altogether different approach by refusing to recognise commercial surrogacy contracts entered into in other jurisdictions.[145]

Under the United States Constitution, the 50 states are bound to give 'full faith and credit' to the judgments of their sister states.[146] Where intended parents have obtained judgment of parentage, they are entitled to recognition of that judgment by the state in which they ultimately settle.[147] Making available a pre-birth declaration of parentage provides intended parents the most expeditious route to parentage recognition[148] because it renders amendment of the birth certificate and adoption unnecessary after the child is born. Petitions for such declarations in states in which surrogacy is treated using an adoption model have understandably been rejected,[149] since the adoption model allows a birth mother a period of time within which to decide to relinquish or keep the child.[150] New Jersey, for example, which requires the commissioning mother to adopt the child, rejects pre-birth declarations.[151] But not every state that allows surrogacy will permit a pre-birth order of parentage if it, like Florida, makes a distinction between traditional and

---

http://www.nydailynews.com/lifestyle/health/surrogate-mom-offered-10k-abort-baby-disabilties-article-1.1279997, accessed 16 June 2014.

141 See, for example, Ind Code § 31-20-1-3; NY Dom Rel Law § 124(1).

142 See, for example, Colo Rev Stat §§ 19-4-103, 106.

143 Kevin Simpson, 'Surrogacy law struggles to keep pace with change', *Denver Post*, 25 December 1998.

144 *Adoption of KFH, 844 SW2d 343 (Ark, 1993); In re Samant, 970 SW2d 249 (Ark, 1998).*

145 Wash Stat § 26.26.240.

146 United States Constitution art IV § 1.

147 See, for example, *Davis v Kania*, 836 A2d 480 (Conn Super, 2003); *In re Doe*, 793 NYS2d 878 (Surr Ct, 2005).

148 *Smith v Brown*, 718 NE2d 844, 846 (Mass, 1999); Andrew W. Vorzimer, 'The Egg Donor and Surrogacy Controversy: Legal Issues Surrounding Representation of Parties to an Egg Donor and Surrogacy Contract' (1999) 21(2) *Whittier Law Review* 415, 426.

149 See, for example, *In re TJS*, 54 A3d 263 (NJ, 2012); *AHW v GHB*, 772 A2d 948 (NJ Super, 2000); *Doe v NYC Bd of Health*, 782 NYS2d 180 (Sup Ct, 2004).

150 *AHW* at 954.

151 *In re TJS*, 16 A3d 386, 391 (NJ App Div, 2011).

gestational surrogacy or, like New Hampshire, grants a surrogate the right to keep the child.[152] Even in the case of gestational surrogacy, Florida requires the commissioning couple to file a petition with the court within three days of the child's birth. Upon the court's determination of the validity of the arrangement, the court orders the issuance of a new birth certificate.[153] This approach is also common in states that require judicial pre-approval of the surrogacy contract. In such states, once the child is born and the child is confirmed to be the intended parents' child, the order for an amended birth certificate issues.[154]

One interesting development in the area of parentage designations in surrogacy cases is the equal protection challenges intended mothers have lodged, complaining that the statutes that presume the paternity of husbands who consent to the insemination of their wives with donor sperm should extend to intended mothers who use surrogates. These complaints have had mixed success in the courts. The Sterns raised this argument in *Baby M.*, but the court esteemed the situations to be far from parallel: '[a] sperm donor simply cannot be equated with a surrogate mother … even if the only difference is between the time it takes to provide sperm for artificial insemination and the time invested in a nine-month pregnancy'.[155] Thus, a justification for the different treatment has been found in the physiological differences between men and women.[156] A later New Jersey decision, *T.J.S.*, emphasised the 'actual reproductive and biological differences, necessitating in the case of an infertile wife, the introduction of a birth mother whom the law cloaks with superior protection'.[157]

Other courts that do equate sperm donors with surrogate mothers[158] may find viable causes of action where officials refuse to place the genetic intended mother's name on the child's birth certificate[159] or the law offers the mother no procedure by which to prove her genetic connection to the child.[160] In this vein, the Court of Appeals of Maryland, whose constitution prohibits gender discrimination, ruled that provisions permitting men to rebut paternity applied equally to a gestational surrogate who wished to rebut maternity.[161] A court in California has expressed similar solicitude toward intentional mothers with no biological connection to the child, ruling that laws governing

---

152 Fla Stat § 63.213; NH Rev Stat Ann § 168-B: 25.

153 Fla Stat § 742.16(1).

154 See, for example, Tex Fam Code § 160.760.

155 537 A2d 1255.

156 *In re TJS*, 54 A3d 263, 264 (NJ, 2012) (Hoens, J, concurring), *In re Baby M*, 537 A2d 1227 (NJ, 1988).

157 Ibid.

158 *Surrogate Parenting Associates, Inc v Commonwealth*, 704 SW2d 204, 211-12 (Ky, 1986).

159 *TV v New York State Dept of Health*, 929 NYS2d 139 (App Div, 2011); *JR v Utah*, 261 F Supp 2d 1268, 1294 (D Utah, 2003).

160 *Soos v Superior Court*, 897 P2d 1356, 1361 (Ariz Ct App, 1994).

161 *In re Robert B*, 923 A2d 115, 125 (Md, 2007).

paternity determination in assisted reproduction may be applied by analogy to establish their maternity.[162] This reasoning was likewise prominent in the opinion of the three dissenting justices in the equally divided decision in *T.J.S.*, discussed above.

VII. The Normative Lens

American reaction to surrogacy has been extremely varied. Commentary ranges from extreme disapproval to measured optimism. Feminist treatment of surrogacy subsumes both evaluative extremes. Gena Corea and Janice Raymond, opponents of surrogacy, view it as just another example of the historical cooptation of women's reproductive power by men.[163] In this view, surrogacy is 'reproductive prostitution'[164] disguised in the language of autonomy, liberation and choice.[165] Corea and Raymond object not only to how surrogacy arrangements oppress and exploit poor, minority women who have few choices[166] but also to how they commodify children,[167] a concern shared by Margaret Radin and Barbara Katz Rothman.[168] In a remarkable stroke of prescience, Corea and Raymond both predicted that Americans would eventually look to women in developing countries to satisfy their demand for lower-cost surrogacy.[169] Anti-surrogacy sentiment is now prominent in scholarship addressing international commercial surrogacy.[170]

162 *In re Buzzanca*, 72 Cal Rptr 2d 280 (1998).

163 Gena Corea, *The Mother Machine: Reproductive Technologies from Artificial Insemination to Artificial Wombs* (New York: Harper & Row, 1985) 221, 223; Janice G. Raymond, *Women as Wombs: Reproductive Technologies and the Battle over Women's Freedom* (New York: HarperCollins, 1993) 31, 99.

164 Corea, above n. 163, 227; Raymond, above n. 163, 144.

165 Raymond, above n. 163, 103.

166 Ibid., 68, 81, 103.

167 Corea, above n. 163, 219; Raymond, above n. 163, 57.

168 Margaret Jane Radin, *Contested Commodities: The Trouble with Trade in Sex, Children, Body Parts, and Other Things* (Boston, MA: Harvard University Press, 1996) 140; Barbara Katz Rothman, *Recreating Motherhood: Ideology and Technology in a Patriarchal Society* (New York: W.W. Norton, 1989) 44.

169 Corea, above n. 163, 215, 274–5; Raymond, above n. 163, 144.

170 See, for example, Natalie Fixmer-Oraiz, 'Speaking of Solidarity: Transnational Gestational Surrogacy and the Rhetorics of Reproductive (In)Justice' (2013) 34(3) *Frontiers: A Journal of Women Studies* 126; Seema Mohapatra, 'Stateless Babies and Adoption Scams: A Bioethical Analysis of International Commercial Surrogacy' (2012) 30(2) *Berkeley Journal of International Law* 412; Seema Mohapatra, 'Achieving Reproductive Justice in the International Surrogacy Market' (2012) 21(1) *Annals of Health Law* 191; Kristine Schanbacher, 'India's Gestational Surrogacy Market: An Exploitation of Poor, Uneducated Women' (2014) 25(2) *Hastings Women's Law Journal* 201.

Counterbalancing the radical feminist stance against surrogacy is the view that surrogacy promotes gender equality by affording some women the opportunity to use their reproductive power as a means of support and other women the opportunity to acquire those services. Marjorie Maguire Shultz, a proponent of this view, has theorised that embracing surrogacy is one way of expanding legal recognition of alternative family forms, including same-sex couple- and single-parent-headed families, wherein parentage would be determined outside the constraints of gender stereotypes and biases.[171] She describes the outcome of *Baby M* in particular as a 'missed opportunity for gender-neutral access to children'.[172] Shultz's views on gender equality are complemented by the work of John Robertson, the foremost American theorist on why resort to collaborative reproduction is a fundamental constitutional right. Robertson believes that curtailing surrogacy would not only deny infertile couples the opportunity to have children genetically related to themselves but 'may also deny women who wish only to gestate opportunities to do so'.[173]

More recent scholarship on domestic surrogacy in the United States acknowledges that just as an unregulated surrogacy industry would likely result in emotional and financial damage to both would-be parents and surrogates alike, an anti-surrogacy stance aimed at stamping out exploitation and commodification leads to other harsh realities with which to grapple. The hallmark of this scholarship is its deep engagement with empirical data showing that the primary factors tending to trigger the fear of exploitation in surrogacy are not present in domestic surrogacy arrangements in the United States.[174] The data reveal that surrogate mothers in the United States are not poverty-stricken but are instead educated women who often prefer surrogacy to the other options they have to earn income.[175] Nor is their bond with the developing foetus particularly confusing or traumatic for them. Indeed, it is the bond with the intended parents, particularly the intended mother, that is the most meaningful to surrogates.[176]

Thoughtful scholars like Pamela Laufer-Ukeles would have us acknowledge that what actually happens in surrogacy transactions suggests the need for a more nuanced understanding that transcends abstract fears or uninformed enthusiasm. The best regulation in such an environment will promote surrogates'

171 Marjorie Maquire Shultz, 'Reproductive Technology and Intent-based Parenthood: An Opportunity for Gender Neutrality' (1990) *Wisconsin Law Review* 297, 315, 344–5.

172 Ibid., 378.

173 See John A. Robertson, *Children of Choice: Freedom and the New Reproductive Technologies* (Princeton, NJ: Princeton University Press, 1994), 131.

174 Pamela Laufer-Ukeles, 'Mothering for Money: Regulating Commercial Intimacy' (2013) 88(4) *Indiana Law Journal* 1223, 1230–35.

175 Ibid., 1235.

176 Ibid., 1233. See also V. Jadva, S. Imrie, and S. Golombok, 'Surrogate mothers 10 years on: a longitudinal study of psychological well-being and relationships with the parents and child' (2015) *Human Reproduction* 30(2) 373.

fundamental expectations so as to protect them from emotional harm, support the other participants in the transaction, and quell the societal fear that surrogacy undermines human dignity.[177] It must ensure that surrogates are receiving complete and correct information about the process, are not experiencing familial pressure, and are not suffering economic or emotional distress.[178] It is not difficult to see shades of Laufer-Ukeles's proposal in some of the early legislation establishing judicial oversight of surrogacy transactions in order to protect the parties involved. More recent legislative schemes – in Nevada and Illinois, for example – appear to conform even more closely to her proposal.

In a departure from existing legislative schemes, however, Laufer-Ukeles urges that a surrogate mother be given the right to claim 'infrequent but potentially ongoing visitation' with the child in the rare event she has difficulty separating from the child.[179] This provision would likely influence the parties at the bargaining stage to reflect more fully on the significance of their intimate undertaking and not to see the arrangement as one that necessarily terminates upon the birth, with no further contact between the surrogate and the child. Such a provision might understandably dissuade those couples desiring more decision-making control from pursuing surrogacy, but this would be an acceptable outcome, as such couples would likely be less willing to acknowledge and honour the intimate aspects of the surrogacy arrangement or the need or desire of the child to have as complete an understanding as possible of how s/he was created.

The appeal of Laufer-Ukeles's proposal is its position somewhere between the extremes of extolling surrogacy as a procreative right and of presuming surrogates to be mere reflections of, as Raymond would put it, 'patriarchal constructionism'.[180] The goal should not be to police reproductive options with a view to channelling people into the most familiar manner of having children. Most people will find their way there without any help from the government. Instead, the state should focus its efforts on constructing a platform from which individuals who need to build their families in an alternative manner can do so without harm to themselves, to those they enlist to assist them, or to the children they wish to create. Once the family building project is achieved, the state should end its oversight and wish them well.

To better achieve this salutary end, it is necessary to dismantle whatever discrimination remains within surrogacy regulation, most saliently the restriction in some states' statutes that only heterosexual married couples may have access to surrogacy. Heterosexual marriage-based restrictions have no place in surrogacy regulation because they do not promote the purposes of marriage or ensure two-parent support for each child.[181] They do unfortunately, however, give the

177 Ibid., 1238–39, 1253–55, 1259, 1262–63.

178 Ibid., 1250.

179 Ibid., 1254.

180 Raymond, above n. 163, 37.

181 Richard F. Storrow, 'Rescuing Children from the Marriage Movement: The Case against Marital Status Discrimination in Adoption and Assisted Reproduction' (2006) 39(2)

misguided impression that married couples are somehow more deserving than others to have access to surrogacy. Equally disturbing is that these restrictions appear geared to create the illusion of legitimacy of birth. If so, they run afoul of what are now firmly established constitutional and social commitments to equal treatment by perpetuating the same distinction between legitimacy and illegitimacy that has been fully discredited by the United States Supreme Court.[182] Thus, the exclusion of all but heterosexual married couples from surrogacy is in conflict with important constitutional tenets and sound social policy.

VIII. Conclusion

Surrogacy in America assumes many forms. Despite the entrenched reputation of the United States as a nation in which consumers are free to pursue commercial surrogacy at will, the truth about surrogacy in this country is a bit less dramatic. Because the regulation of surrogacy lies within the jurisdiction of each of the 50 United States, and since attitudes toward surrogacy vary widely within and across those jurisdictions, it is unsurprising that the United States does not embrace commercial or even altruistic surrogacy uniformly, but instead comprises a variety of different laws that run the gamut from acceptance to prohibition. Furthermore, the availability of compensated surrogacy in certain jurisdictions does not suggest a laissez-faire attitude toward such arrangements. Indeed, even in jurisdictions that are particularly friendly toward surrogacy arrangements, a good deal of regulation, be it of a legal or extralegal nature, goes into decisions about which arrangements will be tolerated and which will not. The legislative trend appears to be toward liberalisation of the law in states that have banned surrogacy, but we still, even as late as 2014, see proposals to ban surrogacy in certain states.[183] Thus, although the United States, when viewed from outside, looks like a permissive, laissez-faire jurisdiction, it in fact constitutes a microcosm of the wider global variation in the regulation of surrogacy, with pockets of prohibition alongside pockets of permissiveness.

U.C. Davis Law Review 305, 318–31.

182 See, for example, *Trimble v Gordon*, 430 US 259 (1978); *Weber v Aetna Casualty & Surety Company*, 406 US 164 (1972); *Levy v Louisiana*, 391 US 68 (1968).

183 See above nn. 44, 46.

Index

For Product Safety Concerns and Information please contact our EU
representative GPSR@taylorandfrancis.com
Taylor & Francis Verlag GmbH, Kaufingerstraße 24, 80331 München, Germany

www.ingramcontent.com/pod-product-compliance
Ingram Content Group UK Ltd.
Pitfield, Milton Keynes, MK11 3LW, UK
UKHW022131190926
475702UK00013B/1753

* 9 7 8 1 1 3 8 7 0 1 7 3 1 *